"Katrina Shawver, a well respected journalist and public speaker, has used her interviewing skills to write a solid biography on Auschwitz-Buchenwald-Death March-Dachau and Communist Poland survivor Henry Zguda. She weaves his memories with historical research to tell an important story of courage and tenacity. It is presented so that everyone will learn, and will not want to lay the book down. Additionally, there are numerous photos that greatly enhance the story, helping readers visualize the people and horrors as well as the beautiful times of Zguda's life. We know that we should never forget the Holocaust, and Shawver is ensuring that we won't."

—JOHN LIFFITON, Professor and Director Genocide Conferences, Scottsdale Community College

"Katrina Shawver has done something rare. With her journalistic eye, she has created a book of outstanding research, divine instincts and the most human of components. Our hero, Henry Zguda, lives an extraordinary life filled with enough examples of strength and loyalty to warrant medals. As a non-Jewish survivor of concentration camps during WWII, this story deserves to be part of history. It is told with urgency and tolerance. A remarkable feat of writing! Bravo for humanity!"

—MARCIA FINE, author of Hidden Ones, The Blind Eye, and Paper Children—An Immigrant's Legacy

"Henry Zguda is a man you would like to know. When you read *Henry*, the interview-based story of his life, you will indeed come to know this hardy and hopeful soul, from his youthful days as a champion swimmer to his post-war life in Communist Poland and, finally, in the United States of America. However, it is the harrowing personal experiences of this Catholic Pole as a prisoner in the German concentration camps of Auschwitz, Buchenwald, and Dachau that yield information found nowhere else and keep the reader riveted to the page. Highly recommended."

> —JAMES CONROYD MARTIN, author of *The Poland Trilogy*, and
> IPPY Gold Medal Winner, *The Boy Who Wanted Wings*

"By painstakingly reconstructing Henry Zguda's remarkable story of survival, Katrina Shawver sheds light on one of the darkest chapters in human history—in particular, on the plight of Catholic Poles who found themselves in concentration camps like Auschwitz and Buchenwald. *Henry* is both poignant and inspiring."

> —ANDREW NAGORSKI, author of *The Nazi Hunters* and
> *Hitlerland*

"This sensitively crafted narrative is a vital contribution to the documentation of the suffering inflicted on Polish people during the Holocaust. Katrina Shawver has collected the memories of Henry Zguda, beginning with his arrest in Krakow in 1942 and ending with their blossoming friendship in 2002. His own words are skillfully sewn together with Shawver's observations and research, and the result is a compelling tale of anguish and the triumph of hope against all odds. This labor of love deserves a wide readership as the last Holocaust survivors pass away, taking their stories with them. We are fortunate that Shawver had the presence of mind to bring Zguda's story to the world."

> —LEONARD KNIFFEL, author of *A Polish Son in the Motherland* and
> the blog PolishSon.com, member of the Board of Directors of the
> Polish American Librarians Association and the Polish Museum of
> America in Chicago

"Elie Wiesel said, 'When you listen to a witness, you become a witness.' Katrina Shawver's luminous non-fiction, *Henry: A Polish Swimmer's True Story of Friendship from Auschwitz to America,* is a beautifully rendered act of witness and love about an extraordinary Pole, Henry Zguda, a Christian, a political prisoner in Auschwitz and Buchenwald. Shawver's compelling narrative illuminates Henry's memories as well as his heart and his enduring humor. She has rescued Henry's vital piece of Holocaust history so that we don't forget, and as an immunization against recurrence. Everyone who reads *Henry* becomes a witness."

—**JACK MAYER,** Vermont writer and pediatrician, author of *Life in a Jar: The Irena Sendler Project,* a non-fiction about the Warsaw ghetto, and a new historical fiction about the rise of the Third Reich, *Before the Court of Heaven*

"*Henry* is an exceptional read! If you are into real life World War II survival stories that are very detailed this is your book! Katrina Shawver's ability to transport the reader back into time is truly remarkable! Every chapter makes you want to keep on reading about this truly remarkable man that survived so much and yet was so humble. Best book I have read on Auschwitz!"

—**J. R. SHARP,** CDR USN (ret), author, *Feeding the Enemy*

"World War II survivors are resilient, unique figures but here, Shawver reveals a remarkable, rare gem of a human who would have otherwise gone unnoticed in the aftermath of German-occupied Poland. She weaves together a riveting, unforgettable tale that captures the unstoppable flight of the human spirit."

—**GREG ARCHER,** author of *Grace Revealed* and Huffington Post columnist

"I worked as a counterintelligence agent in Germany for twenty-five years. During that time, I spoke with thousands of Germans who survived the horrors of World War II. Most claimed falsely that they knew nothing about the concentration camps and never supported the Nazi party. From those who were victims of the Nazis or those who spoke honestly about their experiences, I can attest that Shawver knows what she is talking about."

—**ROBERT DUKELOW**, author of *Four Strong Women: A Glimpse of Germany's Untold History 1938-1957*

"Those brave souls who survived World War II are some of the finest examples of courage in our lifetime. Fortunately, Katrina Shawver knew exactly how to bring Henry Zguda's courage to life. In this fascinating, terrifying and inspiring book, *Henry—A Polish Swimmer's True Story of Friendship from Auschwitz to America*, readers are transported to a time and place where survival seems impossible. What a stellar tribute to Henry and those whose lives he changed."

—**JUDITH L. PEARSON**, author of *The Wolves at the Door: The True Story of America's Greatest Female Spy*

"*Henry: A Polish Swimmer's True Story of Friendship from Auschwitz to America* by Katrina Shawver is the story of Henry Zguda, a Catholic Pole and political prisoner of Nazi Germany who survived Auschwitz and Buchenwald. Based on her interviews with Henry, Shawver tells his first-person account in vivid and, at times, alarming detail. Indeed, Henry serves as a witness to history about the millions of innocent people, and not only Jews, who suffered at the hands of the Nazis. It should not be forgotten."

—**JERRY AMERNIC**, author of *The Last Witness*

"This remarkable true story will take you on a historical journey, filled with a firsthand account of how one man survived the impossible, and then found the love of his life."

—J.L. WITTERICK, International Best Selling Author of
My Mother's Secret

"In recounting the memoir of Henry Zguda, a non-Jewish survivor of Auschwitz and Buchenwald, author Katrina Shawver tells us not only the story of a man who survived the camps. She brilliantly conveys what it meant for her to listen to a survivor who taught her 'Hope was the only incurable disease of Auschwitz.' This memoir is an indispensable book for anyone who wants to learn about the concentration camps, what it took to survive them, and how they continue to touch our lives today. I've read dozens of memoirs of people who survived the camps, and Katrina Shawver's book is among the best."

—JOHN GUZLOWSKI, author of *Echoes of Tattered Tongues:*
Memory Unfolded, winner of the Eric Hoffer/Montaigne Award

Henry:
A Polish Swimmer's True Story of
Friendship from Auschwitz to America

by Katrina Shawver

© Copyright 2017 Katrina Shawver

ISBN: 978-1-7345729-8-8

Published by:

RIBBON
FALLS
PRESS

RIBBON FALLS PRESS
4747 E. Elliot Rd, Ste 29-320
Phoenix, AZ 85044
Katrinashawver.com
Ribbonfallspress.com

HENRY

A POLISH SWIMMER'S

TRUE STORY OF

FRIENDSHIP FROM

AUSCHWITZ TO AMERICA

KATRINA SHAWVER

RIBBON FALLS PRESS
PHOENIX, ARIZONA

DEDICATION

To my husband, Rick, with all my love,
for always being my strongest champion.

And in loving memory to Henry and Nancy.

Ad aspera, ad astra
Through hardship to the stars

"The past actually happened,
but history is only what someone wrote down."

—A. WHITNEY BROWN

PREFACE

This book is based entirely on multiple first-person interviews with Henry Zguda from November 2002–2003. A shoebox full of cassette tapes holds Henry's Polish-accented voice and wry humor. If his English appears simple in this narrative, or not fully descriptive, it demonstrates how he spoke. English was his fifth language, so he frequently mixed up verb tenses or terminology. For the benefit of the reader, I cleaned up some of his "broken" English, or paraphrased slightly where it was needed to keep the tale flowing, yet retaining Henry's spirit and personality. Background context and history are woven into this tale to paint the backdrop and set the scenes for a time and place few people still alive experienced. Every year there are fewer survivors here to tell their stories. Fortunately, I met Henry at the right time, before his tale and artifacts were lost to history.

TABLE OF CONTENTS

PROLOGUE

How did the Henry I know survive *this*?

On a cold, gray, dismal day in October 2013, my husband and I visited the Auschwitz-Birkenau State Museum. After hours of poring through documents in the archives, we spent three hours touring the institution's two primary sites. Auschwitz I, originally a Polish army camp before the Germans repurposed it as a concentration camp, houses the museum and offices. The massive Birkenau, or Auschwitz II— built three kilometers away to hold more than 100,000 people at one time—stands mostly empty and silent, save for tourists.

My husband and I, and our private tour guide Magda, remained the only three humans at the lonely entrance to Birkenau as the camp closed at seven o'clock that evening. Most tourists avoid the uncomfortable cold, not realizing this is the truer experience of a concentration camp.

As we stood near the arched entry over the train tracks to hell, I shivered—not from the fading daylight and rapidly dropping temperatures, but from the chilling presence of the ghosts of more than a million murdered innocent souls.

Each cried out to me . . . *"Do not forget us."*

••

I met Henry Zguda in November 2002, through a phone tip, a call I considered a lucky break. I regularly sought out interesting people, organizations, or events in the community to write about, and was out of ideas for my regular column in the Phoenix newspaper, *The Arizona Republic*. I called him and scheduled an interview for three days later, knowing only that he was Polish, had survived two German concentration camps—Auschwitz and Buchenwald—and claimed to have attended school with Pope John Paul II. He lived a half mile from my home.

After our first meeting, I became fascinated with what instinct told me was a compelling story at risk of being lost forever. Henry had no siblings, and never had children, which partly explained my boldness in calling him up soon after the first interview. There seemed to be no one else to hand his stories to.

"Henry, what do you think if we write a book?"

With that one simple, but incredibly naïve and impulsive offer, Henry and I began a series of twice-weekly interviews that soon became a growing friendship. I developed a fascination for how someone who had endured so much had lived so well, and without apparent bitterness. Henry talked and I listened, occasionally interrupting with questions. We always met at his house on a screened-in patio, seated around a metal table topped with papers, photos, and a strategically positioned bowl of snacks. The patio allowed us to close the sliding glass door to the kitchen, so his wife Nancy couldn't hear the most brutal stories, though I later learned she knew quite a few. The mutual chemistry, and Henry's faith in me, meant we openly discussed almost anything.

"Why bring up all the negative? I am alive. Forget about it." Henry said these words more than once. He expressed surprise at my consistent interest in listening to some of the harshest stories. "Aren't you tired of all this?"

I never was.

Henry and I quite simply clicked, and I basked in the atmosphere of love he and Nancy so clearly shared.

Henry spoke, wrote, and read Polish, German, French, and Latin, and subsequently learned English after he defected to the United States in 1959. But that story comes later. Speaking in a thick Polish accent, he frequently confused his verb tenses, or only knew items and places by their Polish or German names, which led to some interesting guesses on my part as to English equivalents.

Like peeling back the layers of an onion, Henry revealed a few new surprises with each meeting, whether it was an odd story or a surprising cache of original documents and artifacts. A single brown photo album with peel-and-stick pages captured his eighty-five years in aging photos and newspaper clippings that placed him where his stories occurred. Unlike a formal, guided interview, if his thoughts drifted to a tangential story, I went with the flow. Those tangents provided some of the most amazing and unexpected tales.

A modern reality increasingly nagged at me as I worked on this story. Henry was a Catholic Pole who had been arrested, tortured, and imprisoned for three years in concentration camps for one reason only: he was Polish, and Germany had sworn to destroy all of Poland. He'd been a respected survivor in Poland, or "Auschwitzer," similar to how we honor war veterans and former POWs in this country. Yet, no matter to whom I mentioned this gentleman and project, universally everyone responded with a comment akin to, "What? He wasn't Jewish? Why was he arrested? There were only Jews in the Holocaust."

Only one woman's reaction surprised and validated me.

"They arrested him? Well, he must have been important."

She was, of course, Polish.

Besides the need for extensive research and translation of original documents from Polish, French, and German, this story could not be completed without visiting Poland. In the fall of 2013, my husband and I flew there and visited Kraków, Warsaw, Oświęcim, the site of Auschwitz; and Weimar, Germany, the site of Buchenwald concentration camp.

In August 2014, I located 130 documents on file with the International Tracing Service that referenced Henry's camp experiences. I have verified ninety-five percent of Henry's stories precisely as he described. My one research caveat is this: I only read English, so my resources are mostly limited to those written in, or translated into English.

Occasionally, I asked Henry about Polish attitudes between Jews and Poles, as I am neither. I strove to comprehend the social fabric and cultural biases of a pre-war Poland, and a country at war. Why was it, I asked myself, that even now, Henry's story— as well as that of millions of Poland's war casualties and the

near destruction of all things Polish—is specifically omitted
from the definition and teaching of the Holocaust? The answers,
I would eventually discover, are still current and as sensitive and
complex as a doctoral dissertation.

Henry answered all of my many questions in an honest
and matter-of-fact manner as he remembered them. I believe
his observations are important, for they were not said to be
politically correct or incorrect. He simply spoke pragmatically
as he knew life at the time. Each story paints a background of
context, and mirrors a country under siege. My innate curiosity,
the desire to provoke thought, and the need to tell lesser-known
stories, drove my newspaper and blog writing, and has propelled
this project forward.

The French poet George Bernanos wrote, "Hope is the risk
that must be taken." Henry's variation was simply, "Hope was
the only incurable disease of Auschwitz." Henry died one year
after I met him. The stories stopped, and the hole left in my
life yawned larger than I could have foreseen. An unexpected
and extremely close friendship subsequently grew between his
widow Nancy and me. Her death, in June 2013 at the age of
ninety-two, left yet another gaping hole in my life. I still miss
her dearly.

Nancy often called me her angel from heaven.

"Katrina, you have no idea the trust I have in you. Henry
thought you were just wonderful."

Like my talks with Henry, Nancy and I, too, shared a
chemistry that meant we could talk about anything, usually
over a glass of wine. She made me laugh. Nancy offered, more
than once, to give me all the love letters he wrote to her in his
broken English. She laughed every time she read those. I said
no, because I felt too presumptuous as a non-family member—
surely another family member would claim them? I truly regret
not taking them. They were thrown out by someone who didn't
know or care what they were.

Nancy once confessed to me that several people through the
years offered to write Henry's story. He only said yes to me. The
responsibility of holding a man's story in trust hangs heavy . . .
but, first and foremost, we were friends. His story touched me,
has stayed with me, and, for whatever reason fate led me to him,

I believe was entrusted to me for a reason. I did not seek this story; the story chose me unexpectedly, providentially, and, I believe, as the right person to carry it forward.

As I write these words, I gaze at two pictures hanging above my computer. In one, Henry reads to my then fourteen-year-old son Devin, following a game of chess. In the other, Nancy and I raise our glasses of Merlot in a toast to friendship. I smile every time I look at them.

To Henry, I raise a glass of good Polish vodka. Henry, you're the richest man I've ever known.

Na zdrowie! Cheers!

AN UNUSUAL OFFER

Phoenix, Arizona
November 2002

I stood outside a small, pleasant home at the end of a cul-de-sac. The Phoenix sun, blue sky, and cool breeze signaled perfect hiking weather on nearby South Mountain. Winter tourists and mountain bikers filled the trails on weekends. The incessant summer heat had finally receded.

The weathered front door sported a small, beribboned straw wreath adorned with American flags. I was there because, two days earlier, I received a random phone tip about a Polish gentleman who'd survived a great deal. I saw the call as a lucky break, as I was just back from vacation and fresh out of story ideas. I'd reached out and set an appointment right away, always looking for unique stories.

I knocked, the door swung open wide, and a friendly, attractive woman in her seventies gushed a warm hello and ushered me in.

"Hi, doll. Come in. Come in. I'm Nancy. Henry's waiting for you." Her distinctive Bronx accent immediately reminded me of my grandmother Gertrude, who lived her entire life near New York City.

Behind her stood a tall, thin, but muscular, silver-haired gentleman, his pink polo shirt a bright contrast against his tan. Smiling a big welcome, I swore I saw a twinkle in his eyes.

I reached out to shake hands. Instead he lifted my right hand, bowed slightly, kissed the back of it, and said simply, "Hi. I'm Henry." Somewhat startled, I realized the interview had already begun with an intriguing and unexpected greeting.

I followed Henry through an efficient, bright kitchen. The smell of freshly brewed coffee mixed with the vanilla scent of a flickering candle on the counter greeted me as we passed through a sliding glass door to a pleasant screened-in patio. In the far corner, a dusty exercise bike stood next to an aging couch, its brown leather seat cushions cracked like a dry desert wash. Through the screen, I saw petunias and other colorful flowers edging a small rock-filled side yard. Lush bougainvillea climbed the block wall in full scarlet bloom, smiling at the morning sun.

He directed me to one of four chairs encircling a brown, metal patio table. As I pulled the chair out, it squeaked a small protest as it slid across the concrete patio. He pulled out the opposite chair, which squeaked in reply, and sat down expectantly. A small stack of worn paperbacks lay next to a thick file of newspaper clippings. I drew out my notepad, ready to begin our interview.

Nancy still hovered behind me.

"Doll, can I get you some coffee? Tea? Water? Anything?"

"No thanks, Nancy. I'm good."

I'd just finished my second cup of morning coffee, so I wasn't thirsty. Besides, I tended to be clumsy and sometimes knocked glasses over. The last thing I wanted to do was look unprofessional and spill anything in this lovely couple's home.

Satisfied, Nancy slid the glass door closed, waved through the glass, and left to do her own errands.

In sixty minutes, I had more than enough information to fill my allotted six hundred words. Henry spoke of Olympic athletes and a lifetime as a competitive swimmer and trainer. I'd gotten a glimpse of original photos, and he told me a few stories from Auschwitz that I'd never heard before. During our interview, he pulled out a faded photocopy of a magazine article about the liberation of Auschwitz.

"See this? See these skinny people behind the fence. That was me at the end of the war."

For some reason I barely noticed his thick Polish accent. Who cared if he mixed up verb tenses, as do so many immigrants? Like most Americans, I'd never needed a second language outside of the obligatory two years of Spanish required to graduate high school and college. I can manage a *¿Como esta usted?* but not much more. I have always envied and respected anyone who is fluent in at least two languages.

I truly regretted I'd only allotted one hour for the interview, but my to-do list for the day stretched way longer than the few hours available before I picked up my three kids after school at three. I reluctantly said goodbye, gathered up my notes, and promised to let Henry and Nancy know when the story would run in the paper.

The rest of the day passed quickly. I sat down at my computer in the corner of the family room to draft my column, then worked on a myriad of household chores. I picked up my kids from school: Devin, age fourteen; and my eleven-year-old twins, Jamie and Derrick. After a snack, homework began around the kitchen table. I sat down at the computer to polish the article before sending it off to my editor.

As dinner approached, I thought gratefully how I'd pulled a tray of homemade lasagna out of the freezer that morning. While I put the broccoli on to steam, Jamie buttered the garlic bread, and Derrick set the table. Devin would wash the dishes later. All three were eager to learn to cook. The house rule: if you cook, someone else does the dishes. No one liked washing dishes.

My husband, Rick, walked in the door, washed up, and we sat down for dinner. It was Jamie's turn to say grace.

"God is great. God is good. And we thank Him for our food. Amen."

I grew up with that grace, and it's the only one I remember. All the kids know it in their sleep.

"Guess what I learned in science class today, Mom," Jamie grinned. "Mushrooms have sex."

Rick didn't miss a beat. "Then they must do it *very* slowly."

The next morning, after I dropped kids off at school, I came home, threw in a load of whites, and poured myself a second cup of coffee. As the washing machine churned nearby, I sat down at the kitchen table and settled in to read the morning newspaper. A small headline in the "Lifestyle" section popped out at me.

"Auschwitz Survivor Talks to Local High School." The woman was quoted as saying, "It's important to teach the younger generations the real history. My family stays alive as long as I hold up their memory."

An impulsive, crazy idea started percolating. I stared at that headline, wondered if it was a sign, and tried to shake the thought.

My logical self said, "What the hell are you thinking?"

My insecure self said, "No way."

My impulsive self said, "Why the hell not?"

Just then, my good friend Pam knocked on the door and walked in without waiting for an answer, holding her half-empty cup of coffee. For us, a knock was a mere formality.

We both stopped to refill mugs and then moved outside to my sunny patio, overlooking a yard barren of much adornment save plain grass and a swing set at the far end. Pam and I each pulled out two chairs from the round patio table, one to sit in and the other to prop our feet on as we cradled our warm mugs.

Among many things I love about Pam, although she has six kids to my three, she's never stressed. She is the only other mom in the neighborhood I know, is crazy smart, and keeps me sane. We've come to spend a lot of time together. She knows me well and I trust her instincts.

Between sips, I told her about Henry and a couple of the stories he'd already told me. My gut instinct insisted there was a huge, underwater iceberg of unique stories at risk of being lost forever. Besides, I'm a history geek, reader of biographies, and believer in happily ever after.

Pam mused matter-of-factly, "If no one else wants those stories, then you need to get them. There must be a reason you met him."

Two days later, impulse and naiveté won. I picked up the phone and dialed Henry's number. This time, Henry answered the phone.

"Henry, what do you think of writing a book together? You've got the stories and I've got the English and writing skills. What do you say?"

I sensed his surprise, or maybe pride, that a total stranger would be so interested and bold. Only years later did I realize just how unusual an offer I'd made. No one, and I mean no one, just calls up a stranger, offers to write his or her story, *and* work for free.

He agreed and we set up our first official "book" interview. I bought a tape recorder, microphone, and two thin travel guides to Kraków. They were the only Kraków travel guides for sale at the bookstore, both printed in Britain, yet each spelled the name differently. One spelled the city as "Cracow" and the other as "Kraków." Clearly, in 2002, Poland was definitely not the tourist mecca on par with Prague, Paris, and Pompeii.

But, I wondered to myself, *couldn't they at least spell the city the same way?*

As I stood at the cashier and paid for the thin guidebooks, I remembered a lesson my father tried to teach me years ago. Be careful what you ask for. You might get it.

What had I just agreed to do?

ARREST: KRAKÓW 1942

Kraków, Poland
May 30, 1942

HENRY TELLS HIS STORY:

I was walking down the narrow street, right behind the Planty. Someone had told me the Germans were looking for young boys to round up, so I was making a big circle around the Main Market Square. Every single door and window was boarded up, nobody on the street. I was on my way to the YMCA to be with my friends. I didn't make it. All the doors on the street were closed and locked. The people knew to lock the doors before the Germans began arresting.

I come around the bend, and here comes a big truck, with the [German] SS guards walking in front of it, holding big guns. One of the SS waved his hand towards himself, signaling to me. *"Kommen Sie hier. Kommen Sie hier."* [Come here.]

The other three or four soldiers kept their guns pointed at me. What are you going to do? I was twenty-four at the time and they looked to be the same age as me. I felt secure because I had good German papers from working at Freege. I turned and walked right up to face them. They politely asked, "Are you Jewish? Polish? Deutscher? [German?]"

I decided to answer in my best high school German. "*Alt Deutscher Staat. Jawohl!*"

[I'm from old German country. Yes, sir!]

Alt means ancient, almost pre-historic. Why? Because long ago, Germans had claimed Kraków as the old German city. Of course, that was a thousand years ago. Now, Kraków was under German rule again.

So, what do they give me? They give me a punch in the nose and a kick in the ass, and I find myself in the back of the truck. There I find my friends, about twenty of them from the YMCA. The Germans picked up the entire basketball team, a couple guys from the boxing team, and footballers, all strong guys. I was the only water polo player they got that day. We kept whispering back and forth, "Heh, where are they taking us? What are they doing with us?"

So, someone decided we should eat any papers that had names, addresses, or phone numbers on them.

The truck started rolling slowly and didn't drive too long. It came to a stop, we heard some orders, and the truck drove through the gates of Montelupich prison and stopped inside the large courtyard. Some SS guards threw open the flaps, then stood back with guns pointed at us, lights shining down.

I'd been by this building before; it's not far from downtown Kraków. The Montelupich family built it as their manor four hundred years ago; the park across the street used to be the manor's gardens. In the 1800s, the Austrians made it a prison when they ruled over Kraków. They covered the tall windows in bars. Now, all I saw was barbed wire and glass on top of the walls. I didn't have time to look around as the guards pointed their guns at us and shouted, "*Raus. Raus.*" [Out. Out.]

They hurried us into the cellar of the big building. There were about two or three hundred of us in the dark cement room. We kept whispering to ourselves because we had no idea what to do.

The next morning, about forty of us were moved to an L-shaped transport cell on the main floor. The Germans did release three men as *Volksdeutsche* [German nationals living in Poland]. In the corner of the room, there was a barrel of excrement by these big, heavy doors that slid on a track. There was also a big, tiled oven, and only one twenty-five-watt bulb hanging from the ceiling to light the entire room. Everyone take a seat somewhere by the wall. You get nothing to sleep on, but you take up some space and make do, even though the cement was cold. We talked. Some guys still had matches on them, and someone had a stubby pencil, so we pooled the matchbook covers and made a deck of cards to play bridge. It was something to pass the time.

The first day, nothing.

The second day, interrogations.

One by one, we are taken out to the SS room. An SS officer sat at a table and two other guards stood by. I stood facing the table, but not too close. He looked at me with no expression on his face. Then, the questions began.

"Tell us about your underground activities."

I don't know what you're talking about.

Whap! Whap! One of the guards beat me from behind on my head and back with a heavy wooden stick, like he was swinging a baseball bat.

"Did you listen to the radio?"

No! I screamed in pain as the guard beat me again.

My interrogator's voice got louder. "What? You're a high school graduate and you're telling me you didn't hear the BBC on the radio?"

No!

Whap! Whap! Whap! Now, the blood is running down my face. I can barely stand.

"What? You didn't see the notes the BBC drop from the airplane?"

No! By now I almost fainted.

"That's it. Pants off. Now!"

I remember this as clearly as yesterday because it hurt like hell, more pain than I ever have in my life. They had a Pencala brand pen—an expensive fountain pen with a sharp point. You can write with it; it was long and thick like a stick. They kept hitting me down there, with the sharp point. I screamed until I passed out. They throw me out of the room onto the hard cement floor in the hallway and throw my clothes on top of me. I crawled back to the holding room in agony, the guard kicking me if I stopped moving. Behind me, I heard it start all over with the next guy they took in the room.

After the first beating they give us two days to recuperate.

I always looked for a way to get out. I was the one who volunteered to carry the slop bucket out every morning. It meant I got out of the room, even for a few minutes. I was the only one who went outside that came back into the room after leaving. Everyone else, once they left they never came back.

On the third day, the process started all over again. One by one, they dragged us out of our holding room.

I remember when we were waiting for the interrogation, lined up in the hall, they tell us to face the wall, heads to the wall. You don't move or talk or they hit you. I tried to whisper something to my friend next to me but they heard me. Bam! They shoved my head against the stone wall.

Among the forty of us in the holding cell, there were two priests and a famous Olympic skier, Stanley Marusarz. In the 1936 Olympics, he ranked seventh in the world for ski jumping, and now I get to meet him. He also was one of the very few who ever escaped from Montelupich Prison. He survived the war and competed in the 1948 and 1952 Olympics, but I never see him again.

Our holding cell was on the ground floor of the prison. Some windows had bars on them. Someone found a towel, and the two strongest guys soaked it in the slop bucket to get it wet, then wrapped it around two of the bars like a tourniquet. They bent those bars and made an opening just big enough for a grown man to squeeze through. Stan and two other guys decided to make a run for it. Stan jumped out first, ran to a ten-foot high fence that had glass and barbed wire on top. The second guy jumped out the window and ran to the fence. Stan tried to help him up the wall, but he didn't make it up the fence and the Germans shot him in the back. The third one got out the window, but the Germans shot him before he even got to the fence. Only Stanley got away.

A few days after that episode, two kitchen cooks from the SS kitchen came into the room, went to one of the window's bars and jarred one of the bars just a little loose. They were laughing as they did it. They left, and we dismissed it.

Around 10 p.m., just as we're about to sleep, the SS major came in the room drunk like hell. He went straight to that window and demanded, "Who did that?"

One of the professors who was with us spoke up in German.

"*Jawohl, Herr Major,* two German soldiers came in this morning and did that."

The SS major got all red in the face and yelled at the poor guy.

"What, are you crazy? Two German soldiers?"

He grabbed that professor, slapped him up the side of the head, threw him to the ground and kicked him two or three times. As the professor lay there, the SS major then turned his drunken face to the rest of us with his pistol pointed at us.

Suddenly there was one boy in this corner by the oven. He started shaking, and then said, "I know who did it."

The German major ordered him, "Come here."

So, this kid goes to the center of the room. He went into a spasm and fainted.

The drunk SS major starts pointing at us randomly and picks out ten of us. I was holding the bridge "cards" in my hand, so I was sure that's what he saw. Then, he turns and points directly at me with his pistol. I'm a dead guy for sure.

"*Nicht du!*" [Not you!] And he waves his gun behind me.

I'm taller than most of the guys. I didn't know some short guy moved to hide behind me. The major saw the movement and grabbed this small kid from behind me, and marched him out with the other nine he'd already picked out. Ten minutes later we heard *rat a tat tat tat tat* out in the courtyard. We heard the shots, and I just kept shaking. I leaned my back against the wall, slid down to the floor and put my head in my hands. Now, we were down to twenty-four men.

On June 15, they told us to get dressed and line up. The guards marched us out to the courtyard where a transport truck stood waiting for us. We had no idea where we were going. The truck left Montelupich, followed the outskirts of Kraków, heading west through the woods. The drive was no more than an hour. We kept peeking out under the flaps. As we neared our destination, I saw men in blue-grey striped uniforms working along the road. I recognized two brothers who were my friends. Karol and Wilik Tomaszczyk were pulling a wooden cart on two wheels, sort of like a flat wheelbarrow. Wilik recognized me and signaled, "Henry, you're going to be all right," as we drove past. I remember thinking that was a good sign. I tell the other guys,

"If they can do it, we can do it."

As we came through the gates to a camp of sorts with red brick buildings, we drove under a sign in German that said "*Arbeit Macht Frei* [Work Makes You Free]." I had no idea what this place was, but I remember feeling great relief. I'd always been a hard worker. This had to be better than Montelupich prison.

PART 1

THE SECOND POLISH REPUBLIC

1918–1939

Henry Zguda's First Communion. Undated.
Henry Zguda's personal photo album.

HENRY AND I BEGIN

A week after our first meeting, I arrived at nine in the morning and rang the doorbell. Nancy again opened the door wide and ushered me in. I had to smile back at this friendly woman who gushed hospitality.

"Hi, doll. Come in. Come in. I'm so glad you came back. I've been after Henry for years to write his stories, and he never did. We tried, but it's very hard. There are just so many stories, where do you start? Now you're here. Thank goodness."

I followed Nancy out to the same patio where Henry and I held our first interview. Before we even passed through the same efficient kitchen, I recognized the smell of fresh brewed coffee and, that time, a cinnamon-apple scented candle. As I passed by the fridge, I noticed my newspaper column about Henry posted prominently on the refrigerator.

Henry rose to greet me. I, again, extended my right hand to shake as the usual American sign of greeting and also as agreement on our new joint project. Again, he lifted my hand and kissed the back of it.

Nancy still hovered behind us.

"Doll, I have fresh coffee. Can I get you some? I can make you tea, too."

"No thanks, Nancy. I'm good."

"Well then, can I get you some cake? Let me get you a slice."

"No, really Nancy, thanks. I'm still good." I would soon learn that Nancy offered food and drink to anyone who came through the front door. She seldom accepted no for an answer. It was characteristic of growing up in a large Italian family in the Bronx, which she said she always missed.

We both smiled, and she again slid the glass door shut and went on her way. I was instantly glad I suggested this project. Even if the story didn't pan out, I'd met two very welcoming, nice people.

Henry and I took a seat at the patio table.

This time, a bowl of chocolates and nuts sat nearby. The same thick, brown photo album he'd shown me on our first visit rested on the table next to a few well-worn and yellowed paperbacks. I quickly scanned titles such as *The Case Against Adolf Eichmann* by Henry A. Zeiger, *Inside the Third Reich* by Albert Speer, and a few volumes in Polish. Henry turned and slid his chair closer to me until we were almost side by side, and opened the photo album. Forget any thought of archival quality photo storage. The aging photos were all glued on those sticky pages with a peel-back plastic film, already yellowed, the album barely held together with brown duct tape.

I pulled out a folder with my business card, resume, and writing samples to ask Henry's permission to write his story. He asked me what he should pay me. We discussed drafting a formal agreement, and I took notes to draft one for our next visit. As to money, I said we would settle that later, as we worked on the project together. Money never was the goal of this project.

I set up my tape recorder, plugged in the microphone, slid it toward Henry and pressed *Record.* I pulled out my notepad and pen, ready to take notes as he talked.

Henry gave me a big smile. "Very nice article you wrote. I send it to my friends in Sweden, Poland, and Belgium. You're international now."

I accepted the comment as a form of congratulations, and a sign of more international connections in this story.

Left-right, Henry's mother Karolina Zguda, Henry,
Henry's great-grandmother, Henry's Aunt Antonia, 1919.
Henry Zguda's personal photo album.

He lifted up a framed photo of a young boy in a white suit.
"See, wasn't I a nice boy?"

Henry grinned at his own joke as he pointed to his First
Communion photo. He turned to the album and flipped the first
few pages. There were exactly four photos of him before about
age sixteen and they were all school photos. Henry then pointed
to a small, very old, sepia-toned photo. There were two young
women who looked no older than eighteen or nineteen years
old, standing on either side of a seated, very stern older woman.

I doubt a smile had ever graced the woman's face. One of the young women held a young toddler up by his arms.

This is my mother, me, my aunt Antonia, and my great grandmother. When my great grandmother was younger, she was a maid in the czar's palace in Leningrad. I always thought of her as being a hundred years old. For a while, she lived with us. I didn't like her at all. She was always after me. "Henyu don't do this. Henyu don't do that. Henyu clean this." My family all called me Henyu [Hen-you]. My whole life I've never done well with someone giving me orders.

And when she died, at the moment, she had a big coffer, a big trunk, and the black iron bands across it, very heavy. It was the secret of our family. Everyone waited years to see what she has got in there. Maybe money, maybe something. My mother has four sisters, and four brothers—eight together. After the funeral, all the relatives came with the ax and tried to open this trunk. I remember I was sitting in the corner of the room on a stool.

Finally, one of the uncles swings the ax and breaks the lock. First, out comes the dress from when she was a maid. Then, the dress when she was dancing as a young girl. Funny, Russian style.

Next, the relatives found some jewelry, but just some cheap, costume stuff. Finally, there on the bottom of the trunk lay a thick envelope. Ah, so there was the money everyone counted on. Sure enough, the envelope was full of money. Inside, the uncles found 100,000 Russian rubles from 1917 when the czar was still in power. For 100,000 rubles you could have bought two or three villages with all the peasants in them.

Henry had been laughing since he started the story. Now, he chuckled as he recalled the look on his relatives' faces.

Except now the czar was dead and the money was worthless. Everyone was laughing like hell except for my uncle John. Uncle John was the richest one in the family.

Curious, I had to ask something. "Why was he the richest?"

Uncle John was a barber. He was so tough. He owned a barbershop, money coming in every day. You buy a pot, you buy it once. But, when you cut hair, people always come back when their hair grows. It was a good barbershop. I remember he would look at my hair, at the thickness and flexibility, and make predictions. A good barber knows his customers.

He tells me, "Henry, you are very timid. You don't go too far in life. But you're going to go far away from here."

After that, Uncle John was very, very upset and talked to no one for a week.

Henry kept grinning, then turned his attention back to the photo album and continued on.

I did not know my father, Wincenty Zguda, at all. He was made to join the Galician Austrian army in World War I. They were in the trenches near the Po River in Italy, in plenty of mud, water, and rain, with mosquitos big as birds flying around. So, he got the malaria disease.

I wasn't sure I'd heard Henry correctly.

"Wait. Henry, don't you mean the Polish army?"

No, No. There was no Poland then.

At that moment, I truly began to realize how little I knew about Poland, and just how much I'd have to learn. I was not even sure if it was Cracow or Kraków, and Henry just said there was no Poland? Right there in the first interview, the scope of the project doubled. As I mulled the idea of no Poland, Henry continued his story.

He came home from the war when I was about one and a half years old. One day, he's jumping off the bed, you know, like a shake, a seizure. He land on the floor. My mother, Karolina, have to pick him up. She called for help, and orderlies finally come and take him to some hospital in Berlin. She didn't know which one, and we never heard anything again. So, we don't know where he is.

Henry stops, smiles, and points to the ceiling as if to heaven. Well, now we know where he is, but not at that time.

"Do you have a photo of your father?" I asked.

No. No photo. My mother was a very tough lady from the mountains. She came from the *Górale* people, a peasant people from the southern mountains of Poland. *Górale* are poor, but tough. Independent. She survived. I survive. I have her facial features, sort of dark with a big nose. She was very short, not like me. Henry is my American spelling. In Poland my name was Henryk. My mother and friends called me Henyu. Until I was about seven, we lived with my two aunts, uncle, and four cousins in a two-room apartment.

Though Henry had many cousins, the only two he ever spoke of by name were Wladyslaw and Stanislaus, who were like brothers to him. In the album, photos of him with these two cousins scatter across multiple pages in later years.

We live on the nice street in Kraków, Stefan Batory, who was a king of Poland, in sixteenth century, 1575–1586. He was famous for saving Europe from Turks taking over. Eventually, my mother get a job in the state tobacco factory and we moved into a small apartment on Panska Street.

Breakfast is a piece of bread, you wet it a little, and a small sprinkle of sugar on it. You know we have a specialty in Poland I love: kasza. It's a grain. You go to the store and buy the kasza grain, put it on to steam, and it grows big and tasty. Then, you top it with real sour milk, not the buttermilk we have here. Mmm good.

In Poland, sour milk was made from full milk. On the border of the city, when the peasants carried the milk to town, the inspector would test the milk for fat. If there was not too much fat, he turned them away and wouldn't let them sell it. Why? The fat was for the children; they needed it to grow.

At this point Henry chuckled again, shrugged and lifted both his palms up in semi-frustration.

You know, I can't recognize skim milk in this country; it's like water and you pay double. In Poland, if you sold skim milk you went to jail. No one there was allowed to skim the fat for themselves. Children need the fat to grow. Here, people actually give their children skim milk.

I'll tell you what else makes no sense to me at all in this country. You watch television and there are all kinds of ads for weight-loss programs. I don't understand why people pay to lose weight. Losing weight is so simple—stop eating. Then, you save money. Let me tell you, under communism you stand in lines forever just to get food. Why pay more money to eat less food? That makes no sense to me at all.

Henry just held up his hands and shook his head at the twisted logic of paying to not eat, as I subconsciously reached for another piece of chocolate, ignoring that inch I could pinch.

AN OVERVIEW OF POLAND

T he evolution of Poland that led to Henry's statement, "No, no, there was no Poland at that time," deserves a brief discussion. Poland's world position in the twentieth century and many of the biases and cultural divides in place during Henry's life resulted from centuries of conflict.

Poland lies squarely positioned in central Europe, between her two historical enemies, Germany and Russia. Poles have always had to defend themselves against outside powers wishing to annex or destroy their lands. From the Polish Golden Age in the sixteenth century, through 1989, the country experienced dozens of border changes in four hundred years. Like several other countries in Europe, there are no natural geographic boundaries that help define Poland's eastern and western borders, or make them easy to defend. Outside powers have always wanted the benefits of Poland's strategic location along trade routes, rich farmlands, coal, and other natural resources. For centuries, the pattern of all invaders was to commit wholesale slaughter against the Poles and destroy villages, farms, and whatever else they could after they stole anything of value.

Most historians agree that Poland's true golden age stretched from the end of the fifteenth century up until it began to decline in the early seventeenth century, ending in 1648 with the Swedish invasion. Kraków University, which was soon renamed Jagiellonian University, was founded in 1364 as the second

university in all of Europe. Though it struggled for a while, by
the fifteenth century it flourished, attracting students from all of
Europe, and firmly established the city of Kraków as a center of
learning. In 1491, Nicolaus Copernicus enrolled in Jagiellonian
University to study astronomy, later joining the priesthood. He
is known for postulating the heliocentric philosophy that the
planets revolve around the sun, and not the Earth. The results
were quietly published in 1543 after his death, twenty years before
the Italian astronomer Galileo was born. Galileo would later
champion the same heliocentric philosophy of Copernicus, only
to face persecution and condemnation from the Catholic Church.

By 1600, the Polish Commonwealth was the largest state
in Europe, occupying a geographic area nearly three times
the size of Texas. The population of approximately ten million
was twice that of England, or equal to that of Italy, Spain, and
Portugal combined. Poland differed in philosophy from other
European countries led by dynasties, such as the Hapsburgs
of Austria and the Tudors of England. Where the royal leaders
sought to increase control of the individual and maintain their
centralized power, Poles took the opposite approach with the
conviction that no man had the right to tell another what to
do. Noblewomen enjoyed the same property and inheritance
rights as noblemen. The disdain for authority and respect for
the dignity of the individual were evident from the Middle Ages,
and would eventually lead to a short-lived democracy in the
eighteenth century. The ideal of individual freedom, at least for
the nobility, fed a strong desire and belief in an independent
Poland that has existed for centuries.

Unfortunately, an inefficient government structure, and
a lover's triangle would set the stage for Poland's eventual
demise. The Polish nobility considered themselves the highest
authority in the land. Membership in the nobility was inherited,
peasants had few rights, and kings were elected by the nobility.
Any Catholic nobleman—citizen or foreigner—could run for
the position. In the vein of independent spirit, or perhaps a
stratagem by the nobility to ensure no one acted against them,
they eventually instituted the flawed concept of *Liberum Veto*,
or rule by unanimous vote. In the Polish assembly, or Sejm, no
proposal could become law and no decision was binding, if even

one person voted in opposition. The vote for royal elections had to be unanimous. Imagine any government trying to function with unanimity—nothing would get done. Thus, it shouldn't be surprising that, despite a population of more than eleven million people and a large geographic territory, Poland never developed a strong central government, central treasury, or substantial standing army. In the early eighteenth century, ninety percent of Poles lived in poverty or service to nobles. Despite a proud heritage, the country fell victim to stronger powers, though not without a valiant fight.

Catherine the Great ruled Russia from 1762 until her death in 1796 at the age of sixty-seven. She came from a ruling family in Germany, and had strong ties there. She ascended to power after she had her husband arrested, forced him to abdicate, and subsequently had him murdered by the brother of her current lover. She took many paramours throughout her reign. One of her earliest lovers before she took the throne was Stanisław Poniatowski, a member of Polish nobility. He fathered one of her children, then she subsequently forced him out of the Russian court. Sensing he would be an ineffective leader, Catherine maneuvered politically to help get Poniatowski elected king of Poland in 1763, and placed Russian armies in Poland "to help protect" the country.

When Poland enacted a constitution in 1791, it was the first-ever such document in Europe, and only the third in the world, after the young United States ratified its constitution. Prussia, Russia, and Austria strongly opposed an independent country, especially so close to their borders, lest the spirit of independence spread and incite their own citizens to rise up against their respective monarchies. To divide and divvy up Poland, Catherine the Great used her connections to lead a three-way coalition of Russia to the east, the Prussian empire to the west—the precursor to modern day Germany—and the Austrian empire to the south. Russia, by far, gained the greatest amount of territory in the move. By 1795, Poland disappeared from the map of Europe.

When Poland was partitioned, Warsaw and eastern Poland fell under Russian oversight; Kraków came under Austrian rule, and the western areas came under German dominance.

The Austrians treated Kraków far better than the Russians did Warsaw. The Austrians gained land, but were predominantly Catholic—like most of the Poles in their newly acquired territory—and hated the Germans and Russians despite their strategic alliance.

The Austrians modernized the city by introducing running water, electricity, and the first electric streetcars. When the original medieval city walls crumbled, the Austrians tore them down and, by the 1820s, converted the area to a beautiful fifty-two-acre greenbelt known as the Planty, which encircles and defines the original downtown Kraków. The beautiful park is filled with hundred-year-old chestnut trees, lighted walking paths, benches, and monuments. A walk around the entire park is about two and a half miles, and begins and ends at Wawel Castle overlooking the Vistula River.

During World War I, more than 400,000 Poles died and 900,000 were wounded fighting in three different armies: Russian, Prussian, and Austrian. In 1918, one year after Henry Zguda was born, Poland regained her independence as a nation. The newly independent Poland became referred to as the Second Polish Republic.

GROWING UP IN KRAKÓW

HENRY CONTINUES:

My mother worked long days at the state tobacco factory. I was very lonely. After school, I found my friends on the Planty.

"Planty, Henry? What's a Planty?"

That's the park around Kraków.

I pulled out the city guide to Kraków I'd brought, and opened it to a map of historic, downtown Kraków. I held it out for Henry and handed him my pen to mark places as he talked about them.

Here's the Zakopianka where my friends played. There were benches and beautiful *kasztan* [chestnut] trees all around the park. Here's where I live with my cousins.

As Henry spoke, he marked Xs on the map for each place he pointed to.

My mother worked all day. I go to the park. I had many, many friends. I remember one friend, Karol Lolek Swolinski, who lived in my apartment house. We used to play in destroyed houses and crawl around in caves, any place we could explore. He ran away to join the circus. Son of a gun, six months later I get a postcard from Bombay, India, with a picture of a circus, signed Karol Swolinski, Circus Attendant.

Then, I had a friend who became famous. He was Jan Owczazyk. Now, there's a good Polish name for you.

Henry laughed at me and patiently spelled out Jan's last name, as he did with all Polish names. One particular day, when he spelled out about four complicated Polish names in a row for me, I complained about what a hard language Polish was because of all the consonants. Henry had a ready answer.

I know Polish is hard for Americans. But, really, it's Polish that is so simple. It's English that's hard. Why would any language have two and three words that sound the same and mean different things? *Steel* and *steal*. *They're*, *there*, and *their*. *Its* and *It's*. That makes no sense to me. Polish doesn't do that. You should learn Polish, then we could really talk.

Henry returned to his story.

Jan was involved in soccer and sports with me. But he was a very nervous type. He was the only one of my friends who was famous, because he killed his grandmother with the weight of a grandfather clock. You know the weights. He was arrested and went to prison. We never see him again.

I have game for you: *palant*. All you needed was a piece of broomstick, cut about eight inches.

Henry held his hands out to demonstrate the length, then continued his story.

For yourself, you need a good stick, like the length of a table or chair leg, or a piece of branch. With *palant* you need a big field. We played like baseball, except with sticks. So, you hit this piece of wood this way and that. I remember one day I hit that stick right through the window of the Zakopianka restaurant. We ran like hell.

Henry laughed heartily at the memory.

We also played soccer. We make our own balls. You take old socks, rags, and whatever you can find, make it into a ball, get it wet, and go around it tightly with a cord. You do this until the rags are the size of a soccer ball. One of us was always making one. They lasted for an entire game if you make it good enough.

We'd also do running and make marathons around all of Kraków. Once a year we'd have a big race. I lived near the rail station. So, we ran around the entire outskirts.

Again, I brought out the travel guide and turned to the map of central Kraków for Henry to mark specific places.

And then here, and here, and here; those son-of-a-guns cut through.

Henry then referred to the map of Kraków and pointed to where they took a shortcut without running the full circuit.

"They cheated?"

Sure. Everyone did. You just had to do it so you didn't get caught. No one organized it but us. When you went past the Wawel Castle, you could cut and save about a mile. It was worth it because no one could see you take the shortcut. We were all fast runners.

My friends and I had our own circle on the Planty we called the Zakopianka because it was near the Zakopianka restaurant. The real action was *Guziki*. Buttons. We played it all the time. Anytime my mother don't know where I was, she brings the broomstick or the rug beater to the park, give me a beating and chase me home. She was always mad I was sitting on my schoolwork instead of doing my homework.

Henry smiled again.

I liked the rug beater better than the poker—it was softer. There were many times I'd be two or three hours late coming home and then she'd come looking for me.

"I've never heard of Buttons. How do you play?"

They have good buttons, big buttons, like from a winter coat. You know, good size, like two inches thick. What you do then, you rub and scrape them on the street to smooth and polish them on the bottom so they slide easier. Then, you make an even button so they slide.

I handed Henry a blank sheet of paper so he could draw a diagram of the game. I always do better with visual examples.

See here, this is the bench. You make a mark with a scissor or knife . . . here's the goal . . .

He stopped to grin and wink at me. Sarcastically, he offered up one disadvantage. "You know, Buttons was very dangerous. Those benches were old, so many times I go to slide and miss, and get a big splinter in my hand, and then I'm like, 'Aw shit.'"

Henry went on to explain and diagram a simple game, scored like soccer and played with nothing more than a comb, stolen buttons, a slice of cork, and a wooden park bench. Henry demonstrated how to "flick" the comb down to make the "cue ball" button slam a slice of cork into the goal. Like soccer or football, if the cork passed between the other team's goal, you scored.

Of course, my mother always beat me if I tried to sneak buttons because she needed them on the coat. Many of my friends and I didn't have fathers with big coats at home, so we had to attract other boys to steal from their fathers. My team, we always have the best Buttons players, we always beat the other teams because we know how to get the buttons. Sometimes I trade candy for buttons.

"Where did you get the candy?"

Mostly we have to buy it. But my friend, Haubenstauch, his family have a deli. I'd grab a handful of candies for my pocket. But there's another way my team get the best buttons. I don't know if I should tell you.

He looked at me slyly, then grinned.

"Henry, now that you said that, I'm really curious. Go ahead."

We traded used condoms.

I blurted out, "You're kidding. Seriously?"

Yeah. You clean them up and you can make balloons. They were a big attraction for some.

Kraków was very religious. Churches on every street. This corner is Saint Nikolas, this corner Saint John, one block down Saint Whoever. That's a lot. Every Sunday at twelve noon the Saint Mary Church held an obligatory mass—everyone always took their wives, children, and families. Of course, there was the Church of St. John. It always stink back there. What you gonna do? The men, they can't hold it any longer. You sit in long mass, but no public bathrooms. That's also where the cheap prostitutes hung out as well, behind Saint John's.

So, we just go there, and we can find one, two, three condoms every night.

Henry Zguda in front of St. Mary's Church in Kraków. Undated.
United States Holocaust Memorial Museum, gift of Nancy Zguda.

ST. MARY'S CHURCH
AND ALTARPIECE

Henry turned to a new page in his photo album and pointed to a small, wallet-sized, black-and-white photo of himself as a young man in his twenties. He was dressed in a suit and stood facing the camera. Behind him towered a tall, brick church with dual church spires rising up toward the sky. The vertical lines were square and straight, not unlike Notre Dame Cathedral in Paris. But, as I looked at the church, I was struck that the dual towers existed as completely different styles. The left tower appeared to be far more ornate than the second, shorter, plain tower to the right. Henry must have read my mind, as he went on to explain the photo.

You know, St. Mary's Church is a very important church in Kraków. It is the central church in Kraków after Wawel Cathedral. See how the two towers are different: one is higher than the other. When you go right here, you can see the knife on the wall.

"Why would a church have a knife on the outside wall?" I asked.

That's an old story. Two brothers were building this church. Each brother was in charge of a tower. They were very jealous of each other, so each one kept trying to build his tower higher and better. When the older brother built his tower higher, the younger brother couldn't get over losing, so he killed his elder brother with a knife. Then, he was so upset, he killed himself with the same knife. So, still today one tower is shorter.

Inside the church you have a very tall Veit Stoss altar, carved in wood, in the fifteenth century. There's a centerpiece and two sidepieces, and it opens up. It is very famous, worth millions of dollars. It's a very important piece of art in Poland. The faces are all out of wood.

He turned his attention to the picture again. See the taller tower? There's the room for the fireman with the big cornet. My neighbor Cyprian Dultz took me up there many times when he played the Hejnal.

Then Henry shaped his hands like a trumpet and sounded a short tune. Dah-dah, dadada dah, da— He abruptly stopped mid-note.

Cyprian was a member of the fire brigade. He was trained as one of the trumpeters of Kraków—four hours fire brigade, four hours trumpet duty. We'd climb many, many stairs to the top of the taller tower. On each side there was one window. He'd go to one window, open it, play the tune, then pull it closed and go to the window on the next side, until he'd played once each of the four directions.

The song stops in the middle in memory of the bugler the Tatars shot in the throat with an arrow centuries ago. From the fourteenth century, every day, someone plays the trumpet, even during the German occupation. At that time, someone played the trumpet every hour, all day and night.

••

St. Mary's Church anchors the huge Main Market Square in central Kraków. Founded in 1222, it faces east, which is typical of the time. After the Tatar invaders—the precursors to Mongols—burned it down, it was rebuilt on the original foundation and enlarged in several phases. Between 1477 and 1489, the artist Veit Stoss carved its most valuable piece of art: the main altarpiece done in five parts—one central carving, and two side carvings, both front and back. The intricately carved, wooden masterpiece stands a majestic thirty-six feet high and forty-two feet wide, and is the largest Gothic altarpiece in the world. The two sidepiece carvings depict one scene while open and another while closed.

The altar remains a huge symbol of Polish pride and culture. During World War II, Germans dismantled it and shipped it back to Germany, along with other priceless works of Polish art. In his book *The Monuments Men*, author Robert M. Edsel refers to the Veit Stoss altarpiece as one of Adolf Hitler's most cherished objects. Fortunately, it was recovered unharmed in 1946, from the basement of the Nuremberg castle where the Germans hid it.

Today, tourists plan their visits to the church to witness the ceremonial opening and closing of the altar every day at twelve noon. When I later visited Kraków, my husband and I made a point of standing in line early, to be in the front row to witness the ceremonial opening. I was stunned by its beauty, craftsmanship, and immense size. Henry's description was so understated, I realized he probably understated most other descriptions as well. There's a reason every travel guide to Kraków lists it as a must-see. The small, black and white photo in the guidebook gave little indication of its true beauty.

Today, the Hejnal bugle call, which has been a part of Kraków's history for almost as long as the altar, is a major tourist attraction in downtown Kraków. The Tatars had tried to overrun Poland for centuries, so Poles built thick walls around the town and positioned a trumpeter at the main gate to sound an alarm if he spotted invaders. According to legend, under one raid, the bugler sounded the alarm in time for the city to defend itself. Infuriated their attack failed, the attackers launched a barrage of arrows, one of which struck the bugler in the neck, stopping the tune mid-note. In memory of the brave guard who saved Kraków, the bugle call is sounded every hour, and always stops mid-note just as when the guard sounded it. Present-day, tourists crowd the Main Market Square at every hour, just to hear the famous bugle call. The only change in the centuries-old routine came after 2005. To commemorate his death, every April 2, at 9:47 in the evening, the bugler plays the favorite song of the beloved Saint John Paul II, who called Kraków his home for four decades.

There are several recordings of the bugle call on the internet if you enter "Hejnal of Kraków," or similar keywords, into a search engine. I never did see the knife near the main entryway that faces the Main Market Square—but tourists are discouraged from entering through the front entrance. Our walking-tour guide said a knife hangs in the church to remind thieves not to steal. Another travel guide said the knife now hangs in the large Cloth Hall across the Main Market Square. Choose your explanation.

HAPPY BIRTHDAY, HENRY

I arrived for our fourth interview session on December 6, the day before Henry's birthday. To surprise him, I stopped and bought a Happy Birthday balloon-on-a-stick and a small cake. In our short time together, I'd come to truly look forward to our interviews, and whatever new story he had that day. Henry was sharing his life with me one interview at a time, and teaching me about Poland and so many other places I'd either never heard of or only read about in history books.

Henry opened the door and smiled broadly with his usual, "Welcome back!"

I pulled the balloon from behind my back. "Happy Birthday, Henry!"

Henry's reaction wasn't what I expected. He was totally confused.

"What's this all about?"

"Henry, it's your birthday tomorrow. Happy Birthday!"

"No, no it's not my birthday. Why do you say that?"

This was not going like I expected, and I was not sure why.

"But Henry," I explained, "your identity papers all say 'born 12-7-1917.'"

Henry grinned and let out a huge laugh.

"No, no, my birthday is July 12. All Americans make that mistake. Europeans put the month before the day."

Darn it! I *knew* that. But my American brain just didn't register the difference.

Henry laughed generously and called out for Nancy.

"Nancy, Nancy, come in here. Look what she brought me!"

Nancy acted just as puzzled, but we all had a good laugh as we went inside. Nancy took the cake into the kitchen, sliced it into three pieces, and we sat down at a small, round, dining room table to share.

Henry saved that balloon for months until his J-U-L-Y birthday. Nancy later told me he smiled every time he looked at it.

A BEAUTIFUL VIEW

HENRY CONTINUES:

I lived at Panska 9 near the train station. There were two levels—all built around a central courtyard—and a roof. I figure out a shortcut to my friend on the second floor. I took the key to the attic, opened the door, walked through attic to the other side, crawled out a small window, and slid down the eave by the chimney. One day I am walking across, I slipped and then saw the most beautiful view. I see a small window, half covered in something, and inside there's the action. Such a beautiful view. A very famous painter, Wicenty Wodzinowski, lived in the apartment, and he had two daughters. There in the kitchen they are taking a shower.

I was so pleased that I tell my friends from school. The next day, they came with me when I went through the attic. There was almost no space for four of us to sit there on the eave; we almost fell. But my friends were very grateful to me. I should have charged admission, but I didn't. The girls were in their twenties then and very beautiful. It was worth it.

COWBOYS AND INDIANS

My mother was a good mother. She had no money, but she sent me to a good high school, a very expensive Catholic school on Sienna Street associated with the Dominicans. My school was known as the best humanistic school. We attended Holy Cross Church nearby. Around the Holy Cross Church at a certain time of year, there were beautiful, beautiful lilacs. Everyone come just to smell them and enjoy them.

"How did your mother pay for such an expensive school?"

She wanted me to associate with a better class of boys than the Planty. She worked very hard and found a job as a housekeeper for the Freege family. The Freeges were one of the richest families in Kraków at that time. They were very good to her and she was grateful. They owned a huge seed farm that shipped seeds all over Europe. Today, it would be Freege Dot Com. You know, that dot com business makes me nervous.

In school, we studied Greek, Latin, German, religion, gymnastics [physical education], math, physics, and chemistry. German was very important to know. I always liked the languages, especially Latin. You know, half of Polish is based on Latin. I still have papers with favorite Latin sayings they use right now in this country. *Si vis pacem para bellum.* If you want peace, prepare for war. That's still true today.

Morituri te salutant. We who are about to die salute you. This was the saying of the gladiators before they fight.

De mortuis nil nisi bonum. Only the good is spoken of the dead.

I didn't do too well in mathematics or sciences. On a scale of one being the best, I'd get twos in the languages, and fours in math and science.

During my high school years, about 1933 to 1937, school usually got out around 2 p.m. We'd pass Szpitalna Street where you could find old or used books and translations of our schoolbooks in Greek or Latin. They were used and cheap. The shop was full of books from floor to ceiling. The Jewish owner knew where every piece of paper was located. You ask for *Commentarii de Bello Gallico* by Julius Caesar and he just gave you the ladder and pointed to the shelf. Ask for books on Agamemnon and the Trojan War, the same. But what I mostly bought in this shop were supplies of Karol May books.

Across the railway station from my house, there was the Kino Corso, on the bridge across Lubicz Street, next to the chestnut trees. *Kino* means movie, so it was a movie theater.

It was the only one close to us, and I only saw movies in the winter. Why? Because it was dark early, about four o'clock. That's when you can climb on the big chestnut tree, go on the first balcony of the Kino Corso, and you were inside without them knowing. I saw all the movies with Tom Mix. If there was a Tom Mix movie, we couldn't wait to get on this tree and get inside.

Movies were twenty-five *groszen*—that was expensive for us. My only entertainment was the Kino Corso.

I made a mental note to figure out the currency equivalent of twenty-five *groszen*, but then another question came to me and I had to ask. "What other movies did you like? Do you remember any besides Tom Mix?"

No. I only wanted to see the cowboys and Indians.

Clearly enjoying the memory, Henry held his hands up to mime holding a rifle and aiming across the room, then grinned.

Bang, bang, bang. Those are the movies we liked. I always dreamed of seeing the land of cowboys and Indians, and now I live in Arizona, only one hour from where Tom Mix died in a car accident in 1940. He made it to age sixty, but I am still here at eighty-five. Who is luckier? I went to see the memorial they built where he died in a car accident in 1940, down by Florence [Arizona]. They say he was even wearing his big, white, ten-gallon hat when he died.

KARL MAY

I didn't recognize the significance of the name Karol, or Karl, May at the time or realize that when Henry said "Karol" he was using the Polish variant of the author's German name, Karl. Intrigued, I later looked him up, and it gave me a keener insight into some European attitudes towards the US. Virtually unknown to English audiences, Karl May (1842–1912) was a prolific writer, and is considered the best-selling German writer of all time. His books have sold more than one hundred million copies and have been translated into thirty languages. In a recent comment on Amazon to a May book, a German reviewer said simply, "The Germans have a saying: 'We know Goethe, but we read Karl May.'"

May named his main character Winnetou, "the noblest of all Red Warriors." Even Adolf Hitler admired the books about the Apache hero and never banned them, even though they glorified a man of color. Ironically, May never visited the American West, yet his writing strongly influenced how most Germans think of the "First Americans," even today.

In yet another connection to Arizona, the Chiricahua Apache Indians lived in the southern part of the state, in an area known today as the "Land of Standing up Rocks." The picturesque, remote area contains large expanses of pinnacles, spires, and interesting rock formations, not unlike the sandstone spires of

Bryce Canyon in southern Utah. Today, about eighteen square miles of the area are preserved by the National Park Service as the Chiricahua National Monument. The San Carlos Apache Nation now calls southern Arizona home.

Apparently, a fascination for Native Americans continues. When we visited Poland, we observed that street performers are very common in downtown Kraków, hoping to capture a few *zlotys* from passing tourists. Situated between a traditionally dressed Polish couple playing the accordion and bass, and someone posing as a still, silent, silver statue, there was a pair of Native Americans performing for a small crowd. Dressed as plains Indians with long feather headdresses, they stood in front of an eight-foot-tall teepee in the background. The vision startled me in the middle of Poland. One played a melodic native flute that sounded just like recordings I've heard of Navajo songs. The other danced in the background. What I viewed as a caricature of Native Americans apparently looked like the real thing to others around me. Their bowl on the ground in front of them was filled with *zlotys* and *groszen*.

1936 YMCA Kraków. Henry is in the back row center, with a small plus sign on the photo. *Henry Zguda's personal photo album.*

Henry Zguda and friends. The back reads: 20/8/1933. Kocjan, Zguda, Sala, Resich, Laska. Henry is the second from left. *Henry Zguda's personal photo album.*

Undated news article. The caption reads:

"Lodz. February 7. The swimming competition between two representative teams of YMCA Lodz and YMCA Kraków took place in the winter-indoor pool of YMCA Lodz. The guest team from Kraków won for a ratio of 78:50. The Kraków swimmers showed very good shape, which contributed to setting a few new regional records. They took all first places and most of the second ones. Besides, they won both medley relays. The best swimmer in the guest team was Zguda." *Henry Zguda's personal photo album.*

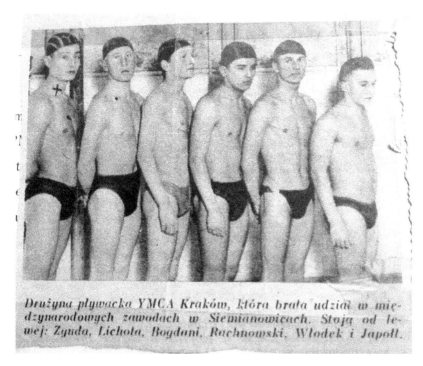

Undated news article. The caption reads:

"The swimming team from Kraków that participated in the international competition in Siemianowice. From the left: Zguda, Lichota, Bogdani, Rachnowski, Włodek, and Japoll." *Henry Zguda's personal photo album.*

Na basenie warszawskim zakończono pierwszą rundę rozgrywek o mi-
strzostwo ligi waterpolowej. Zwyciężyła drużyna „Elektryczności",
którą widzimy na zdjęciu w składzie (od lewej): Cygański, Gumkowski,
Karpiński, Jabłoński, Szypko, Zguda, Dzięgielewski i Czuperski

Undated news article. The caption reads:

"The first round of games in the Water Polo League Championship
ended in the swimming pool in Warsaw. The picture displays
the winning team 'Electricity' with the participants (from the
left): Cyganski, Gumkowski, Karpinski, Jablonski, Szypko, Zguda,
Dziegielewski, and Czuperski." Even though the arrow points to
the swimmer second from the left, the caption correctly states that
Henry is third from the right. *Henry Zguda's personal photo album.*

Front page of the sports section of the *Illustrated Daily Courier* newspaper, dated March 3, 1937. The headline above the photo reads: "Krakow Winter Swimming Championship." The caption below the photo reads: "As it has been already reported, on Saturday and Sunday, the winter championship of the Krakow District competition took place in the swimming pool of Krakow's YMCA. Present were swimmers representing teams from YMCA, Cracovia and Makkabi, whose large number is shown in the above picture." *Owned by MHK [Historical Museum of the City of Krakow], ref. no MHK-Fs1989/IX.*

SWIMMING MAKES YOU DUMB

HENRY CONTINUES:

When I was sixteen, some of my friends told me about the YMCA. It was one of the biggest, most modern places in all of Kraków at the time. The Americans built it in 1927, and it had an indoor, twenty-five-meter swimming pool. When I first joined the YMCA, I played basketball because I was already a good runner, and played it in school. I also liked volleyball very much.

One day, someone posted a sign that the YMCA was promoting the swimming section. If you joined the swim team, they waived your membership fees. I never swam in my life. For free dues, now I am a swimmer. That was the beginning of my career as a swimmer. Water has always been good to me. We also played water polo, which is a very physical sport.

My favorite reason I liked swimming was that I'd never been able to take a shower before. Now, I could get all the way in the water for the first time.

I held up a hand to interrupt him. "Wait, Henry. What do you mean you hadn't had a shower before?"

Henry shrugged.

We had no shower at home. Most houses didn't have showers at that time. Our apartment building had been built in 1550, but when I lived there it was practically falling down. The building was old. There were balconies inside the house along the first floor and second floor, with like a courtyard in the middle. There were two floors above the street. Each floor was spanned with an iron belt to keep it from falling apart. The walls had cracks that kept opening. Sometimes I thought I might fall asleep and wake up in the street.

If you wanted to wash yourself at home, you heated warm water on the coal stove. Then, you set up a metal tray in the kitchen. You stood in it and poured the water over yourself and washed. There were six apartments on each floor, and one bathroom at the end of the hall for all six apartments. There was often a line of people on the balcony waiting to use it.

Henry opened his photo album and pointed to several pages of newspaper clippings and photos from swim competitions in Lodz, Warsaw, and other cities. He pointed to one clipping pasted below photos of several young men in racing bathing suits.

See here? Zguda first in 100-meter freestyle. That was my best event. I was a sprinter.

Henry then translated the Polish text for me.

"Lodz. February 7. The swimming competition between two representative teams of YMCA Lodz and YMCA Kraków took place in the winter-indoor pool of YMCA Lodz. The guest team from Kraków won for a ratio of 78:50. The Kraków swimmers showed very good shape, which contributed to setting a few new regional records. They took all first places and most of the second ones. Besides, they won both medley relays. The best swimmer in the guest team was Zguda."

Henry paused and stared off into space for a minute as if remembering something specific. Then, his focus again switched to the news clipping. He thumped it a couple of times with his index finger, then looked up at me with a grin.

Swimming makes you dumb, dumb, dumb.

Henry was most certainly not dumb. Even more confused, I asked what he meant by that.

Think about it. Imagine playing water polo. First, you warm up with an hour of swimming. Then, you practice passing the ball for one hour. *Then,* you play an hour-long game against your opponent. So, what does the coach make you do afterward? To relax and wind down, you swim another 800 meters. So, what you think of? You think of nothing. You just swim. Do you understand? You do this every day, and finally, you are dumb. You just push through without thinking.

In 1936 after the Olympic Games in Berlin, some members of the American swimming team came to Rabka Zdrój, Poland, as part of a goodwill tour and held some swimming workshops and such. I represented the Polish team against the USA. I remember swimming against Peter Fick; he placed sixth overall in the men's 100-meter freestyle in Berlin. Jack Medica came. He won the gold medal for 400-meter freestyle and the silver medal for the 1500-meter freestyle. Ralph Flanagan also came. He won a silver medal in the men's relay, placed fourth in the men's 400-meter freestyle and fifth in the men's 1500-meter freestyle. They were all good freestylers and very nice guys.

I smiled big, and asked, "So, Henry, did you win, swimming against the Olympic swimmers?"

Henry looked at me with an expression that clearly communicated the message: *Did you really just ask that?*

No. No way. Fick was swimming 100 meters in one minute; I was swimming in one minute eight seconds. But I remember he and I had a great time laughing together. He even made it easier. He swam the full 200, and my friend and I each swam 100 meters, but we still lost by very much.

Henry laughed as he remembered and pointed back to his photo of the athletes.

Here I am. I'm nobody, and I'm swimming with Olympic athletes!

Visiting US Olympians Peter Fick (in USA sweater) and Jack Medica (in dark bathing suit) with unnamed Polish swimmers. 1936. *Henry Zguda's personal photo album.*

Left to right: Kazimierz Szelest, unnamed woman, Henry Zguda.
Undated. *US Holocaust Memorial Museum, gift of Nancy Zguda.*

A DINNER WORTH TEN *ZLOTYS*

Another problem with swimming—you spend all your time swimming and you come out very hungry. Herr Stein, you know he was Jewish, he always invited us for the sausage on Sienna Street. He owned the Willshein restaurant. It was thirty-five *groszen*. We borrow, beg, steal, but we have to have the hot dog, the sausage, with sauerkraut and red sauce. It was heaven in the mouth.

Henry raised his right hand up, kissed the fingertips, and flicked his hand in the air.

Pyszne! Delicious! You go home, all you get is beans, macaroni, or sauerkraut. I eat whatever I could find. You see an apple in the street somebody threw there, you brush off the dirt and you finish it. You don't care; you're hungry. I think I had more antibodies in my body than others who only have good food.

At the YMCA water polo is a very tough sport. Not only do you have to swim and stay on top of the water, you have to fight the other team. Elbows jabbing at you, guys pushing, there's no limit on the number of personal fouls. We had a powerful goalkeeper, Kazimierz Szelest, on my water polo team, and we were very good friends. I called him Kazio, and he called me Henyu.

Henry pulled out a small wallet-sized photo of Kazio, Henry, and an unnamed, attractive woman standing in front of a train.

Henry and Kazio appeared dapper in tailored suits and ties, and the woman appeared equally well dressed. I was struck by how good looking all three of them were. Henry appeared to be wearing the same suit as in the earlier picture taken of him with the twin steeples of Saint Mary's Church in the background.

See—look at Kazio. John Wayne had nothing on him. Kazio looked like a movie star . . . see his blond hair, fair skin, and beautiful straight, white teeth? He was all muscle, 220 pounds. He came from a good family and was in perfect health. This is the only picture of Kazio I ever had. Kazio saved my life, but I tell you that part later.

Because Kazio was very handsome, there were several times the entire water polo team did very well because of this.

Again, Henry smiled and gave a good chuckle at the memory.

Near the rail station, there was an old palace that belonged to Earl Dzieduszycki. The palace was a big corner building, two stories high. It was a very nice place. He liked boys. Now and then, in 1936, the earl would come to the YMCA just to hang around and talk to the guys. Twice, the earl invited the entire water polo team to his house for dinner. He was always insistent that Kazio Szelest had to come. The earl always seated Kazio next to him.

I remember we'd sit there in this beautiful palace and be served by a butler. Can you imagine? It was one of the few times I ate very, very well. We always had to coach Kazio in advance and get him to hold back. Why? Because the earl would keep grabbing Kazio's leg under the table.

All through dinner the earl would try to make conversation with Kazio. "How do you like the dinner, Kazio? Can I get you anything else, Kazio?"

It was very, very hard for Kazio to sit there and not to reach up and punch the earl in the face. Kazio only needed one punch and the other guy is down. He went for only one reason—so his friends could eat well. We were very grateful to our friend. That kind of dinner would have cost ten *zlotys* per person. At that time a good meal at a very nice restaurant cost one *zloty*. The earl was willing to feed the entire team just so he could sit next to Kazio. I specifically remember eating at the earl's two times in 1936.

"Can you describe a good dinner back then?"

First, you start with a good soup. Mushroom soup. Polish mushrooms are different from American mushrooms. You pick them in the forest, you dry them on a string, and hang them in a circle in the kitchen by the stove, and they keep for years. They keep the smell of fresh mushrooms for years. The mushrooms are dark, not like the white mushrooms that are grown in dark, dank places. The soup with mushrooms would have a little rice or wild rice in them. Then, usually pork chops, potatoes, and boiled sauerkraut. At the end of the meal you have vegetables, followed by an apple compote.

"Does Polish sauerkraut taste the same as here?"

Henry gave me a look of sheer disgust and practically spat at the thought.

What? Are you kidding me? Uncle Ignacy was the family specialist in sauerkraut. Uncle Ignacy, that's short for St. Ignatius, was a little guy and tough. He was not educated and could barely write, but he was smart. Very smart. Every year, sometime before winter, we'd buy the regular cabbage, we'd shred it on the board with the knives, and load it into barrels. You put a bottom on a wooden barrel, then put some cabbage in. Then, Uncle Ignacy comes along, washes his feet, and he starts thumping and thumping and stomping. Then, they put in black salt, then another layer of cabbage, then another layer of salt, and he keeps stomping.

Everybody had to watch him when he stomped. We'd get him tea, sandwiches, whatever he wants. He sweats and works hard for two to three hours stomping the sauerkraut. Nothing goes in the barrel except cabbage, salt, and Uncle Ignacy's feet. When you squeeze out the cabbage there is liquid; it just gets sour by itself.

Then, you put a board on the top of the barrel, pound it with a heavy, heavy rock to push the lid closed. Then, we rolled the barrel into the cellar and left the rock on top to hold the lid. When the mildew starts growing white on top of the cabbage, then the uncle and I would go down, take a dish, everybody taste it. Um, delicious. We mix it up, skim off the white stuff, stir, then every dinner we had sauerkraut. Sauerkraut in this country smells of chemicals. Chemicals are worse than Uncle Ignacy's feet.

THE BEGINNING OF THE YMCA

The YMCA came to Poland in 1919 as a humanitarian mission from American YMCAs. In 1922, an organizing committee worked to establish the Polish national movement. The main aim of the newly established Polish YMCA was "the reconstruction of intellectual and spiritual life of Poland." Its motto, "Serving Poland through Character, Education, and Health," was in tune with what the recreated nation needed at the time. The YMCA outreach program helped the poor, the illiterate, the hungry, and the unemployed.

Two Americans played a key role in helping build the Polish YMCA, including Sereno Fenn, who founded the Kraków YMCA. Fenn was vice-president of the Sherwin-Williams paint company from 1921 until his death in 1927. He also served as the director of the Cleveland Ohio YMCA from 1868–1920. With American help, the Polish YMCA built a beautiful facility in Kraków that housed clubs, hostels, gymnasiums, and promoted sports— especially basketball, volleyball, and swimming. The Kraków YMCA housed the first indoor swimming facility of its kind in all of Poland. Eventually, facilities in Lodz, Warsaw, and Gdynia were also built with American help.

From 1933–1942, Henry trained and competed regularly in both swimming and water polo. Competitions in both sports took him to other major cities in Poland where either a YMCA or other swim club might hold such a competition. I began to understand why he had some notoriety, especially with athletes in other sports clubs and cities. His name appeared in the sports section of the newspaper, and he traveled to other swim competitions throughout Poland for several years. Like many other sports, athletes usually learned the names of regular competitors.

Henry's photo album held quite a few copies of newspaper clippings, some with photos of the swimmers, and some just printed scores from meets. Most show Henry in first or second place. Similarly, Kazio Szelest frequently came in first or second in the same meets they competed in together. Unfortunately, none of the clippings showed dates, but all appeared prior to 1939. When the Germans invaded Kraków in 1939, one of the first things they did was shut down Polish information sources, such as the newspaper.

BLIND MARIE

HENRY CONTINUES:

Kraków is a very old town. But you find every kind of person or history of people in Kraków. Old professions never die away, like old generals.

Blind Marie was a prostitute who lived nearby. For as long as I could remember, the street corner across from the Earl's Palace belonged to Blind Marie.

Henry looked at a map of Kraków and pointed to the exact intersection.

She had blond hair and was solid; you know, tall, heavy, thick-waisted like a cow, but not fat, just strong. She could take on any soldier. She wasn't exactly blind. But one of her eyes always had this funny twitch that made her look kind of funny. She was very demanding from her corner. She'd hold out her hand with fingers gesturing towards herself. "Hey, come on, boy, what can you teach me? Two *zlotys*. You come show me."

Henry raised his arm in front of him, then waved his fingers toward him, like calling others over. He made me laugh as he tried to wink, twitch, and scrunch one side of his face all at the same time, in his best imitation of his friend.

Marie was tough. She never let competitors move onto her corner. But I built a little business with Marie. Once a week when she had time, I taught her to read and write. I earned one *zloty* an hour teaching Marie to read and write. This was good money, though she usually made about five *zlotys* an hour. She made good progress with me and after a while, she could read and write her name.

She was our neighbor, and my mother was nice to her and talked to her on a regular basis. She was a nice lady. It's not the same like here in this country. Go to Amsterdam, on Canal Street, there are plenty of ladies in the window, they are knitting. You go in, they close the curtains, do the business, and they are respected. They are mothers, and voters, and they have a store selling their body, but it is a business.

When war broke out in September 1939, the Germans tried to bomb the Kraków rail station. They missed; and instead, the first bomb landed squarely on Marie's corner. The bombs fell at ten in the morning, when she was home sleeping. Otherwise, Marie would have been one of the first casualties of war. She somehow survived the war. Years later, when I returned to Kraków, there she was on the same street, the same corner, still making a living.

HELENA WEISS

I was in love with Helena Weiss. Everyone was in love with Helena Weiss. Her father owned the swimming pool and tennis courts in Park Krakowski. I started working there on Saturdays and Sundays as a ball boy on the tennis courts, for one or two *zlotys*. Helena tried to swim, so we swim together sometimes. I try to teach her swimming. I remember she was very nice, pleasant, and talkative. I thought I had a chance with her, even though she was the owner's daughter, and I had nothing. But my friend Panska was faster with Helena than me, so I had to look elsewhere. Panska was a good swimmer.

Henry stopped and sighed for a moment.

He was shot on the street during the war by the Germans.

Then his thoughts returned to his story.

I remember holding the white tennis balls—we played only with the white, not today's yellow balls. They played tennis until the white turned dark from the dust. The Slazenger balls came from England and were very expensive. I met many good tennis players there, including Jadwiga Jędrzejowska. Her name was hard to pronounce for some, so she went by Jed. She was from Kraków, and a few years older than me. At that time, she was ranked in the top ten tennis players in the world. I think, in 1937, she make it to number three player in the world. She was very nice to talk to.

I was too poor to own my own tennis racquet, but people let me borrow theirs sometimes, and I became a pretty good player. Tennis was good recreation. After that, I play tennis all my life.

FREEGE SEED COMPANY

My mother recommended me for a job at the famous Polish seed company, Emil Freege, Hodowla I Skład Nasion. She was a housekeeper for the Freege family. She was to take care of the two ladies in the house. They need something to clean, she do it. They send me over to their warehouse and give me the job that I was very good at.

Freege shipped seeds to Denmark, and many other countries in Europe. They sell whatever seeds the farmer needs to sow, you know, like wheat, linen, or flowers. I supervised the ladies from the village. One room, twenty-four ladies, they sit twelve and twelve on each side of a long table. They have thousands of the little bags like you buy in the store, tiny bags like when you are buying the seeds, and there's a big barrel of seeds.

Henry pantomimed the following steps as he described the activity.

The women take a bag—*pfft*—blow in the packet to open it, then they dip a little spoon in the seeds exactly for whatever amount the seeds that day called for, and then seal the packets. All day long they do this, not talking much. They don't read or write, so it's important I make sure they get the right seeds in the right bags, you know, make sure they get the petunia seeds with the petunias, and not the sarsaparilla or something else.

Most of the seed names were in Latin, but I learned Latin in high school. Even now when I go to the store to buy flowers I want to buy them by their Latin names. I don't know the English names, like geranium or petunia. It was very helpful to my employer that I could spell in Latin if they have a problem.

In 1936—I was nineteen then you know—I worked there all day, and then went to swim and train at the YMCA in the evening. I was very fortunate to have this job. I had to be strong to carry hundred-pound bags of seeds. I'd carry them from the warehouse to the wagon.

"Henry, when you say wagons, do you mean trucks?"

No, no. Horses. Wojtek drives the horses and wagon. I still remember a funny story when they experimented with gene crossing. Karol Korohoda was a good botanist, but he almost poisoned the whole town. He crossed a tomato with a potato. He grew these beautiful tomatoes except they were paler in color—more of a yellowish-white, not healthy-looking. Peasant boys kept sneaking into the fields to steal something to eat. They got very sick, and I think at least one died. When the townspeople finally figured out what the boys had eaten, the farm workers they had to keep running the boys off until the whole field was plowed under.

I learned that science behind crossing a potato and a tomato supports Henry's story. Tomatoes and potatoes are of the same nightshade family and can't cross-pollinate. Occasionally, potatoes may produce a flower and a fruit that looks like a small tomato. The flowers and resultant fruit are indeed poisonous.

Henry's identification card, issued the summer of 1939.
US Holocaust Memorial Museum, gift of Nancy Zguda.

THE JEW BEATERS AT PARK JORDANA

In the summer of 1939, I was crazy in love with Gena Pietrzykowska. She was my first love. She was the secretary at Freege. She had beautiful, beautiful breasts I could hardly look at without touching. I asked her for a rendezvous one Sunday afternoon. We went to Park Jordana, a beautiful park near Kraków. We were sitting there on a park bench enjoying the conversation and beautiful summer day. Then, along come the anti-Semites. They were just a bunch of young students, walking through the alley. They saw me sitting with Gena, and then approached us very angrily and stood over us.

"Hey. You Jew, you get out of here!"

They shouted and pointed at me. I stood up to face them. They started to circle around Gena and me. I looked right back at them.

"Hey, do I look like a Jew? I'm no Jew," I said. I don't know, maybe I did look Jewish. I have dark coloring like the *Górale* and I have this big nose. Gena screamed for help, but no one came.

There were four or five guys and they gave me a nasty beating before they ran off. I had a broken tooth, my lip was cracked, and I had a huge black eye. I was very embarrassed and in a lot of pain. But Gena loved me so much, she felt very sorry for me with my black eye. She didn't know what to do so she took me home. The next day I went to the ambulance place.

After the clinic, I went to the YMCA. I looked like hell. Kazio saw me right away and hurried over.

"Henyu, what happened to you?"

When I told him he said, "Henyu, don't worry. We fix it."

Kazio went and found two big weight lifters and a couple of other big guys from the water polo team, and the six of us went back to the park. We split up into pairs and went walking around the park. Sure enough, we saw a couple of guys walking down the alley. I don't know if it was the same group that beat me, but we saw them.

So, we went up to them and casually asked, "Heh! Which of you is a Jew?"

They protested and whined, all excited, "No, no. We're not Jews. We're here beating Jews!"

"Oh yeah? Well then, come here."

I don't remember who, but one of us threw a solid punch that landed on the guy's face. All it took was one punch before they run off like little cowards. We split up into groups and went around the park. When we found any other anti-Semites we beat them up worse than they'd beaten me up. We do the same thing they did. We go up and start talking to them, "Come here guys, what are you doing?"

"Oh," they say, "we are beating the Jews!"

"Oh yeah, we do beating, too." After that, we didn't see those groups around the Park Jordana for quite a while.

WHY DID PEOPLE HATE
THE JEWS?

"**H**enry, I don't get it. Why did so many people hate the Jews?"

My question may seem extremely obvious to those who have lived in Poland, or around anti-Semitism their entire lives—especially in larger cities—but it wasn't to me. I've only had three Jewish friends in my life, never set foot in a synagogue, and other than the fact that I celebrated Christmas, while my few Jewish friends celebrated Hanukkah in December, it didn't seem like a big deal. Nor did they look different to me, like the Jew-beaters assumed Henry was Jewish just by his looks. I don't remember anti-Semitism being raised as a civil rights issue in the United States in the 1960s, 1970s, and 1980s when I was growing up. My memory was the fight for civil rights and affirmative action for Blacks and Latinos, as well as equal rights for women.

Whether it was simply the demographics of my childhood neighborhoods, or that the question never came up in my parents' social set, I simply was never exposed to the Jewish faith in any depth whatsoever during my solidly Protestant upbringing. I certainly never learned much in Sunday School beyond the Old Testament stories of Moses, and the ten plagues sent against Egypt. I knew Jesus entered Jerusalem on the

Jewish Passover, before he was crucified with a sign that read the "King of the Jews."

With Henry, I also sought a simple and straightforward answer to why Hitler was determined to erase the faith from Germany and Europe, beyond: "That's just how it was and always had been."

I also wanted Henry's perspective. So far, all of his explanations had been honest and frank, if high level. I focused intently on his answers, as he explained what it had been like then.

Anti-Semitism was very big in Poland. Many people didn't like Jews, like I told you. There were guys fighting on the stores or breaking windows in the Jew-stores, anyplace someone make money, like the kiosk for the newspapers and cigars. I don't know why and I don't care. Not everyone held a grudge. Athletes don't care about such things. My friends didn't care; we were all the same. I swam with other swimmers who were Jewish and had friends who were Jewish.

In school we had Jews. Like I said before, on a scale of one being the best, I'd get twos in the languages and fours in math and science. Only the Jews worked hard enough to get all the ones. The best grades were always for the Jews: Weisberg, Weisman, Greenberg, Silverman, and so forth.

I didn't have to join the Polish army. I was a good Catholic boy supporting my mother, so they give me an exemption. If I had had a brother, one of us would have had to go. Soldiers in the army often stayed in primitive conditions, away from home. You didn't see many Jews in the Army, and people began to resent that, too.

At that time, Poland was a poor country. I was poor; my friends were poor, we were the same. But always the Jews have something. If you needed money, the moneylender was Jewish. The storekeeper on the corner was Jewish. The jeweler was Jewish. And their sons always went to school to become doctors. The kiosks were run by Jews. Sometimes, I'd help my friend at his kiosk, and sell newspapers for him when he had to go someplace. He sold papers in Hebrew and Polish, and he taught me a little bit of Hebrew. I remember he was always very, very careful with his money.

I think if Poland was a rich country like America, people might not care so much, because everyone have the opportunity to make it here. But what most ordinary Poles didn't understand is that Jews became doctors and were successful because they worked very hard and studied. The Jewish families believed in study and hard work, and they encouraged their children to develop. The Jews always did so well because they work hard and don't waste their money. Then, they became the leaders who have something, and leaders are always resented by those without. It's still true today.

••

Henry's response to my basic question on Jewish relations summarized a high level of attitudes, but I also struggled with a secondary, intertwined difference in the European thought process. As I researched further, and looked at concentration camp and war statistics, I didn't understand why the counts of "Jews" and "Poles"—or Germans, Czechs, Russians . . . pick your country—were mutually exclusive, in terms of both self-identity and war casualties. As an American, I still find this odd and different from how my country breaks down subpopulations. War casualties are first "American" casualties, and census populations are sub-categorized by ethnicities such as Hispanic, Black, Asian, and so forth, not by the religious categories of Jews, Protestants, and Catholics, etc.

Looking at history through a European lens requires a shift in viewpoint to gain a greater grasp of the prevailing attitudes and political undercurrents of Henry's time, as well as the years leading up to World War II. The original Pilgrims to the Americas sought religious freedom, and separation of church and state forms one of many basic tenets of the US Constitution. Conversely, for centuries, religious differences in Europe factored into a greater divide in self-identity, and to be Jewish was its own distinct and separate identity, ethnicity, and culture, regardless of country of origin.

Religion has always played an important and contentious part in Poland's history. As early as the tenth century, Jewish merchants traveled on trade routes that passed through Poland. Where other countries discouraged Jewish settlements, Poland welcomed the Jews. This, in turn, attracted an ever-larger Jewish population. In 1264, the Duke of Greater Poland, Boleslaus the Pious, issued the Statute of Kalisz, also known as the General Charter of Jewish Liberties. The statute granted unprecedented legal rights to Jews. They were allowed to settle, follow their religion, be protected from harm, engage in various occupations, and even play a role in the minting of coins. Subsequent Polish kings also ratified it again in 1334, 1453, and 1539.

Where Poland practiced a tolerant, welcoming attitude towards Jews, other European Jews, especially in Spain, began to suffer greatly. Until 1391, Spain had the largest population of Jews in Western Europe. After that year, Dominican friars began forcing conversion to Christianity through forced baptism of Jews, orders to destroy their neighborhoods, and the imposition of harsh penalties. In some cases, they kidnapped Jewish children so Catholic households could raise them as Christians.

On March 31, 1492, King Ferdinand and Queen Isabella issued an edict of expulsion, known as the Alhambra Decree, ordering all Jews to leave Spain by the end of four months unless they converted to Christianity. At the time, the Jewish community in Spain numbered 200,000 people. The royal decree forced those who refused to leave to convert to Catholicism. Jews who chose to stay and converted became known as "*conversos*" or "new Christians." Jewish neighborhoods were destroyed, and other Spaniards profited greatly as Jews were forced to liquidate their possessions and homes, and sell their businesses at ridiculously low rates. Many ship captains charged exorbitant sums to ferry escaping Jews to Portugal or other Mediterranean countries such as North Africa, Italy, and Turkey.

Even worse, trials by "inquisitors" sought to prosecute nonbelievers as heretics, and in some cases inflicted brutal forms of torture. One of these methods consisted of binding prisoners to a rack, trussing their hands, and stretching them. Another brutality inflicted on prisoners took the form of an especially painful form of hanging, the *garrucha*. A prisoner's hands would be bound behind them, and then slowly strung up, leaving the prisoner to hang only by the wrists. Three hundred years later, the Nazis would utilize on many prisoners the same incredibly painful method of hanging.

Though Jews have suffered expulsions throughout their history, the Spanish Inquisition remains the most infamous. The Second Vatican Council did not revoke the edict until December 16, 1968.

Then, as now, an influx of new immigrants challenges any country either to welcome foreigners—especially those of a different culture—or to put up legal and social barricades to discourage, if not prohibit them, and chase them out to other countries. As Spanish Jews migrated eastward into other European countries, they encountered the same hostile attitudes they'd left behind. Besides the predominantly Catholic countries, the Protestant Lutherans and Calvinists of Germany also chased the Jews out of their cities.

Many escaping Jews moved to northern Italy, including Venice, even though Italy was solidly Catholic, and home to the Vatican farther south in Rome. As with other European countries, Venetian leaders gradually became concerned by the large influx of Jews and, at the same time, began to receive pressure from the Vatican to the south to act against the ever-increasing population of outcasts. In response, they established a forced resettlement of Jews into a special neighborhood: essentially a small, dirty island near a foundry. They built gates at the two bridges to the island, and locked them at midnight. Guards ensured the Jews could not leave at night, with the exception of doctors. Jews could not own land and were restricted to merchant professions such as money-lending, tailors, printing, and medicine. However, unlike the deadly ghettos established by the Germans during WWII, Jews were allowed to roam freely throughout the city during the day, in part so they could spend their money outside their community. In turn, Christians crossed the bridges to shop in Jewish stores. A rich Jewish culture developed with synagogues, a school, theater, and literary salons. Still, Jews were given no choice where to live and conditions grew ever more crowded. The gates of the ghetto would not be torn down until Napoleon Bonaparte arrived in 1797. The term "ghetto" became the slang term for the area, based on any number of Italian words, depending on which version of Italian etymology is attributed. It would be 425 years before the invading Nazis of World War II established the

Jewish Ghetto in Kraków in March 1941.

While Poland practiced a more tolerant and welcoming attitude than most of Europe, it still encouraged strong Catholicism. Though not asserted to the point of strictly forced uniformity like Spain or Italy, Christianity was, by far, the dominant presence and philosophy, even though religion in the large Polish Commonwealth was split between the three different denominations. These included long-time Polish Catholics of central Poland, German Lutherans to the west, and the Orthodox Christians of Ukraine and Russia to the east.

The Polish ruling class never identified a "Jewish problem" or implemented forced conversions though, by choice, many Jews lived in completely separate towns or *shtetls*—a Yiddish term for a small town. They spoke Yiddish and, in essence, lived apart from the mainstream population. In the larger cities, Jews often prospered financially, but were rarely permitted to own land, and never attained the higher social status reserved for the Polish "nobility."

By 1772, the Polish Commonwealth sheltered eighty percent of the world's Jews. In 1795, when Poland disappeared from the map of Europe, the fate of Polish Jews grew ever more difficult. Prussia disdained Jews, Austria wanted them to assimilate into society, and Russia barely tolerated them, restricting most Jews to the same lands they'd lived on before, rather than permitting them to immigrate farther into the country. Catherine II of Russia forced the Jews to stay in their *shtetls* and forbade them from returning to the towns they occupied before the partition of Poland.

Between 1881 and 1921, Russia launched three different waves of *pogroms* against Jews. The Russian word *pogrom* designates an attack of such ferocity that an entire village could be looted and destroyed, while its inhabitants endured rape, murder, and banishment from their homes.

Less than one percent of Jews earned their living in agriculture, while sixty-two percent made their living from trade. According to the 1931 census, 3.1 million Jews lived in Poland, representing nearly ten percent of the entire population of Poland. In Warsaw, Jews comprised more than thirty percent of the city's population. Even though many Polish Jews were caught in a poverty trap, during the same census, Jews comprised forty-six percent of all lawyers and nearly fifty percent of all doctors in Poland.

Even in large cities, Orthodox and Hasidic Jewish men dressed in long, black gabardine coats, grew beards, and wore black hats and prayer shawls. In short, they stood out, were easily identified as "different," and primarily identified themselves as belonging to the Jewish community rather than the country of Poland. Many spoke Yiddish as a primary language, and those who spoke Polish treated it as a second language.

Catholicism remains extremely important to Poles, even to this day. After centuries of living side by side, Polish Jews in many ways assimilated better than in other countries. As the Great Depression spread through Europe, many Jews remained successful and prosperous, while the majority of Poles labored in poverty. This nurtured the seeds of hate and jealousy founded in a centuries-old resentment of Jews. In 1937, the Polish government resurrected an idea first promulgated by a German anti-Semite in the nineteenth century. They strove to expel the Jews to the island of Madagascar, a French colony off the coast of Africa. The Polish government actually negotiated an agreement with France, known as the Madagascar Plan, to do just that. In 1938, the Nazis even explored the idea of exiling four million Jews to Madagascar. Neither plan came to fruition.

It would be overly simplistic and highly inaccurate to say that, during World War II, all Jews were successful, all Christians practiced anti-Semitism, and no Jews acted against their own people. Certain members of the *Judenrat*, the Jewish council in the Ghettos, assisted the Nazis in deportation of their own people. Yet, during the nearly six years of occupation by German and Russian/Soviet forces, more Poles helped their fellow Jews than any other country. Yad Vashem, in Israel, recognizes more than 6,600 Poles as "Righteous Among the Nations" for their part in rescuing or saving Jews. Due to the stiff requirements of nominations for Righteous Among the Nations, including nomination and testimony of a saved survivor, many Poles estimate the number as possibly thousands more.

This high number is especially significant for two key reasons. First, many Poles themselves struggled to survive the ravages of war. Germans arrested and murdered Poles, Russians evicted and deported more than one million Poles to slave labor and gulags in Siberia, and both the Russians and Germans murdered Polish military and civilians indiscriminately. How are you in a position to save Jews if you yourself have been deported? Secondly, the German penalty for helping Jews was highest in Poland than any other occupied country: death to you and your entire family. If, for instance, the Germans discovered a family or person helping Jews, the Jews were usually executed first, followed by the rescuer's family, and then the rescuer. If there are no survivors, then who is left to nominate you?

For centuries, the Jews have been treated separately and differently from other countries and communities. This makes it clearer why many Jews identify first as Jewish, then their nationality. Eastern European borders changed multiple times over the centuries, redefining national identities; each country considered the Jews a predominant ethnic minority. Some of the worst actions against Jews occurred in the far eastern part of Poland where the Cossacks of the Ukraine and Russia conducted wholesale massacres. Father Patrick Dubois, a French priest, has dedicated his life to locating witnesses and identifying execution sites in the former Soviet Union. He's recorded thousands of testimonies that document villagers assisting the Nazis and identified hundreds of previously unknown or hidden execution sites. Truly, evil is its own ethnicity and knows all cultures and countries.

Polish and Jewish relations in any century remain a complex topic that continues to stir strong emotions from both Poles and Jews from Poland.

PART 2

POLAND AT WAR

1939–1942

SEPTEMBER 1, 1939: SHOCK AND AWE

HENRY CONTINUES:

In the YMCA, there were dormitories that were mostly rented to students at the Jagiellonian University. Jagiellonian University is a very good university, the second oldest in Europe. Many students came from across Europe to study there. Kraków has always had many universities, but Jagiellonian is the oldest and most famous.

We had a little buffet or dining area for the students who lived upstairs. I remember, during the summer of 1939, there were mainly ten or twelve German students staying there who were attending university. My friend Nowak was working in the buffet, and they were always busy eating there. One day the Germans got very demanding and kept saying, "Give us that kasza! We demand you give us some kasza!" For whatever reason, Nowak decided he didn't want to.

"No. No way I'm giving good Polish kasza to Germans."

Then someone else in the dining room said, "Oh, just give it to them, they deserve it."

The Germans went back to their rooms after getting their kasza without making too much of a fuss.

I was at work when bombs fell on Kraków on the morning of September first. I didn't know what to do or where to go, so I ran to the YMCA to be with my friends. I'm standing there with my friends and, son of a bitch, all those same German students reappeared in their Gestapo uniforms. Every damn one of those students was an officer of the Gestapo spying on all of us at the YMCA. The Germans had been planning that invasion for a long time. Those soldiers spoke very good Polish, and now they knew who everyone was in the YMCA.

I was standing there when they marched in and grabbed one of my friends roughly. Stefan Sala, I think.

"Where is Nowak?" they demanded

"I don't know!" said Sala.

"*Ja?* Well, you go find him. Either you bring him to us or we'll find you."

Just as they released Sala, my other friend grabbed me and we ran out the back door damn fast. We didn't wait for any more questions. Nowak had already left to hide in the forest, and we weren't far behind.

The Germans were almost to Kraków. Kazio had told me to head east, towards the Russian border. So, as soon as I could get to my mother, I told her I was leaving. She give me some bread, and then I left with my friend Tadeusz Glab.

••

Germany employed a new form of ruthless "shock and awe" warfare when it invaded Poland. Hitler had planned the *Blitzkrieg,* or lightning war, for some time with the full intent to simply "run over" Poland. By late August of 1939, even the Polish army became aware of the large amassing of German troops and equipment near the Polish border, and tried to maneuver equipment into place. At dawn on September 1st, some 1.8 million German troops, supported by 2,600 tanks, invaded Poland in a three-pronged approach. The Polish army's contingent of tanks numbered a mere 180. The German *Wehrmacht,* or army, quickly bulldozed its way into Poland, easily overwhelming Polish forces.

The German *Luftwaffe,* or air force, comprised the second lethal component of invasion. More than 2,000 aircraft ruthlessly dropped bombs on cities—showing no distinction for schools, hospitals, or churches—and flattened anything in sight. The 420 planes of the Polish air force were simply no match for the massive attack. Poland had only regained her independence twenty-one years earlier. The country had made great strides towards rebuilding its military while facing huge obstacles and a worldwide Depression, but knew it was no match against Germany.

Six months earlier, Germany had demanded more land for the Third Reich. In response to the aggressive stance, Britain and France formed a full military alliance that guaranteed Poland's borders. The agreement stated that, in the event of an attack by Germany, Polish forces only needed to hold off invading German forces for a period of two weeks. Poles fought valiantly for four weeks trying to hold off the Germans, fully expecting Britain and France to come to their aid with divisions, tanks, and planes. In a bitter betrayal, though Britain and France declared war on Germany on September 3, 1939, neither country sent a single soldier to aid in Poland's defense. Poland quickly fell, as German nationals who lived within Poland's borders cheered the invading German army. Germany lost more than 50,000 men, 697 planes, and 993 tanks and armored cars against defending Poles. But the effort cost Poland nearly 200,000 in dead and wounded.

On September 17, 1939, the Russian army, under the direction of Józef Stalin, surprised Poles and invaded Poland from the east. This invasion negated a non-aggression pact signed in 1934 between Germany, Russia, and Poland. A larger geographic portion went to the Soviet zone, and about thirteen million Poles came under Soviet Rule. Beginning in February 1940, thousands of Poles living in that portion were evicted and forcibly transported in frigid cattle cars to labor camps in Siberia, or even farther north in Russia. The estimated number of deported Poles ranges from one to two million people. At least 130,000 officers of the Polish army came under Soviet jurisdiction and were imprisoned. Russians separated the officers and enlisted men. In March and April of 1940, nearly 22,000 Polish army members, including some 14,000 officers, were summarily executed in the Katyn Forest.

Germany incorporated the western part of Poland into the Third Reich, and organized the central part of Poland into the *General Gouvernement*. Hitler installed his lawyer and friend,

Hans Frank, as leader of the latter. Frank chose Kraków as his capital and the historic Wawel Castle for his headquarters and personal residence. Frank's concept of Poland was simple: erase Poland from human memory. Any Poles not eliminated would be shipped back to the Third Reich as slaves. Ironically, the one reason almost all of Kraków's historic buildings survived the war was that the Germans did not bomb their own headquarters in Kraków.

Conversely, the Germans destroyed more than eighty-five percent of Warsaw by the end of the war. Heinrich Himmler, director of the dreaded SS, an acronym abbreviated from the German term *schutzstaffel,* or protection squadron, advocated that "all Poles will disappear from the world . . . It is essential that the great German people should consider it as its major task to destroy all Poles." The Germans immediately attempted to destroy all symbols of Polish culture, closed all secondary schools and universities, and dismantled or shut down any information systems. Radios were no longer permitted, nor were newspapers, theaters, cinemas, or cabarets. Polish businesses were transferred to private German ownership. Hans Frank declared all works of Polish art, including private collections, be confiscated to "safeguard" them. The famous Veit Stoss altar from Saint Mary's Church was one of the first works appropriated and sent back to Germany.

In a lesser-known action—yet equally sinister—throughout the war, the Germans kidnapped up to 200,000 young, blond, blue-eyed Polish children who looked sufficiently Aryan in appearance, and sent them back to Germany to be raised by good German foster families. Most would grow up with no knowledge of their Polish heritage. While the exact number of kidnapped children will never be known, I rely on Halik Kochanski who, in her thoroughly researched book, *The Eagle Unbowed, Poland and the Poles in the Second World War,* used the number 200,000. Few humans in Kraków went unscathed.

Nearly seventy thousand Jews lived in Kraków at the time of the German invasion, and they became immediate targets of mocking and mistreatment by German soldiers. By November, Frank ordered them to wear the Star of David, and their plight declined quickly. By March of 1941, all remaining Jews in

Kraków—who hadn't fled or been evicted—were ordered into a ghetto established in Podgórze, a suburb of Kraków. Roman Polanski, film producer, writer, and actor, lived with his family in Kraków in 1939. Though only six years old in 1939, he remembers his father being marched off to Mauthausen, a concentration camp in Austria, and his mother shipped to Auschwitz. He was able to escape the Kraków ghetto in 1943 with the help of a Roman Catholic family who sheltered him for the remainder of the war. Only about two thousand Kraków Jews survived the war.

KAROL WOJTYLA

In our interviews, Henry's stories mostly skipped from the beginning of the war to 1942. He made brief mention of an unsuccessful few weeks running from Kraków with his friend Tadeusz Glab following the encounter with the Gestapo students at the YMCA. Thousands of fellow citizens fled their city and headed east, following the Vistula River, seeking safety from the Germans in Russia.

However, Russia invaded Poland from the east on September 17, 1939. Like Henry and his friend, most people turned around and headed home, with nowhere else to go. Seemingly overnight, Poland was once again divided between her two historical enemies, and subjugated to either Nazism or Communism. Once again, the proud Republic disappeared from the map of Europe.

I interpreted Henry's omission of detail during that time frame, whether intentional or unintentional, as an unspoken statement that his life had settled into a routine, with fewer memorable stories. He worked at Freege during the day. In the evenings, he spent much of his time at the YMCA with his many friends, training regularly in swimming and water polo. Weekends meant working at the tennis courts in Park Krakowski. Somehow, he obtained work papers from the Germans that permitted him to continue working at Freege as a supervisor during a time when other young men were rounded up by the Germans or simply disappeared.

He claimed he attended classes at a clandestine high school after the war started. The Germans closed all Polish schools, but classes continued in secret locations. Of course, any records kept by these underground schools would have been destroyed during the war.

While I have few details for these three years, I later discovered a nugget of information that offered a greater window into his wartime activities and character. In 2012, I began in earnest to translate many of Henry's papers from Polish and German. This sworn, notarized statement was among those papers:

> *I certify that, well-known to me colleague Henryk Zguda, born on July 12, 1917, in Kraków was a member of the Youth Division in YMCA in Kraków in the years 1932–1939.*
>
> *During the Hitler's occupation in the years 1939–1942, the above-mentioned colleague— Henryk Zguda—led an underground action by distributing bulletins and conspiracy-like correspondence/newspapers, such as "Poland still alive" and "White Eagle," as well as participated in the meetings that condemned racism and Nazi ideology.*
>
> *Japoll Kazimierz, Kraków*
> *March 1, 1958*

Henry always claimed he attended school with Saint John Paul II, née Karol Wojtyla. They were close in age though Henry was three years older. Several times he reminisced about Wojtyla.

"He ran in different circles, always praying with the priests, and in theater. I was sports all the way. Who knew he would be pope one day?"

••

In 2013, I visited Wadowice, Saint John Paul II's hometown, a small city located an hour's drive east of Kraków. There, I spent a half-day with our interpreter at Wojtyla's high school, the *Gimnazjum w Wadowicach*, trying to verify Henry's supposed connection. There is no record of Saint John Paul II ever taking high school classes in Kraków, nor of Henry taking high school classes in Wadowice. Henry finished high school in 1936. Saint John Paul II finished high school in 1939, then moved to Kraków.

The school director graciously took time out of her busy schedule during my visit, and researched every professor at the school, and the class roster of every class the sainted pope had taken. She proudly ushered us into the *Aula Papieska,* or Pope Hall, a modern classroom added on to the school in recent years. The room is dedicated to learning and the memory of Saint John Paul II. Displays of memorabilia surround the room, including photos of his teachers, class rosters, and other mementos that detail his life during his school years and his youth in Wadowice. All religion classes are taught in this room. Students and staff are, of course, very proud of their connection to such a special person. Wojtyla often said the school was an important influence in his early life. Per the director, "It is easy to teach children in such a place."

A sizeable canvas portrait of the pope, painted in oils by a student, stood prominently near the entrance and bore this famous quote: "Wadowice is where it all began. Life, school, university, theater, and priesthood began here."

No records remain from Henry's high school. The building still stands exactly where Henry said it did, in downtown Kraków, not far from the Main Market Square. Today it is home to a cooking school. One of the first actions the Germans took after invading Poland in 1939 was to close all schools. Following the war, the communists converted it into a cooking school, and all school records were destroyed in the process.

Without documented school records, could the two men have crossed paths in Kraków? Absolutely. Kraków was a small town in terms of knowing people, and Henry always knew a lot of people. Both young men lived in the same Catholic parish, and priests were known to have held underground classes. Henry was never particularly religious, but he loved studying Latin, and talked about attending underground classes during the war. More than once, he said, "You know, those classes helped many, many people." Henry insisted he remembered the pope from his Latin class, because "Wojtyla came before Zguda" during roll call. In 1978, when Karol Wojtyla became the first non-Italian pope in four hundred years, and took the name John Paul II, Henry recognized him immediately.

(I can't confirm the school connection through records. Yet, in a simple analogy, I remember many names and faces of people from my high school with whom I was not close friends. I can name three who later went on to some level of renown.)

Henry once told me he sent a personal note of remembrance and congratulations to the pope, prior to a vacation in Italy. Henry requested an audience to say hello. In Henry's papers I found a letter in Polish dated July 1, 1984, from an advisor to the pope, that confirms Henry's letter. It reads:

> *His Holiness John Paul II thanks you for your letter, compliments and kind memory. However, the enormity of the tasks and responsibilities prevents him from giving private audiences, about which so often is asked. Therefore, I encourage you to take advantage of the general audience held every Wednesday. For information and tickets, please apply directly to the Prefecture of the Pontifical House, Vatican City, or also take advantage of the services of the Polish benevolent pastoral center in Rome on Via delle Botteghe Oscure 15.*
>
> *The Holy Father recommended the matter to God in prayer for all those who turn to Him and sends His Apostolic Blessing.*

Whereas some people might have waited to see such a prominent former classmate, Henry skipped the general audience; his vacation schedule in Rome didn't fall on a Wednesday.

OF SUGAR AND MOUSE DROPPINGS

HENRY CONTINUES:

After 1939, there was always at least one German guard on the premises of Freege ensuring we were working, and I tried to stay on good terms with one of the guards. I knew some German from school, so I could communicate. I was very lucky. People who spoke German did much better during the war. They give me good German work papers with a seal to keep working at Freege, since I know Latin and German.

I remember the Germans came upon some sugar and vodka, so they hid it at Freege for themselves. *No one* had sugar at that time. The sugar came in hundred-pound sacks in heavy, heavy paper, and they stored twenty sacks there.

Wojtek, the wagon driver for Freege, had beautiful, strong teeth. He and I worked together and collected mouse droppings from various places until we had a good amount. My friend who ran the store on the corner gave me some paper sacks about the size that would hold two pounds of sugar. Wojtek managed to get into the large sacks of sugar that were underneath and against the wall, where you couldn't see the sides. He chewed holes in several bags. The bags had to be bitten and chewed to look real. He then made a small trail of sugar, as if rodents had been spreading it. Then, we skimmed off sugar from several bags into the paper sacks I had. After loading up the sugar, we scattered mouse droppings in and around the sugar. I had sugar for my mother, my cousins, my friends, and for my girlfriend Gena. The Germans didn't notice the holes until they went to carry the sugar. It spilled out and made a huge mess, mixed in with the mouse droppings. Boy, were they mad, but they never suspected anyone but mice got into the sugar.

Henry laughed heartily at the memory.

PART 3

KL AUSCHWITZ, OŚWIĘCIM, POLAND

JUNE 1942–MARCH 1943

Henry Zguda, Prisoner 39551, June 1942. *Used with permission of the Auschwitz-Birkenau State Museum, Oświęcim, Poland.*

ABANDON ALL HOPE, YE WHO ENTER HERE

I arrived one day to find Henry thumping his fingers on a book about Auschwitz. He pulled out a set of three two-inch-square prisoner headshots taped together in a row. A young, bald Henry, facial features chiseled like a fit athlete, stared into a camera in one. Another showed his right side, and the third captured his left profile. In the side shot, his head was clearly butted up against a large nail. He wore a prison uniform with an upside-down triangle above his left shirt pocket. In the left side of the photo, I read the inscribed words, "Polen. 39551. KL Auschwitz." The photos bore several layers of yellowed tape, as if to laminate and protect them. Henry handed them to me to look at. I held them carefully and looked at both sides. I realized they were original camp photos from 1942. I cringed inwardly at their condition, as probably any museum archivist would.

"Henry, how did you get these photos?"

Simple. I went to the Nuremberg trials and they have these books of photos. I see mine and I take it out of the book when no one was looking. I figure it's mine anyway.

I watched Henry pick up another book, and a single sheet of typed phrases fell out. He smiled with recognition, and looked back up.

Here's something else I find. I love the Latin, so I made a list of phrases I like.

He ran his finger down the sheet of paper and until he found a phrase that sparked a memory. His face turned angry, and he thumped the paper a couple times. He looked up and stared off into space. Then he looked me straight in the eye. He read the Latin and immediately translated the saying to English.

Lasciate ogni speranza voi che entrate. Abandon all hope, ye who enter here. I like this saying much better than *Arbeit Macht Frei.* This is what really should have been over the entrance to Auschwitz. This is the sign at the entrance to hell in Dante's *Inferno.*

Arched sign over the entrance to Auschwitz I. *Used with permission of the Auschwitz-Birkenau State Museum, Oświęcim, Poland.*

THE BEGINNING OF AUSCHWITZ

The Germans formed a plan in January 1940 to build a concentration camp in the vicinity of Oświęcim, Poland. Jails overflowed with arrested Poles and Jews they had no intention of releasing. The Germans chose to repurpose an abandoned Polish army camp for a new concentration camp. The relatively remote location contributed to the secrecy of the camp and its true mission. The army camp included a group of two-story, red-brick structures, and other existing facilities that could be adapted, cleaned up, and occupied in a relatively short time period. The location offered accessibility to water and rail lines and was centrally located in Europe. Even better, it was on Polish soil, and only forty miles east of Kraków, the new capital of the *General Gouvernement*. Like every other city the Germans claimed in Poland, they renamed towns from Polish to a German variant. The Germans named the camp *Konzentrationslager Auschwitz*, abbreviated as KL Auschwitz.

The German high command chose Rudolf Höss, a fervent and early member of the Nazi Party, as the first *Kommandant* of Auschwitz. He had already demonstrated his loyalty by participating in a political assassination, for which he was arrested in 1923, and not freed until 1928. He had held positions in two other concentration camps, Dachau and Sachsenhausen, understood a harsh prison life, and seemed to thrive in the military atmosphere.

Höss arrived in early May of 1940 and appropriated not only the Polish army camp but a nearby lovely, fourteen-room home, newly built in 1937 by a Polish soldier. He evicted the Polish family living there and claimed it as his personal family villa. All construction and modification of the camp came from slave labor. The German mayor of Oświęcim, at Höss's request, ordered the local Jewish community to supply three hundred laborers who were worked hard and beaten for the slightest infraction. A contingent of Polish prisoners sent from Dachau was assigned the task of building a provisional fence. To make room for the camp and a wide swath of land outside the camp, Höss evicted Poles and Jews, and destroyed approximately a thousand homes and farms, leaving their occupants with nowhere to go, and no means of earning a living.

For staffing, Höss brought with him SS Sergeant Gerhard Palitzsch as his direct subordinate. Palitzsch, a good-looking German, ranked as especially evil because he enjoyed executing prisoners. Palitzsch hand-selected thirty hardened criminals to come to Auschwitz as "kapos" in a misguided concept of "prisoner self-government." These thirty kapos ran the various blocks in the camp, with little supervision from the Germans. Prisoner number one, Bruno Brodniewicz, was appointed the "camp senior." Henry knew these people only as Kapo Bruno, Kapo Arno, Kapo Michael, and so forth. In the case of Kapo Jakub, Henry was insistent he was in Block 11 when he arrived in June 1942. Even though other accounts refer to a Kapo Jakub who arrived later, in this account, I'm using Henry's recollection.

Kapos held the most important jobs, ran the day-to-day lives of prisoners, and were highly feared for a very good reason. I asked Henry where the word "kapo" came from. He explained to me that it came from the Italian word for head, chief, or boss, though why Germans chose an Italian reference was beyond me. They assigned one kapo to oversee each prisoner barrack, or "block."

Höss ordered an arched, metal sign placed over the entrance to the camp that reads *Arbeit Macht Frei*, a phrase he borrowed from Dachau, where it was first used. When translated into English it sarcastically means "Work Shall Set You Free."

The Germans devised a quick and visual identification system for prisoners in all the camps: they sewed colored triangles on the upper left front of each uniform indicating various prisoner categories. Henry always referred to them by their German name—*winkel*. Prisoners wore "red *winkels*," "green *winkels*," and so forth. Political prisoners wore a red triangle, criminals wore green, the "anti-socials" and gypsies wore black, homosexuals wore pink, Jehovah's Witnesses wore purple, and Soviet POWs wore yellow triangles with the letters "SU." A single letter in the middle of the triangle indicated the nationality of the prisoner: P for Polish, D for Deutscher [German], C for Czech, F for French, and so forth. Political prisoners were generally communists, ordinary citizens, clergy, and anyone else who didn't fit the other categories. The kapos, as criminals, wore green triangles. They assigned nearly all non-Jewish Poles red triangles. The Poles comprised the highest percentage of the prisoner population until June of 1942. At that time, of the 23,070 prisoners, forty-six percent were Jewish, and forty-one percent Poles.

Each registered prisoner received a successive number and was thereafter known by his number, not his name. These numbers were sequential and never reassigned, so those prisoners with smaller numbers soon attained a certain status and respect among other prisoners simply for surviving longer than so many others. The last stage of registering prisoners involved taking photos. Auschwitz records show approximately 405,000 prisoners registered during its existence.

Polish and German, and eventually Yiddish, became the primary languages in camp. Anyone who spoke German fared better since the guards spoke in German and severely punished those who ignored their commands.

One day Henry summed it up perfectly:

These people all speak different languages. But one language is international—a punch in the face.

••

I asked Henry what I considered a basic question, though it was still something I didn't understand.

"So, what did Hitler have against the Poles? Everyone knows he targeted Jews, but why the Poles and Poland?"

Henry helped clarify the situation.

Hitler claimed that the land occupied by Slavs and Poland was really German—at least it was about a thousand years ago. Polish and Lithuanian armies defeated a Teutonic order of Prussians in the 1400s.

The Germans remember everything and remember we always hate them. Every war, we fight against Germany. Russia, too. For a hundred years we were in the slave of these three countries: Germany, Russia, and Austria. We are no good to them, we are not Aryan, we are Slavs—or really slaves—we should be destroyed. Same with the Russians. There was historical hatred of the Polish nation.

They needed our land to expand Germany. Germany thought all our land to the Ural Mountains should be in their possession. It's like the Palestinians and Israelis—everyone want something from the same place. For generations, they never agree and there is resentment. But we Poles always come back.

Inmates reading the inscription on barrack no. 9: "There is one way to liberty: Its milestones are: obedience, diligence, honesty, order, cleanliness, sense of sacrifice, sobriety, truth, and love for your Fatherland." Sachsenhausen concentration camp, 1938. Unknown photographer. *Used with permission of Süddeutsche Zeitung Photo, Munich, Germany.*

PRISONER 39551

When we came in, first they take our names, give us our number, then we go to the washroom where we got our prisoner outfits—the jacket and pants and shoes, which were stolen right away. We have to steal back. The shoes were just a wooden sole with a strip of leather on top. No socks. They shaved our heads. Then we go to the camera. Head up against a wall with a large nail on it. Left. Right. Center. Bam, bam, bam, done in thirty seconds.

You know, they didn't order the tattoos right away. That's why they took photos. Once I thought about paying ten dollars to get a number—nice and neat. People ask to see those, you know. They're always disappointed when I hold out a blank wrist, like I wasn't really there. But I changed my mind. Forget it. I don't need a tattoo to know where I was. I'll tell you a funny story about the SS and their tattoos.

The Germans thought they were so smart. Many of the SS and other Germans had their blood type tattooed near their left armpits. That was so a medic could give an unconscious soldier the right blood transfusion. But they regretted those tattoos after the war. If the Americans or Russians arrested some guy they thought was SS, all they had to do was say "raise your arm," to know they got the guy. Mostly the Russians just shot them.

Everything happened for a reason. You know, we admired them [historically], but they despised us. When they shaved you, it hurt like hell because they don't care. I say shaved, but the razors used too much electricity, so they used scissors instead. Being a barber was a good job in camp—I would have liked that job.

After that picture, we go straight to Block 11 for quarantine. We didn't know yet it was the Dead Block.

Block 11 sat across from Block 10, like across a courtyard. These blocks were two-story brick buildings. All the windows facing the courtyard were covered, either by being bricked up or with wooden shades, so you couldn't see out. On this Block 10 was the experimental block. Through these windows, I hear it—these Jewish girls crying for their mother and grandmother over and over. But the opening was only toward the sky, not down. "Mommy, Mommy! Help me! Help me!"

At this point, Henry just shrugs and holds up his hands.

But what can you do?

The kapo in charge of Block 11 was a big guy. He was the heavyweight champion boxer in Holland and had been the boxing champion of Poznan. He was a swimmer too . . . not a great one, but he knew me. His duty was to keep us from the window. He and I talk a little.

Every few hours, Kapo Jakub would say, "Everybody together in the middle of the room, don't go to the windows. Stay there." He and the guards watched us with the sticks to make sure we stayed there. We can hear the SS walking, or laughing in the courtyard. That's when I learn there's a wall down below in a courtyard where they kill prisoners by firing squad.

The SS come down and tie the hands of the prisoners behind their backs with the wire. The SS was standing there. Oh, that depends, because he was walking, laughing, talking to the other SS guys. We didn't hear gunfire—it was more of a *spfttt*. Kapo Jakub explained they used what was like a nail gun—that way the Germans saved their ammunition. They just shot them in the back of the head. Sometimes the men screamed. Some went silent, some managed to get out a "Long Live Poland."

I asked Jakub, So, how do we get out of here?

"Henry, do you know what block this is? This is the dead block. Outside, they shoot prisoners. They kill people every morning and afternoon in front of that wall down there. They kill ten, five, one, two, or three at a time."

Kapo Jakub takes me to a window and pointed to the

crematorium chimney, smoking like hell.

"Henry," as Jakub points to the chimney, "that is the one sure way to get out of here."

Somehow, I'd managed to hang on to a gold pen on the way from Montelupich. So, I asked him, I have a gold pen. Do you want it? I give it to you.

"Yeah, sure. Now listen, I tell you something. Anytime the work squad leader asks for workers, whatever kind of worker he asks for, you tell him you are the best." So, I remember that.

After quarantine, we get moved to new blocks. The first day on the regular block the oldest German on the block gives the speech to new inmates. So, two hundred of us stand there, at attention on the block. We had to look like we heard and obeyed, just like God Himself is standing in front of us talking. Prisoners and peasants who didn't understand German would just shake their heads and hold their hands up.

The foreman started his speech with, "There is only one way to freedom. You must follow these milestones."

Then he barked each number before saying the milestone.

"One! Obedience."

Bam! He bangs the bunk with the stick.

As Henry said the word "bam," he banged the patio table hard, shaking the contents. I jumped at the sudden noise, just as the scared men in the barracks would have.

"Two! Diligence."

Bam! He bangs the table again with the stick. He just keeps counting.

"Three! Honesty."

Smack! He bangs someone on the head with the stick. Hard.

"Four! Order."

Smack! Another guy gets it on the head. After each milestone he hits or kicks someone new.

"Five! Cleanliness. Six! Sacrifice. Seven! Veracity. Eight! Sobriety."

All the time he's talking, he's walking around with a long stick in his hands, enjoying himself. These milestones were very famous. There was a pamphlet in every block with these. You do something wrong, the SS calls you over to repeat these. The peasants just shake their heads and hold up their arms.

They don't understand German. They get hit for being stupid. I remember these milestones very clearly.

Then he orders: You have to be clean. You may only use the restroom one hour a day. No water, only one hour a day. He kept on with more rules. The Germans give you no opportunity to clean yourself. But, I learn later, the cleaner you are, the longer you live. Germans like it clean.

In the morning, the SS roused us. "*Schnell, schnell, raus, raus.*" Everyone out.

We have five minutes for three hundred guys to use a latrine and stand outside in nice formation. *Appells* [roll calls] were early, like before six o'clock in the morning.

Every morning, the guards would count: *Eins, zwei, drei, vier . . .*

The *schreiber* [block clerk] would call out, I have 200 inmates listed. The *rapportführer* [block leader] would call back, I only have 178. Twenty-two are missing.

Then the kapo would grab a couple of guys and go back to the block. One by one, he'd make the prisoners drag out the missing twenty-two—all dead in the night—and stack their corpses in a pile. Every morning the *leichenträger* [dead patrol] came with the roll wagons to cart off the morning dead pile. You know the Germans never touched the dead. Prisoners just grabbed the dead by the legs and hauled them out to a roll wagon. Another prisoner grabs the arms to throw them on the pile of dead in the cart.

Then we'd hear the block clerk give the all clear. "*Rapportführer*, everyone is accounted for." Only then can we be dismissed for our work assignments.

Sometimes at the roll call, if the Germans decided something wasn't right, if somebody hides, or die in the bushes and we can't find him, we have to stand one hour, four hours, eight hours, or more. It didn't matter if was raining or snowing. I don't remember twelve hours, but I remember four hours standing there, with snow down your back, with the SS walking around. The SS were mad because they had to go in the rain, too. They have to be alert for hours because he is gone.

In the evening, the roll call routine was the same. If people die at work, everyone must carry their bodies back to be counted. The cadavers who died that day were counted and the *rapportführer* smiled because he knew there would be extra bread that night. The kitchen cooked for the quantity of morning roll call—more dead at the end of the day meant extra bread for who the *rapportführer* like, or who could steal it.

BUILDING ROADS

The next morning, after the roll call here comes the *arbeit scharführer* [work section leader]. He announced, "I need cement mixers."

Right away, I speak up. "Oh, ho, *Jawohl, Herr Scharführer.* I am good cement mixer."

"*Ja*, where'd you work?"

"I work five years in Kraków as a cement mixer."

"*Ja*, Kraków is a nice town. Come on."

This was a killer *kommando*. We carried the heavy bags of cement for the trenches and heavy blocks for building more buildings.

On the third day, I dropped a column of concrete on my fingers. One finger was flat, completely flat. The bone was broken and coming out of my finger. I didn't know what to do and it hurt like hell. I think it was about eleven o'clock in the morning. So, I got permission to go to the prisoner hospital. But they just tell me: No way you're sick. Out. Back to work. *Schnell.*

So, what do I do? I go back to the work crew, hold it in front of the guy next to me so he can urinate on it. The ammonia in the urine sterilize it. I also had a little bit of paper from the cement bags that I had hidden to put under my shirt to stay warmer. I tore off a little piece and I wrapped my finger.

You know, paper is the best protector of the cold. Paper from those cement bags saved many lives in Auschwitz. They'd put it under their shirts, and back to front. Of course, if you got caught stealing the paper there was a severe penalty. But you still have to live, so you try.

In the beginning of Auschwitz, the roads and grounds were full of mud and holes. Auschwitz was constant rain and mud. There was a river there like the Colorado River. We had plenty of mosquitoes; they were the only things in Auschwitz you can kill.

To flatten and level these roads, the Nazis ordered a large, heavy roller, weighing about two tons. They also used it to clear the big roll-call area. The roller had no engine and had to be pulled manually. The Kapo Krankemann was in charge of the roller. He named this activity "Invitation to the Waltz" because the word waltz in German was the name for the rollers.

Each morning he gathered prisoners, put them in front of this large roller and, with the help of sticks and ropes, these prisoners had to pull the roller. The kapo himself would sit on top of these rollers on a specially built bench. Seated next to him was a *pipel* who carried a harmonica. On command from the kapo, the young homosexual boy had to play the *Blue Danube* waltz, the favorite melody of Kapo Krankemann.

The prisoners usually fell first under the rollers and were flattened. After about two hours of this work most had fallen to the ground. This continued until all the men either collapsed or died.

When the lunch-hour siren sounded, the corpse carrier *kommando* would come and take the dead people to the crematorium. Then, the next group would be called up for an "Invitation to the Waltz." This was in the early days of Auschwitz.

Building the new blocks was a slow process. The Germans never meant to keep us alive for long, but if they worked us to death first, they got some benefit. Sometimes the materials to build with were delayed so, to keep the prisoners busy, the Germans invented special sports for prisoners. There was always an audience consisting of the SS men on duty, laughing and joking at these. They used mostly Jews. Many were well-educated men who weren't used to physical labor. I see them from my *kommando*. We get hit if we look, but I look anyway.

For one sport, they would just have prisoners jump up and down from a bent knee to upright, for many hours until they collapsed.

Hüpfen und rollen was a combination of leapfrog and rolling on the ground. First, you had to leapfrog across an area and then roll back. Always the Germans would stand back and watch, or laugh. Once someone fell, they were pushed and kicked by the guards for falling.

The most primitive of their sports was the jogging stick. The Germans would put a stick of wood in the ground, and call up thirty to forty prisoners. They were ordered to jog around the stick, going in the same direction for one hour. Then, on order, they would have to turn around and jog the reverse way for another hour. There was no walking, no standing, no stopping. The ultimate end of this sport was the same of leapfrog and rolling. The main idea was *complete* elimination of all prisoners.

Henry emphasized the word "complete" when he spoke, to emphasize the brutality of the sports and the camp.

You have no food inside you, no strength left, nothing to give. You're wearing wooden shoes. No one can run constantly in that condition.

Another sport I watch was . . . they'd have prisoners dig two holes, some distance apart from each other. Often the material was more mud than dirt. The guards would force the prisoners to remove their jackets and put them on backward.

They buttoned the jacket up the back and in front, your arms reach through the sleeves. Prisoners hold out their arms with the jacket draped over both arms. Another prisoner filled the front full of mud and made the prisoner carry the mud from one hole to another. Once the prisoner reached one hole he'd dump the mud into the hole, then wait while another prisoner refilled his jacket with more mud to carry to the opposite hole. The whole thing was so pointless—it only moved the same dirt back and forth. It was only to wear out and humiliate the prisoners.

German guards played another game. They earned a reward if they killed prisoners trying to escape. Any guard who shot an escaping prisoner got at least five *marks—reichsmarks* [German currency]—for reward, and one or two days off work. But the Germans were smart. Prisoners had to be shot in the *back* to be "escaping." Back then, five *marks* was a full day's pay.

If there was a lull in a work detail, especially if the detail was outside the camp perimeter, the guards would have fun. A guard would pick a prisoner, point them to some trees in the distance and order them to walk towards the trees. Or they throw a prisoner's hat towards the tree and send him to get it. After the prisoner took a few steps, he'd be shot in the back.

The camp was surrounded by an electric wire. It was double at that time between the block and the outside. You grab it and you're done, dead, out of there. But it was hard to get to the wires. The SS had orders to shoot any prisoner before they reached the wires. The SS hated it when someone got caught in the wires. The body would get all twisted in between the wires, and it would cost them time and money. They would have to shut off the electricity to get the bodies out. Any guard on duty was penalized if someone made it to the wires.

I remember one of my friends from Kraków. He was a very nice guy. He worked as a cashier in the Bank of Kraków. He had a wife and three kids. One night he came over to talk to me.

"Henry, I can't walk any more. My hands are cracked up and swollen and bleeding. I am not going [to work] tomorrow. I'm done."

"So, what are you gonna do?"

"Henry, I am going to the wire."

He ran out to the electric fence. I watched him get electrocuted and machine-gunned by the SS at the same time. He made me promise that if I ever made it back to Kraków to let his wife know he loved her. But I never did. This happened at the beginning of the war and I forgot his name. Too much happened for me to remember his name.

TYPHUS

Even the Nazis called Auschwitz *Annus Mundi*—the world's asshole. The whole situation was so bizarre with people dying all around you. Always there were lice and fleas like hell.

The louse is like an ant, only white. They are smaller than ants, but fat from the blood they eat. If you have lice and you scratch, then the head stays in the body and you scratch the body. They itch like hell. Lice were the carriers of typhoid bacteria. One bite you're dead.

Henry stopped and held up his thumb and forefinger to demonstrate how tiny they were. Then, he began laughing.

Every few days they had the *läuseappell*, the lice roll call. You had to take your clothes off to kill the lice. You should see the barracks of two hundred skinny naked men scratching or jumping, trying to pick the vermin off themselves and the clothes and kill it. It was hell, but so crazy you have to laugh. You're so tired, what else you gonna do? No one ever talks about when you laugh in the camp. You laugh or you cry. Laughing is better to survive.

Maybe every month they exchange clothes. All they do is take louse X and give you louse Y. The regular Jewish prisoners never got new clothes, because the Germans know they will die in a month anyway.

We got wooden sandals with some fabric stapled across the top for shoes. Some came covered in blood, and they were all filthy. These shoes were hard to walk in since, in the rain and mud, they'd get heavy and stick to the ground. Few of us had socks. We always seemed to shuffle. After working all day you're so exhausted you don't have the energy to lift wooden shoes, especially if you've been working in mud. You drag your feet just to move. We called this the Auschwitz shuffle.

So, imagine I'm sleeping on one wooden bunk with three other guys. Two heads here, at one end of the bunk, two sets of feet at the other end of the bunk, and one filthy blanket over us. So, I'm on the bunk with my friend from high school, I forget his name, then Górny, Iman, and myself.

Then, one night, Iman says, "Oh God, I have a headache."

"Aw shit. What, do you have temperature, too?"

"I think so. Maybe 104. I'm really hot."

What can you do? You're sick, you're out. You have to die. Because you cannot work, you have to stay on the barrack. The *blockältester*, or the block kapo, would come along and say: "Throw him out, get him in front of the barrack."

Then the patrol comes along with the *rollwagen*. In front of every block there was a pile where they throw the dead and typhoid fever people. They go straight to the crematorium. There was *no other* way. They had to kill the typhoid fever plague. We keep Iman in the bunk between us for the night to keep us warm. We said goodbye to our friend in the morning.

COLLECTING *RINDE*

One morning, after I was done with the cement *kommando*, we were standing at roll call and along comes the *arbeit scharführer*. You know, the work squad leader.

"Who speaks German?" he asks.

About ten of us raised our hands. So, he said, "Come with me."

They took the nice small group of us in a truck about twenty miles outside Auschwitz to the forest. That forest reminded me of the Amazon forest, it was so wide and thick with trees. There were many hectares of forest. The Germans were collecting *rinde* from the trees to color the shoes in the nearby shoe-making factory. Each of us spoke a little German, so we could communicate. We were split into two groups. One group cut the trees, and the second group used shovels to peel the dark bark off the cut trees.

A Polish army captain was there, and I was on the end. We were supposed to somehow load several of the tree branches in our arms at one time. Each strip of tree bark weighed about fifteen pounds, maybe more. Then, you had to carry the stack about two hundred meters to the truck. This bark was flat and long, and the tree sap oozing out make them very slippery and hard to carry. The first load, I didn't even make it halfway before I dropped the bark.

This SS guard comes over and kicks me in the ass. I picked it back up and carried the bark about ten to twenty feet more. I dropped it again and fell. The guard took his rifle and started kicking me in the kidneys, all the time yelling at me.

"You don't even deserve a crust of bread for this kind of work!"

Then he kicked me in the face until my lips cracked. As I'm lying on the ground holding my bloody head, he raised his rifle and took aim at me, ready to shoot. Just then, the foreman, a Silesian who spoke good German, came running from the truck to see what was going on. Silesians were usually in good position in the camps because they spoke very good German. The area of Silesia in western Poland was part of Germany for many, many years.

In perfect German, the Silesian faced the guard. "Hey, hey what's going on?"

"Hey, this *arschficker* can't even carry ten pounds. Don't give him no bread or nothing."

"Oh yeah?" Then the Silesian pointed to my legs. By then, I'm so skinny my Achilles tendon was standing out.

"Look at his legs. He couldn't screw anything if he wanted to."

The German laughed, lowered his gun, and gave me one last kick instead of shooting me. With a grunt, he turned and left me lying there, completely smeared in blood, and in extreme pain. My nose was broken and a front tooth was knocked out. I don't remember if I ever saw that Silesian again. But I owe him my life.

The next day I take lots of bark, but I filled it with branches, so it looked like a lot of bark, but it was only about two pounds. That is how I learned to not work so hard. We were far enough away from the camp, there were people who had houses nearby and would sneak some bread and sausages to the prisoners. It was a good *kommando*, but it only lasted ten days. On the tenth day, we hear a car coming. The guards order everyone to come stand at attention. Then comes the aumeier [deputy kommandant of the camp]. We stand there and he makes a speech.

"Damm it! You lazy people, you don't bring any bark to the factory. This is absolutely stealing time, stealing the food of Germany. And, guards, you'll be fined a penalty for such a soft *kommando*. Everybody out. *Raus. Raus.*"

STAY IN THE MIDDLE

O ne day, the SS took us back to the camp from the forest detail earlier than usual. Usually, at six in the evening, the camp bell would ring to signal the end of work. Well, this day we got there before the bell rang and we were sitting there in front of the block, next to the gutter. There were about thirty of us sitting there.

Along comes the crazy kapo *ältester,* the oldest of the block kapos. He was older than old. He was responsible to the Germans for what the prisoners do on the block, reporting how many people died, were killed, and why, and so on.

He sees us sitting there by the side of the road, stops, and then yells: "All right. Everybody up. Now!"

Why? I asked. What did we do?

"You ask me what you did? The bell tells you when you can sit. The bell didn't ring yet, so you have to work. You lazy people are just sitting there on your asses. This is a workday for Germany. Get up. Everybody—twenty-five hits on the ass!"

So, he and the German guards marched us until we were in back of Block 16, with two lines of fifteen guys each, standing in a row. Along comes the kapo from my block, Bloody *Mietek.* Bloody Michael. He was the worst kapo there. He didn't talk to you, he just hit. He had sympathy for no one. He takes over.

"Who plays the harmonica?" he demanded.

There were a few Jews mixed in with us. So, some poor Jew raised his hand.

Bloody Michael pointed to him and ordered him to play "whatever."

As he told this story, Henry held his hands up, imitating someone playing the harmonica. I swear he recalled the exact song as he hummed a cadence.

Michael cursed at him, then shoved him out of the way.

"Aw, get out of here. You don't know how to play good. Next! I need somebody who plays good this time! I want the *Blue Danube*."

No one else volunteered. Bloody Michael wouldn't give it up, so he went after that first Jew and ordered him to stand in front of this barrel of excrement. It stunk like hell.

The kapos used different things to beat prisoners with. Sometimes they used a piece of rubber like from a bicycle, or a hard rubber baton like police use. Sometimes they just used a piece of wood about the size and length of a table leg. It was always very powerful, hard wood. This time Bloody Michael had a long piece of wood. Then he ordered that poor, damn Jew, "Okay, lean over the barrel. Count."

Eins.

Then comes the first hit.

Henry banged the metal table. Hard. I jumped out of my chair, knocking over some papers.

Michael swings hard, and you can hear a solid WHAP as the stick makes contact. The poor guy screamed, Yeow!

Zwei!

"Count louder! I can't hear you!"

The kapos always made prisoners count their own hits—in German. If you couldn't count in German, or lost your count, sometimes they'd make you start over at one again.

As Henry got into the story, he howled in perfect imitation of severe pain. As in real life, his voice grew more pitiful as he acted out each hit.

Zwei. Whap. Ooowww!

Drei. Whap. Ooowww!

Vier. Whap. Ooowww!

The more the prisoner screamed, the stronger he hit. Bloody

Michael got all excited, he was having so much fun. The more he hit, the more he smiled. That poor Jew fainted at about twenty-one hits, and almost dropped his head in that horrible muck. Then, Bloody Michael shoved him out of the way so he could lean the next guy over the barrel and start over.

"Next." And the next man in line leaned over the barrel of shit.

Eins! Whap. Ooowww!
Zwei. Whap. Ooowww!
Drei. Whap. Ooowww!
Vier. Whap. Ooowww!

After twenty-five hits, that guy got shoved out of the way and the third guy got shoved over the barrel. I was in the middle, lucky as usual. By the time Michael got to me, he was tired, so what does he do? He calls over another kapo to take over since he was tired. At least that foreman took pity on us. The rest of us got about ten hits. I think I only got about six hits. But, even with that, there was a huge black mark on my ass. I couldn't sit for a week and I was in a great deal of pain.

I didn't understand until years later what Henry meant when he said "in the middle, lucky as usual." Whether prisoners were marching or lined up, it was easier for guards to swing out or kick the guy they could reach first. Henry learned quickly to position himself in the middle whenever he could. The less the guards noticed you, the better.

A GROWING FRIENDSHIP

I'd met Henry in November 2002. By December, we were already chatting about my kids, my family, and other things in my life. I got the idea Henry got tired of only talking about himself.

The previous summer we'd taken our first big family vacation—a trip to Italy. My niece is an Army wife, and she and her husband were stationed in Vicenza, an hour from Venice. Truly, the trip was a one-time opportunity, we made it happen, and I have a shoebox of photos from the trip.

I'd used a photo from Italy for our Christmas cards, and included Henry and Nancy on my Christmas list. On the following visit as I passed through the kitchen on our way to the patio, I noticed it proudly posted on the refrigerator, next to a copy of my newspaper column.

Nancy came out and she and Henry both "oohed" and "aahed" over my family. The card represented the first family picture I'd shared with Henry and Nancy, and the beginning of their adoration for my kids.

"Look, your boys are handsome. And your daughter? Beautiful. And that's Rick, your husband? Very nice. Very nice."

We talked about my daughter's newfound love of ice skating, and the joy in having twins, and other various current events.

Then Henry surprised me. "Today, it's time we toast our progress. I have good Polish vodka. You want some? I get two glasses."

Caught off guard, I laughed and smiled inwardly. The taste of my morning coffee still lingered, and I'd never taken straight shots of vodka. Henry was different from anyone I'd ever met. At nine in the morning he proposed straight vodka. I declined and promised we'd toast when the book was done. Years later, I regretted turning down the chance to toast with Henry.

We settled into our usual interview spot on the patio. With thoughts on family, I turned the conversation back to Henry.

"Henry, how did you meet Nancy?"

I fell in love with Nancy like nuts. She and I worked at the same hospital in New York City. She was the secretary to a very famous heart surgeon, and I worked in the physical therapy department. She was always very nice to me and helped me with my English. I didn't understand much English, but she had the most beautiful blue eyes and was very lively.

For our first date, I invite her to Jones Beach. We get there, and I take off my street pants so I'm in my bathing suit. She just stared at me, then came and pushed me down into the sand.

Then she screamed at me, "Don't get up! Don't get up!"

I didn't know what was going on. I looked all over to see

what happened. Then, I figure it. She was embarrassed at my French bathing suit—it wasn't much wider than this pencil.

Henry laughed in between his words.

I paid five *francs* in France for the most modern, fashionable, swim pants at that time. In France, the girls don't think of wearing almost nothing. I was very fashionable over there. Once I got an American swimsuit, Nancy was okay.

Years later we vacationed in Nice, France. We saw the nude girls taking a shower, right there in front of you and nothing happen. Everybody survive.

Henry turned to Nancy and grinned as she entered the patio at the end of the story. "See? Nancy loves that story."

View of the kitchen at Auschwitz from outside the camp.
To the far left of the building is the main entrance to the camp.
October 2013. *Photo by author.*

AUSCHWITZ IN OCTOBER 2013

T he drive from Kraków to the Auschwitz-Birkenau State Museum took about an hour. On that chilly fall day, our interpreter, Piotr, drove and answered some of my many questions. I'd allotted a full day at the museum to pore through records, meet with the archivist, and take a private three-hour tour at four in the afternoon. The skies threatened rain, but held back. As the car neared the museum, I grew quiet, not knowing what to expect, yet anxious to find the answers to the many questions registered in my brain. I remained grateful I didn't have to drive, so I could focus my thoughts.

From the parking lot, visitors entered the reception building, which ironically had served as the "reception" building for incoming prisoners. Somber photo displays introduced visitors to the history and stories for this place. I knew instinctively that visitors would leave changed, taking home shocking memories seen only there. Holocaust museums do their best to keep the history saved for teaching current and future generations; but there's no substitute for visiting a concentration camp in person.

Exiting the reception building, visitors walked down a well-trodden path, headed to the camp's main entrance, marked by the famous arched sign: *Arbeit Macht Frei*. We passed a former guardhouse on our left that served as a small bookstore. Just inside the main gate and perimeter of the camp, bordered by a double electric fence, a long, single-story, rectangular, brick building stretched to the right. Twelve chimneys punctuated the roofline with windows overlooking the front of the camp. The sight of chimneys probably brings to mind one thing— crematorium. However, this sizable building was the kitchen. Cooking food, however meager, for a population up to 20,000 prisoners posed a significant and important daily task.

We entered the building to our immediate left, home to the museum administrative offices, which also served as administrative offices during the operation of the camp. I looked down the road lined with three-story, red brick buildings separated by grassy areas. If you ignored the electric fence and photos, it didn't look that ominous. Visitors received a visual grasp, but missing from the experience was the sight, smell, and sound of filthy, ill prisoners, walking past daily piles of freezing corpses. I came full of firsthand stories of a survivor, fully aware and respectful of its horrific past. Yet, I still remember, somewhat sadly, observing a busload of Asian tourists walking quickly in crowds, snapping photos in front of the buildings, and returning to their buses in a very short time. They came, they saw, they snapped, they left, one more tourist destination checked off their vacation itinerary. But did they really *see*, I asked myself?

I had a nine o'clock appointment that morning with Dr. Wojciech Płosa, Head of Archives for the Auschwitz-Birkenau State Museum. He was extremely gracious and helpful, and had set aside relevant materials in another room for us to view, as I had requested he try to locate some specific prisoner names and numbers. Many original materials mentioned Henry, or other prisoners he knew. When something specific didn't appear in the documents, Dr. Płosa patiently and thoroughly answered my questions. We met near his office on the second floor of a former administration building immediately to the left as you enter the main gate.

From the bright windows, we looked down on the kitchen, directly opposite us and just inside the main gate. As I settled in to pore through a larger stack of materials than expected, my husband settled into a corner with a science-fiction paperback, prepared to patiently let me explore Henry's history. I later wished I'd allowed more than one day on our itinerary to explore and verify facts. Piotr helped me comb through the many records, and my excitement rose as so many records did indeed verify Henry's presence, his stories, and those of three of his compatriots, who shall be named later in this story.

Later, as we chatted in Dr. Płosa's office, I noticed a few words in Polish hanging on the wall above his computer monitor, so he could look at them every time he sat down to work.

Nadzieja to ryzyko, ktore trzeba podjać. Our Polish interpreter gave it these words, a quote from French writer Georges Bernanos: "Hope is the risk you must take on your back."

I asked Dr. Płosa a question he has been asked many times— how can he work full-time conducting research at a concentration camp. His response was simple, heartfelt, and resonated with purpose. Per Dr. Płosa,

"I have been working here since 1997. I know that behind each record, each document, each photograph, there is a special kind of human life story. Alive. With plans for the future . . . We know one day there will be nobody. No survivors. So those documents, those materials, texts of stories, they are very important. They will be evidence and very important voices for the next generation, when there will not be a possibility to meet a survivor. Any survivor.

"We know that we do our job not only for us, but also for the future."

At four o'clock, we met Magda, our private tour guide, and began the tour. She was also extremely gracious, knowledgeable, and helpful.

We visited the basement of the infamous Block 11, the brutal prison block within a brutal prison. As we walked down the cement hallway, I asked our guide about Kapo Jakub. She was familiar with Jakub and she even wrote down his full name in my notes as Jakub Kozelczuk. Surprised I would know the name, Magda quietly steered us to a wooden cell door, with a two-foot square piece of clear Plexiglas nailed to it. As I peered closer, Magda pointed out a nearly invisible, but distinct drawing of a man's face and shoulders carved lightly into the heavy wood. The image depicted a man just like Henry described—not much hair, but strong looking like a boxer, with a thick neck. Solid. How strange to see a visual of Kapo Jakub. Stepping down the cement stairs to the basement—a place better described as a dungeon than prison—was sobering, and filled with few other people. I observed a pipe running the length of the hallway ceiling between heavy, wooden, barred doors. Block 11 was the only block with central heating—for the comfort of the SS who worked in the building, of course.

We finished up at Birkenau, a ten-minute drive from the main camp. I stood there in the growing dark of a cold dusk, shivering. I truly wished I had packed gloves and a heavy winter coat. The next moment, it dawned on me that few prisoners were dressed even as warmly as we were. Polish winters routinely drop to subzero Fahrenheit temperatures. My husband Rick, Magda, and I were the only people there. Visiting Birkenau impressed on me the sheer enormity of scale of the operation, despite the fact we had run out of time to fully explore its grounds. We toured one wooden building that looked like a horse stable. Instead of fifty horses, hundreds of women had occupied this crude space with a dirt floor. The grounds seemed to stretch the length of multiple football fields. I could not see the opposite side. We returned to the entrance, and I stood silently, reluctant to leave a place I'd traveled so far to see. I listened for voices and heard only whispers in the wind as I sensed the true magnitude of human darkness in this place. Then, unlike the doomed 1.1 million people who perished there, we exited, climbed in our car, and drove silently back to Kraków and a warm hotel room.

HUNGER

HENRY'S STORIES CONTINUE:

T he camp commander used to say, "If you live longer than forty days you are a thief."

It was true. I went in strong. They called me *Der Lange*, the tall one, and put me in front of the food lines. They give me double soup because I was strong. But only for a week.

Henry stopped.

No way . . . (he greatly exaggerated these two words) you can work twelve-hour days without much food for very long. By the third week, I was already getting weaker.

Hunger was terrible. Auschwitz had no grass, nothing that grew. Today there's grass. Not back then. Prisoners were so hungry, they'd pluck it and eat it.

What do you get to eat? Nothing. For breakfast you'd get a one-fifth loaf of bread three fingers square, and a bowl of brown water they called coffee, made out of chestnuts. Lunch was soup. It was nothing but water, potatoes, beets, leaves, whatever they decided to throw in that day.

In the evening, you get another cup of coffee, another ladle of soup, bread, and a finger of marmalade or margarine, one-sixteenth of the brick. Sometimes, you got like a finger-length of sausage. That was all that you got. According to the Germans, you got 1,500 calories a day. Bullshit. After twelve hours of hard labor, you're exhausted.

I had my metal bowl for soup. You lose your bowl you die. Why? Because the main food you get is hot soup —you can't hold that in your hands. You sleep with the bowl under your head so no one steals it from you. If it was really good food, the kapos got to it before it ever reached prisoners.

You can't imagine what hunger does to people. I saw a guy catch a mouse, bite off the head, and squeeze the blood out. But he was already a *musselman*, almost gone. He's living, but dead. The other prisoners killed him in the night because he was going crazy.

I fainted once. I was sick with a fever, 102 or 103 maybe. You're sick, you work. When I washed the metal canisters for soup, there was a little water in the bottom of the kettle, like a mirror, and I see myself. I was so scared at what I saw I fainted. We had no mirrors, so this is the first time I see myself. On my head there was no hair. I had blue veins sticking out. I look like a skeleton. My friends took me out and carry me to my block. Even now, I never look in the mirror when I am sick.

Imagine you see a pile of bodies; they died at work. One day, I was working with my friend and I looked at the mountain of cadavers. One is hit in the mouth or gun butted, another is shot in the back. They are put in a pile about eight feet tall, maybe twenty to twenty-five people. Then, we see the pile was moving. One cadaver tried to eat a piece of bread from his pocket. He has no mouth, but he try to eat anyway. Then, I see another cadaver next to him who senses bread and they fight for the bread, squeezing it until the bread dissolved into crumbs. It was so hard to watch—these guys are already dead. And you know what we thought about? We had no pity. We were just sad for the wasted bread.

Finally, after about six weeks in the camp, I was done, finished, kaput. I almost looked like a *musselman*, barely thinking, a living skeleton at the end of my limits. My weight was down under 100 pounds. I was so skinny I could hang my hat on my shoulder bone. One morning after coffee and roll call, I walked out in front of my block, laid down with my face in the gutter, and closed my eyes. I was ready to die.

KAZIO

I don't know how long I lay in the gutter. I don't care. Then, I heard a voice I hadn't heard in two years.

"Henyu, what you are doing down there?"

Sure I was dreaming, I laid there.

"Henyu, I said what are you doing down there? Can you hear me?"

Then someone bent down and nudged me.

I'm done, Kazio. I'm ready to die. *Let me go.*

"Henyu. You gonna make it. Leave it to me. Get up."

Kaz gave me his hand and pulled me up. Then, he said something I couldn't believe. "Now, go get the Kapo Michael for me."

What? You're crazy. I can't call Bloody Michael. If I even lift my head up to look at him he'll kill me right away with the leg of a chair. Let me die, Kaz.

"No, no. Everything will be fine. Trust me. Just go to him

and say Kaz sent you, and I want to see him."

I got up and went to the Bloody Michael Kapo, shaking like hell. He stared me down because I dared to talk to him.

"Yeah?"

Kapo Michael, Prisoner 39551 here. Kaz wants to talk to you.

"Kaz? Okay."

Right away, Kapo Michael runs like hell outside the block to find Kaz. I followed and watched.

Kazio grabbed Michael roughly by the collar and pulled him up, then pointed at me.

"See my friend Henry, here? Henry is my friend, and he has to live. Do you get that?"

Bloody Michael was like, "Sure, sure, sure, Kaz. Whatever you say."

"I'm going to send you a few pounds of sausage every day. Keep one pound for you and one pound for my friend." Kaz points to me. "No more, no less. Do you understand?"

Everything changed that day. I was moved to Kazio's room and given a good bed on the bottom deck until I could get my strength back. I didn't share the bed with anyone. Suddenly, I was the favorite prisoner. Right away, I did not have to work. They give me a broom and I swept the block, but did not have to go outside to a job. Within one month, I was back to one-hundred-sixty pounds, just eating nothing more than two soups a day, a piece of sausage, and a double portion of bread. No one stole from me again.

That is how I survived the camp. Not because I was special or smart. I survive for one reason—I was lucky and I know somebody.

Kazio arrived at the camp in August 1940 only two months after it opened. He was number 3454, and somehow he became chief of the storeroom. They had everything there—the sugar, salt, margarine, and staples, whatever they need . . . sausages, yeah. Everything we need for breakfast, Kazio got that. He was not the head of the kitchen, but the head of the supply pantry. That was how he could send sausage to Bloody Michael for me.

I wondered why everyone was afraid of Kazio.

Kazio was one of the strongest men in camp. He and another guy from Warsaw could carry the wooden case of sausage, all four hundred pounds. The box had wooden handles on either side, and they each carry a side. Besides that, he was good friends with Teddy Pietrzykowski.

"Who?"

I'll tell you later. After about a month of recovering in Kazio's room, and having enough food, I was healthier and able to work again. Kazio came to me one morning. "Henyu, let's go meet the kapo I told you about."

I can't remember the kapo's name, but he was in charge of the *kartoffelschäler*, or potato peeling *kommando*. I remember he had been a captain in the Polish army. Kaz took me to the *kommando* and introduced me.

To the kapo he says, "See my friend Henry, here? Henry is my friend, and he'll be a good potato peeler. Make sure he is looked after."

"Sure, sure, Kaz."

And with that, I had a new job under the roof. You know, indoors. I sat next to other preferred prisoners and peeled potatoes. I made many friends there. I was so happy to be peeling potatoes. Kazio made sure I had sausage. And, here I am, just some ordinary Polak. On my left is the future premiere of Poland, Józef Cyrankiewicz. On my right, are two university professors. I meet Professor Nycz there. As we peeled potatoes, we'd reminisce.

The professor told me about the *Collegio Novum*. Two months after the Germans invade Poland, the Germans ordered all the professors at Jagiellonian University to come for an assembly at the *Collegio Novum*. They gonna be instructed how they teach Polish kids at Polish schools.

"*Collegio Novum?*"

New College. It is the Latin name for that part of the university, the main building. The story is that they called all the professors—names like . . . eh, you don't know them, but in Europe they know them because they was making lecture all over the universities of Europe. One hundred eighty-three professors and helpers, vice professors, and adjuncts, and so on. They gathered in a lecture hall. All around them, and at every exit there are plenty of SS, all with guns. And here comes Mr. Bruno Müller, the Gestapo chief in Kraków:

"Sit down, everybody. As you know, you are not doing a good job. We know everybody is nationalistic for Poland.

Therefore, everyone is an enemy of the university. We need to take all of you out to teach you the proper way to teach the future Polish youth."

Suddenly the Germans take everyone out to trucks behind the lecture hall. Everyone was forced to get in the trucks. The Germans took them to Sachsenhausen concentration camp near Frankfurt. All the intelligentsia had to go. They died like flies. That winter was one of the coldest in a very long time. A very few were released after an international outcry.

That was a huge hit on the Polish intelligentsia. That was the Germans. They closed the schools and removed the thinkers. The teachers. Anyone in authority. What do you do when you invade a country? First, you kill the leaders.

THE *FRAUENLAGER*

The first women arrived at Auschwitz in March 1942. The Germans partitioned off some blocks and surrounded these blocks with the electric wire to create the *Frauenlager* [the women's camp]. They brought in about 990 Jewish girls from Ravensbrück. Two hours later about a thousand Jewish girls arrived from Slovakia. They squeezed more than three hundred women into a block. They had to sleep in wooden barracks, very primitive, on top of each other, just like the men.

Not too long after I started peeling potatoes, Kazio came and found me.

"Henyu, you're going to help me tonight. I'm going to see the girls in the *Frauenlager*."

I looked at Kazio like he had totally lost his mind. What? Are you crazy? How are you gonna get there? There's electric wire, there's a tower every fifty meters, the soldiers in the towers have guns.

"Don't worry, Henyu. It's fixed. Just bring this barrel with you when you come tonight. Make sure you leave out the bottom."

I knew from working in the kitchen how to roll the barrel. You had to roll it at just such an angle. And they were big, heavy, and wooden. You roll with it and go with it.

After dinner, when it was dark, but before lights out, I met Kazio behind my block, 16. The fence to the women's camp was right there. Kazio went outside to the wire and motioned me over. So, here I come rolling the barrel.

What does Kazio do? He lifts up the electric wire and we stick the barrel between the wires. Kazio crawled through the barrel and was in. He motioned for me to follow him and I crawled through the bottomless barrel to the other side of the fence.

Kazio had found out that Goldwasser's daughter, a prominent Jewish jeweler from Grodska Street in Kraków, had been on the last transport to the camp. I remember her as very beautiful and a lot of fun. I don't remember her first name.

At this point, Henry stood up, excused himself, and left the patio to go inside. He came back shortly and handed me a solid, twelve-inch-long silver sword. It sat solid and heavy in my hand. I recognized the head of the Polish eagle at the end of the handle. One side of the flat blade was engraved in Polish writing. I asked him what it said.

This is my favorite swimming prize. It's a silver letter opener. It reads 'Gift from Emil Goldwasser Jewelers, Kraków, Grodzka 25.'

I don't remember exactly what we took to Goldwasser's daughter, maybe nylons or perfumed soap, maybe chocolate from the Canada *kommando*. I didn't ask Kazio how he knew she was on the transport. He had his ways. We talk with her a bit, and did what we could to help her, but I don't think she survived.

On the way out of the women's camp, we took the barrel out from the wires. Kazio looked up at the guard tower and gave one of the guards a short wave. He gave a small wave back at Kazio. I don't know how he fixed it, but he did. That was Kazio; he helped who he could, but you couldn't help everyone.

We only went to the women's camp one time. Shortly after that, Birkenau was finished and the women moved out of Auschwitz I, in August.

I interrupted to ask him about something he'd mentioned in passing. "What do you mean the Canada *kommando*?"

They had a special outfit, the Canada *kommando*. They were the people who sorted through the goods brought in by the Jews. They were very guarded because of the goods.

"Why was it named Canada?" I wanted to know.

Because Canada was the land of riches and hope. My friend Wilanowski worked on the *kommando*, so he told me about it. Sometimes they would sort and find diamonds or other jewels. Anything of value was supposed to be turned over to the SS—they were all thieves. That was Auschwitz . . . everyone steals from everyone else. The SS was always walking around and guarding the workers closely.

MUSIC IN THE CAMP

Auschwitz had a wonderful orchestra. Kapo Franz Nierychło was the kapo of the kitchen, and he was the *kapellmeister* of the *lagerkapelle*, or camp orchestra. Go figure. He was a real son of a bitch and he leads the orchestra. He claimed to have been born in Germany, and he obeyed the Germans exactly what they say. He was a postman before the war and led the postal orchestra in Łódź Poland. So, when he came to Auschwitz, the Germans let him organize the orchestra and he picked his guys to play. There were many famous names from all over Europe, Jewish and otherwise.

"But, Henry, where did the instruments come from? I didn't think people brought their instruments to Auschwitz."

No, no, no. The Germans bought the instruments. The Germans would buy a trombone. Then, they looked till they found a trombone player. And so on, till they filled the orchestra. Kapo Nierychło would sit with his boys right there, just inside the main gates to the camp. The orchestra played lively music like marches in the morning as the work crews left camp for the day. It was supposed to give you the energy to work. Yeah, right. The kitchen was next to the main gate, so he just had to walk outside the kitchen.

The smirk Henry gave me expressed more sarcasm than his voice as he remembered the orchestra. Then, he began to hum a tune I didn't recognize.

I specifically remember the Boccaccio operetta—it was a very lively piece. Kapo Nierychło was no good. If you played one note extra he'd hit you in the head or kick you. But Kapo Nierychło was nice to me because I am friends with Kazio Szelest. Kazio was in charge of the pantry, and Nierychło was in charge of the kitchen and the cooks. Kazio was more important since he controlled the food.

In the evening, the orchestra would assemble again and play as prisoners returned to camp from working all day. These poor guys would come back to camp, dragging shovels and bodies. Every day people died, but they had to be counted at the end of the day, so if someone died, the other prisoners had to drag them back. When you get back to camp, you throw the dead on the dead pile by the corner of the kitchen. When the last dead guy had been carried in, the SS guard would give a sign, and Kapo Nierychło always stopped the orchestra on whatever note they were on.

The Germans liked their music. On Sunday they held concerts, and people would come from as far away as Berlin to hear Nierychło's orchestra. The SS officers would bring their wives and families, too. They'd have picnics and listen to music. Sunday afternoons were quieter in the camps because most of the guards were off on Sunday afternoons.

"So, I'm confused. Where did the families watch the orchestra? I mean, I wouldn't take my family to a prison camp."

No, they didn't come to camp. Outside the gates, there were about two hundred fifty acres of ground between Birkenau and Auschwitz. They had many things for the officers. There was a farm where they raised pigs and horses. You were a lucky prisoner if you got to help on the farm outside Auschwitz. Sometimes you could sneak a tomato—but if you got caught, you got shot. On the farm outside the gates, there were SS barracks and a movie theater.

PRISONER MAIL, PACKAGES, AND MONEY IN AUSCHWITZ

Henry and I became good friends after only a few meetings. When someone entrusts you with his life stories, an unspoken connection develops. His willingness to share openly was so different than my family, I just absorbed story after incredible story, even the harshest ones. He used to ask in surprise, "You're so interested. Are you sure you want to hear more?"

I always did.

On one visit to Henry's house, he led me to a compact third bedroom he referred to as his office. As I entered the room, a small wooden desk covered in neat stacks of papers stood immediately to my right. He had already pulled out a thick file of World War II-era articles and news clippings. Above it, a bulletin board held various photos and newspaper clippings from the Arizona Senior Olympics for swimming and tennis. A warped black-and-white photo showed a young, serious boy in a white suit—his First Communion photo. A photocopy of a magazine article showed an older Henry and Nancy sitting lovingly arm-in-arm. The headline read, "How I Met Mr. Right." I smiled inwardly, but for now that article would have to wait as my gaze circled the room, cognizant that what someone keeps and displays in their private spaces reveals a visual depth of character in a single image.

My eyes continued around the room to a four-tiered set of shelves displaying a crowded array of tennis trophies, medals, and various knick-knacks. Henry pulled out a shoebox packed full of neatly organized postcards from around the world. He explained he had a good friend who worked for Lufthansa—she used to send him postcards from every place she visited. After setting the shoebox back in place, he pulled out a large, pale-green, hardcover book, opened it to a random page, and began reading poetry. I can't remember the name of the Polish poet, but Henry insisted the poet was very famous in Poland, and he admired him a great deal. The entire book was a single, long poem, beautifully illustrated. The pages turned easily, as in a book that has been read many times.

Lastly, my eyes came to rest on a poster directly in front of me, clearly made by a young student for a school project. An armband in blue and white stripes, with an upside down red triangle in the middle, was stapled in one corner. In another corner, I saw a yellowed sheet of paper with handwriting in faded pencil, glued to the bottom and hanging loose. I looked closer and read the word "Auschwitz" in the preprinted text, and saw a red postage stamp with the image of Adolf Hitler. It looked yellowed, old, and original. I'd never seen anything like it.

Intrigued, I gestured toward it. "Henry, what's this?"

That's a poster my great-nephew did for a school project.

"I meant what's this piece of paper?"

Henry shrugged.

That's one of my letters from camp. I give it to him.

"What do you mean, one of your letters from camp? Prisoners didn't send letters home from Auschwitz."

Sure, sure we had letters. I have more of them. Do you want to see?

Henry moved to a desk drawer and brought out a weathered, brown envelope with about a dozen more of these letters, all addressed to his mother: Karolina Zguda, Panska 9, Kraków. As he flipped through them, I either saw the words Auschwitz or Buchenwald pre-printed above German text on the fronts. Each letter consisted of a single piece of paper, printed on both sides, that also formed an envelope when folded a certain way. I counted two postcards. The penciled handwriting was more faded on some than on others. He must have sensed my curiosity, because he turned and left the room, taking the letters with him. I followed him back to the patio table to continue this unexpected conversation. Ever so gently, I picked up the fragile documents one by one to examine them. They were clearly authored in German.

Henry told me about these letters.

Once a month, or every six weeks, you could write a letter. These were official letters on camp paper. They gather us all in one room and give us like ten pencils for three hundred guys. You cannot write whatever you wanted to. Every letter had to begin with: *I feel good. I am very glad I am here.* It was such bullshit—here I am dying, skinny, hungry, but you couldn't say that. So, I have to figure out what to say. How are you? How is the uncle? I had many uncles, but 'the uncle' was the phrase I used to refer to the underground. Or I ask about my girlfriend Gena, and so on.

Henry searched through the letters and pulled out one with some text crossed out in pencil.

See, in this letter the censor crossed something out. Here's the censor stamp—*Geprüft 5 KL Auschwitz*—in blue ink. I don't remember what I wrote he didn't like.

If the other guys couldn't write or read in German, they had to pay someone to write, so sometimes I got extra bread if I wrote their letters. I used simple German words I remembered from my high-school German classes. The Germans charge prisoners for that damn stamp of Hitler. For that stamp, you have to give up a piece of bread, and so I am hungry after that.

"Did your mother read German?"

No, no. She had to pay someone to translate.

Still absorbing this new piece of history, I knew one thing immediately. "Henry, these must be very valuable. I've certainly never read about any prisoners sending mail. Have you ever checked?"

These? No one cares about these. They're just old papers, who cares about my story? I've told Nancy to throw everything out when I'm gone. No one will care. Besides, the nephew got an A on his project.

As Henry talked, I kept looking at the papers. In some, the

penciled writing was more faded, in others the handwriting resembled scribbling . . . perhaps indicating a more difficult time? I also looked at the signature and noticed Henry had adopted the practice of signing his name as the German variant "Heinrich." I also began to recognize one word in several letters: Gena, the name of his girlfriend. Sometimes I saw it as Gena, sometimes as Jana, which could also be attributed to poor handwriting.

I was curious about her. "Whatever happened to Gena?"

Do you know she kept going to the Germans to secure my release so many times, she kept seeing the same German officer. They started getting together, and guess who she gets engaged to? This same German officer she was trying to get to help her win my freedom.

"You mean your girlfriend married a Nazi?"

Henry's face quickly turned angry. No! I *never* said he was a Nazi, I said he was in the German army. Not everyone in the German army was for Hitler, but if you're German you had no choice. In fact, he was Austrian. When Hitler invaded Austria, the men had no choice whether to serve. You served or went to prison. Or worse.

Henry turned to several pages in the ever-present photo album, and pointed to a picture of a lovely couple, circa the mid-1950s.

See. That's Gena. Isn't she beautiful? After the war, I visited her and her husband in Austria. He was a very nice guy. We stay friends. He ran a Mercedes dealership.

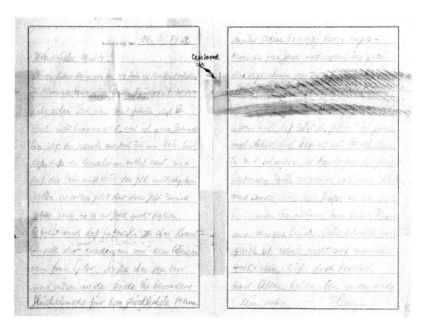

Inside of letter from Auschwitz dated August 16, 1942.
US Holocaust Memorial Museum, gift of Nancy Zguda.

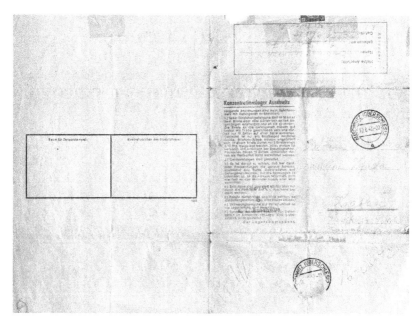

Front and back of letter from Auschwitz dated August 16, 1942.
US Holocaust Memorial Museum, gift of Nancy Zguda.

Henry let me borrow his letters to make copies. I made photocopies and also scanned digital versions using my home scanner, and carefully protected the letters until they could be returned to Henry at a subsequent interview. Though he seemed nonchalant about them, they were not mine to keep.

The next day, I sat down at my computer and searched the internet and several online auction sites. It surprised me to discover camp letters and postcards from prisoners in many concentration camps are regularly bought and sold as World War II memorabilia, most for between one hundred and two hundred dollars apiece. Yet, what Henry had in his possession, and what I had copies of lying next to my computer, comprised a completely different and historical treasure than what I saw online. I quickly realized collectors randomly buy and sell papers of unknown provenance, and probably never translate the contents to determine the context or message contained within. They collect bits of history, but I had been handed a *story*. I was interviewing the author of a set of them who could explain the content and circumstances of each one.

I still couldn't understand why Henry didn't care whether they were valuable or not, beyond the memories they evoked. He had kept them in a safe place since the war, but only for himself. They survived because he sent them to his mother. What mother wouldn't save every precious letter from an imprisoned son? Could there have been more correspondence from Henry that somehow got lost years ago?

Next, I wondered what did people write or send to *him*? It would have been impossible for him to save any of the letters he received. Partial answers came in subsequent letters when he thanked his family for specific items they sent.

My brain raced to the letter Henry let his nephew glue to poster board. Clearly Henry had no idea of the value of these rare documents or, if he did, he didn't care. Why, oh why, couldn't the nephew have used a color photocopy instead of using one of the originals? Where the letter was glued to the poster, the writing was obscured, and it couldn't be removed for preservation. These belonged in a museum. While there was no point in lamenting the near destruction of one of these precious and expensive letters, I made a mental note that neither Henry nor his family had any idea of the dollar and historical value of his papers. I became determined to make copies of as many other papers and photos as Henry would let me borrow, and work to safeguard them as best I could.

What else did this man have hidden away?

I subsequently invited Henry over to my house to show him what I'd found for sale, specifically on eBay. As a bonus, Henry enjoyed being around my children, and they liked him. As I showed him around my house, he came to know my family better as I identified members of my relatives in various portraits hanging on the wall. Any stories of war faded into the past.

Like many seniors in their eighties, Henry had never learned to use a computer and saw no need to at this point in his life. I pulled an extra chair over in front of my monitor for Henry to use, opened up eBay, and entered in a search phrase. Page after page of letters, and other miscellaneous camp artifacts from Auschwitz for sale appeared on the screen. The prices per letter ran as high as three hundred dollars.

Henry's reaction to seeing the letters scroll by on the monitor was completely unexpected. He leaned in closely to read the screen and ignored any concept of pricing. I scrolled somewhat rapidly through them, to show him how many there were. His reaction surprised me, and further validated his connections with many people. He only wanted to read the prisoner names and numbers on the letters.

"Go back. Go back. Slow down. Slow down. I want to see the numbers. Maybe I know him."

●●

Soon after I had made the letter photocopies, I approached a German woman I knew only as a distant acquaintance from my church and asked if she'd be willing to do a small German translation for me. I chose a letter from Buchenwald at random, and asked for two things. I wanted to know what the pre-printed German text read, which I presumed were camp rules. The second request was for a translation of Henry's handwritten cursive German. I explained very little about where I obtained the document, wanting her reaction to be the same as others who had never seen these—which was everyone I knew. I returned to her house a week later.

"Katrina, I read this, but the translation makes no sense. He mentions receiving shoe polish and toothpaste in a package from home. It might be a code or something. I don't know where you got this. In Germany, everyone grows up learning the history of the Holocaust. I know for a fact that prisoners never received packages."

I was as surprised as she was by the translation. Shoe polish and toothpaste? How truly odd. I made a note to ask Henry later. Due to her skepticism, and lack of an offer to translate any more, I politely thanked her, gave her a small gift for her time, and left. Other than that stationery text and the one letter she translated, I did not have the rest of the letters and documents translated until many years later after Henry passed away. At that time, I requested a new translation of the same letter as a cross-verification of its meaning. Because that first translated letter was from Buchenwald, I'll save its specific discussion for later. However, this new and unexpected revelation further intrigued me. Interspersed in the mandatory "I feel healthy" and daily chatter, there were comments thanking his relatives for things like money and stamps, which begged the next question—did he *receive* mail from home as well as send letters? The answer is yes.

Left inside stationery, page one of
letter from Auschwitz dated June 28, 1942.
US Holocaust Memorial Museum, gift of Nancy Zguda.

Right inside of stationery, page two of
letter from Auschwitz dated June 28, 1942.
US Holocaust Memorial Museum, gift of Nancy Zguda.

LETTERS FROM AUSCHWITZ

I include two translations below. The first is of the pre-printed text on the camp stationery. The second is Henry's first letter home to his mother.

Concentration Camp Auschwitz

The following orders are to be followed in written exchanges for prisoners:

Each prisoner in protective custody is permitted to receive two letters or two cards per month from his relatives as well as send two letters or two cards. The letters to the prisoners must be written legibly with ink and may only contain 15 lines on a page. Only a standard-sized sheet of paper is permitted. Envelopes must be unpadded. A letter may contain 5 postal stamps worth 12 Pfennigs. All other items are prohibited and may be seized. Postcards have 10 lines. Photographs may not be used as postcards.

1. *The sending of money is permitted.*
2. *It is to be noted that money or postal mail should contain the correct address comprised of name, birth date, and prisoner number. If the*

address is incorrect, the mail will be returned to the sender or be destroyed.

3. *Newspapers are permitted. However, they may only be ordered through the postal location/office of the concentration camp at Auschwitz.*
4. *Packages may not be sent because prisoners may make purchases in the camp.*
5. *Petitions for release from protective custody to camp managers are useless.*
6. *Speaking with and being visited by prisoners in the concentration camp is generally not permitted.*

Henry wrote his first letter two weeks after he arrived at Auschwitz. Unfortunately, it is the same letter the nephew glued to poster board for his class project so it was the most damaged of all the letters.

June 28th, 1942

Dear Mother!

Since June 10 I'm in the concentration camp Auschwitz. I'm letting you know that I am healthy. I hope you are also healthy. You shouldn't worry and cry, instead worry about yourself. I hope you have enough money and food, if that's not the case, you can pay from the money that is owed to me XXXXX [paper torn] like from Micia and XXXXX [paper torn]. My suit may be picked up from the tailor. He lives on Zwierzynieckastrasse 7 or 8, his name is Wojtas. When you write, pay attention to the instructions on the first page. Lastly, I kiss you with love, my dear mother, and also Ms. Jana. Kindest regards to all acquaintances and relatives and for all in the Bude where I worked.

Henryk

T here was a time in 1942 and 1943 we get packages. The packages help you to survive a little better. One month, I get a package for Christmas from my mother. It was a little package, because my mother didn't have much. She sends me some cookies and a pair of woolen socks. It was cold like hell at that time. She included a big darning needle and a little yarn to mend them later. I give the paper with all the crumbs to my friend so he can taste a little bit. Only, he was so hungry, he just gulped everything including the paper. Then, I see wool sticking out of his mouth. I didn't know until then the needle fell off the ball into the cookie crumbs. I try to pull on it to get needle out, but he swallow it. Oh man, what could I do? I was sure it's goodbye Charlie. Then, two days later, he comes to me. "Success, a bowel movement." Normally, if the doctor ask you about if your bowel movements are regular, I say, What do you mean regular?

Every six or seven days was regular, because you have no food going in. But he was early, and he calls to me, "Henry, guess what I found?" He holds up a two-inch darning needle. How on earth does this needle go through his system and it comes out without killing him? Crazy things happened there.

••

- 2 -

Konzentrationslager Auschwitz
Häftlingsgeldverwaltung

Auschwitz, den 23. Oktober 1942

Einzahlungsliste

Häftl. Nr.			RM.	
		Übertrag:	427.—	4455.—
37584	Sarnowski	Wladisl.	17.—	
37617	Baczkowski	Wladisl.	20.—	
37621	Benerat	Stefan	20.—	
37624	Chrust	Leo	30.—	
37624	"	"	20.—	
37638	Kluczny	Ceslaus	20.—	
37638	Kluczny	"	20.—	
37647	Miller	Wladislaus	40.—	
37655	Przepiorka	Miecisl.	25.—	
37664	Wozniak	Eugen	30.—	
37700	Stachurski	Ceslaus	20.—	
37714	Bros	Johann	20.—	
37848	Ignatowski	Andreas	50.—	
37966	Moskal	Stanisl.	25.—	
37986	Owczarek	Thadäus	20.—	
37994	Cencel	Wenzel	40.—	
37996	Czubala	Josef	20.—	864.—
38025	Szwedowski	Johann	20.—	
38077	Blaszczyk	Ignatz	20.—	
38077	"	"	5.—	
38087	Kornacki	Miecisl.	30.—	
38090	Krolicki	Marian	20.—	95.—
39209	Koscielniak	Alex	10.—	
39209	"	"	10.—	
39232	Pazdziora	Leopold	10.—	
39247	Woycicki	Alfred	50.—	
39252	Michajluschkin	Ignatz	100.—	
39271	Elbl	Ulrich	20.—	
39297	Jerousek	Alois	50.—	
39307	Kotzmann	Johann	20.—	
39339	Sypien	Rudolf	40.—	
39367	Noga	Adam	5.—	
39371	Teileis	Heinz	20.—	
39375	Kaufhold	August	10.—	
39376	Guth	Vinzent	20.—	
39406	Roman	Josef	20.—	
39408	Burchacki	Wieslaus	8.—	
39421	Babicki	Josef	30.—	
39430	Dziemba	Gerhard	20.—	
39431	Faber	Siegmund	40.—	
39453	Bak	Josef	20.—	
39457	Basta	Wladisl.	25.—	
39457	"	"	40.—	
39482	Gren	Adolf	25.—	
39485	de Ines	Miecisl.	20.—	
39525	Orlowski	Josef	15.—	
39538	Skoda	Theodor	30.—	
39542	Urbaniak	Johann	30.—	
39551	Zguda	Heinrich	10.—	
39557	Dalowski	Kasimir	20.—	
		Übertrag:	719.—	5414.—

Page 5 of the Prisoner Money Management Deposit list for October 23, 1942. The second line from the bottom reads 39551, Zguda Heinrich, 10 *Reichsmarks* (deposited in his account.) *Used with permission of the Auschwitz-Birkenau State Museum, Oświęcim, Poland.*

When Auschwitz was established in 1940, it was designed as a prisoner detention and concentration camp. When prisoners received packages, the Germans also benefited. Prisoners' families were encouraged to send money, which was deposited into a prisoner's account. Guards opened and searched every incoming package for contraband or items of value. Some prisoner memoirs do report surprisingly intact, if opened, packages. In his memoir, *War in the Shadow of Auschwitz*, John Wiernicki recalled receiving his first package from home. Even though it was previously opened by censors, he found bread, fat, sausage, and a small cake. He considered himself very lucky, especially when he began to receive regular packages from his grandmother. With food, you could trade for almost anything. Interestingly, in this same memoir, he referred to "Kaz" as one of the "good" prisoner functionaries from the early Polish transports who tried to help everyone regardless of race or national origin.

The letters offered a "small" deception that detained relatives were "healthy" and "well-treated" in the camps, if families believed it. When Henry said "you pay" for the stamp of Hitler, I'd assumed that meant in bread, a true story for many. Clearly, Henry had no money when he sent his first letter home. Honestly, the concept of prisoners and money never entered my thoughts as a camp reality, until I delved into more scholastic research at a later time.

Auschwitz also provided a prisoner commissary, where prisoners who had money in their accounts could purchase such things as toothpaste, camp stationery, or perhaps some goods such as pickled beets. These items added a small point of light in the dreary day-to-day struggle to survive, while giving the Germans ways to siphon off prisoners' funds. Soviet POWs and Jews, who occupied the lowest ranks in the camp, were rarely afforded this privilege. However, as a significant exception to this rule, Ann Kirschner wrote a fascinating account entitled *Sala's Gift, My Mother's Holocaust Story*. Her [Jewish] mother survived five years as a slave in seven different Nazi work camps. She had saved more than 350 letters, photographs, and a diary she did not reveal to her family until 1991 on the eve of heart surgery. The letters were later donated to the New York Public Library. As to the commissary, Henry never mentioned the commissary in our talks, and I only learned of it later in my research.

Prisoners could send mail to only one person, and that address stayed on file at camp. Thus, prisoners also faced the dilemma: do I tell the Nazis where my family lives?

Germans kept detailed records of prisoner funds, which I find ironic, as all prisoner funds eventually ended up in German hands. They simply found a way to "charge" prisoners for small things not provided to everyone, and deducted the funds from their accounts. The Auschwitz-Birkenau State Museum showed me a copy of a page from an *Einzahlungsliste*, or Deposit List, dated October 23, 1942 that cataloged a daily record, by prisoner number and name, of the amount of money received that day. The last column is for *reichsmarks*, German currency.

Henry's name appeared second from the bottom as *"39551, Zguda Heinrich, 10."*

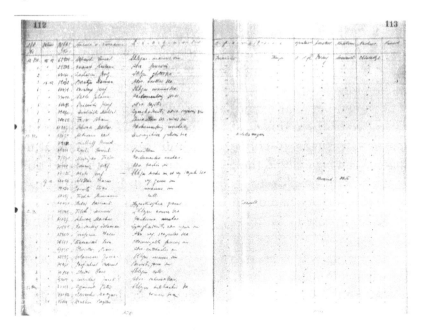

Page from the book of operations of the Surgical Division of the prisoners' infirmary at Auschwitz between September 9, 1942 and February 22, 1943. Line 12822 indicates a date of 16-12 (December 16), for prisoner 39551, Zguda, Heinrich, (illegible.) *Photo 531773_0_1/ITS Digital Archive, USHMM.*

THE CAMP HOSPITAL

HENRY CONTINUES:

When I was on the *kartoffelschäler kommando* peeling potatoes, I got a very large infection in my finger.

Henry paused and gestured to demonstrate a swollen finger with a large bump on it.

I remember that experience vividly. At that time, I'd see Kazio two or three times a day when he'd take the wagon and deliver salt, sugar, or coffee. So, I said to Kazio, "Look at my finger. I can't even hold the peeler. I can't work. What do I do?"

Kazio told me, "Go to the hospital. Go to Dr. So-and-So." I forget the doctor's name, but I remember him.

Kazio insisted. "He is my friend. Go to him and tell him Kazio sent you."

So, I went over to the infirmary in Block 19 to see the doctor. I was living in Block 17 then.

"All right, I see you got this carbuncle. Oh, don't worry about it. Do you want to be awake?"

No, I don't want to be awake. Give me something.

Henry gestured around the small, screened-in patio we sat on.

We went to a room the size of this patio. Maybe it is a little wider. There were maybe one or two tables in there. As I was going in, I saw an old Jew with a huge carbuncle on his neck. He was bent over, the lump was so big. You know, those abscesses can kill you if you don't kill them first. He was just standing there and, on the way to the table, here comes the *pfleger*. The male nurses were inexperienced. They have no medical training, but you say you're a nurse, so you're a nurse. He had a knife and a small round bowl shaped like a kidney to collect the water and pus. He put that bowl up to the man's neck, cut, cut, cut, squeeze it two or three times and he was done. The nurse turned him around, wrapped about two pieces of toilet paper on it, kicked him in the ass, and sent him back out. Before I made three steps across the room, they were done.

I never saw that poor old Jew again. I'm sure he died. You know the carbuncle is right on the nerve system, big and bold like that, with pus. Imagine it. They just cut, squeeze, put paper around, and out he went. No disinfection, no nothing. And only toilet paper. That was it.

I followed the doctor to a table and he told me to lie down. While I am lying down, I saw a second man with a carbuncle come in, get treated like the first Jew and sent back out.

But, for me, the doctor says, "I'm going to give you chloroform. Start counting."

I started counting one, two, three, ahh . . . That's all I remember before I was out. When I woke up, I had a very nice bandage. My carbuncle was gone and done very nicely. All because I was a friend of Kazio. You needed someone to help you to survive.

I remember one Jewish water polo player we tried to save. Kazio put him in the hospital and changed the names on the beds. His name was Stazio Rosen—he was the goalkeeper in the Jewish swim club, Makkabi. Good swimmer, too. He was already weak and sick. We did what we could, but it only worked for about two weeks.

The Germans were scared like hell of typhus after [SS Gerhard] Palitzsch's wife died from typhoid fever. They don't know how she got it, but we think maybe a prisoner carried it into their house while it was cleaned, as an attempt to infect Palitzsch, but they never proved it.

Henry's voice continued with a hard edge to it.

Palitzsch loved the killing in Block 11. He was one of the worst killers there. Later, after his wife died he was caught in relations with a Jewish woman and was arrested. It couldn't have happened to a nicer guy.

Sometimes we try to save someone by hanging a typhus sign over a prisoner's bed in the hospital. Germans stayed away, but sometimes the guys were so sick they die anyway.

PROMOTION TO COOK

Kazio convinced Kapo Nierychło and the SS man that I was ready to become a cook. I had put on some weight. You had to be strong to be a cook, to maneuver the heavy kettles of water. In the kitchens we had forty huge kettles, each with one hundred liters capacity, and we would cook all day. Sometimes the Polish underground tried to save priests or older professors by getting them positions as cooks. I remember one of the laborers in the kitchen was the ex-archbishop of the Ukrainian Orthodox Church. But it was still very hard work, and most couldn't keep up. They didn't last long. Always the SS were walking around watching us so we don't steal.

As a cook, I had a white outfit. Germans were very insistent the kitchen be clean. When I passed by other prisoners, they stand aside to let me pass. I was prominent. I was *somebody*. A cook was *somebody* in Auschwitz, and it was a very good job. The cook was above the potato peeler. We had food, and better food than other prisoners, like marmalade and margarine from the prisoner barrels. Cooks lived in Block 25, next to the kitchen. We had only a few steps to reach work, but we had to get up very early to prepare morning coffee for the camp and start the soup for the day.

There were about forty cooks for twenty kettles of soup and three helpers for each cook. For breakfast, prisoners get coffee. It was nothing but brown water—no sugar, no nothing—and a piece of bread. Then, lunchtime was soup. I made the soup, so I know what was in it. Water, a few potatoes, beets, leaves, something like that. Everything went in the soup—dirty leaves. Maybe some powdered chestnuts or a little flour to thicken it. You know, you boil it down.

As more Jews were shipped to the camp, we'd get barrels every morning of whatever food leftovers were found on the prisoners. Jews could only bring twenty pounds of luggage, so what did they put in their luggage? They brought the best of what they had. You'd find diamonds hidden in toothpaste, dollars tied and hidden in coffee. Whatever I find went in my soup—toothpaste, marmalade, mothballs, anything. The SS gets the barrels with unbroken jars for the SS kitchen and dining room. We got the broken jars so you had to pick the glass out.

Henry broke out in a big grin.

One morning I sat down with a broken jar of marmalade to have a taste, and there's something in it that looks like a finger. I found a condom in my marmalade. It was the size of my pinkie finger, rolled and tied, sewn shut so it's waterproof. I looked around quickly to make sure no one was watching. My friends would be jealous because I am so lucky to get a condom for breakfast. I broke it apart and I found five one hundred US dollar bills. Those poor damn Jews. They were smart. They tried everything. Someone was smart enough to know that Polish *zlotys* were no good outside Poland.

Another time I found a good gold watch in the bottom of my pot. I still remember the brand—CYMA—very famous Swiss watch. Anything I found, I hid for Kazio to come get later. He used it to help the underground, you know, bribe guards for favors, or whatever else he did. What was I going to do with five hundred dollars in that place?

Around the kitchen, there was like a drain in the floor. The grate over it was about three inches on either side that fit over the channel. When I'd find something valuable in the barrels, I hid it under the same grate every time. I had to be very careful because there was always an SS guard walking around the kitchen, constantly watching us. If he caught me, I'm dead. I never saw anyone remove things from the drain, but whatever I put there always disappeared. That was the thing about Kazio. I never asked him for details, and he never volunteered the information. It was safer that way.

Undated photo from Auschwitz. When Henry saw this photo, he immediately recognized the two-wheeled cart as his *rollwagen*. In this photo the *rollwagen* (two-wheeled hand cart) is being used to transport a kettle of something, perhaps coffee. This was the same style cart used in many camps to carry many things, including corpses, or *leichenträger*. On the four-wheeled wagon, the steam rises from a barrel of soup. *Used with permission of the Auschwitz-Birkenau State Museum, Oświęcim, Poland.*

When my discussions with Henry reached Auschwitz, I checked out a sizable and heavy book entitled *Auschwitz, A History in Photographs* from the Phoenix Public Library. The graphic, no-holds-barred photo album of hell was not in high demand. I seemed to be the only person in the entire library system requesting this book, since it was the only copy in the entire system, and I kept renewing the checkout for six months, the maximum checkout period for any item. Had anyone else requested it, the renewals would have stopped. By the time I returned the book, it was well worn, with a nearly broken spine from opening, closing, and flipping through so many pages, so often. For most of those six months, various yellow post-it notes marked multiple pages with Henry's comments.

While I regret the damage, the book was invaluable for me, providing visuals of a place I'd never been. Henry was never a descriptive storyteller; he focused more on the people and their stories. Like many storytellers, he already had the visual memories in his brain, and forgot the listener can't see what he does. If I interrupted him and asked for more details, he always complied and gave simple and direct descriptions that helped my understanding. Still, I needed to balance between requesting more details, and not interrupting his storytelling.

Sometimes when I flipped through the pages of the book with Henry, he'd stop and point to a picture with recognition. "There's my *rollwagen* [two-wheeled hand cart]" or "There's Block 11 like I told you." He reacted with instant recognition to every photo in the book, except for places that were built after his time there.

"I know this guy, 76824—this face is very familiar. These young boys I don't recognize. Not the Jude. Here. I recognize this guy too."

Some photos triggered tangential stories to our current discussion. When the conversation diverted to another story, I could have redirected him back to our current story thread. That I chose not to was, in hindsight, a wise decision. Those conversations in a different direction provided some of the more colorful and unexpected stories in this narrative.

The Auschwitz photo album, as I still refer to it, was certainly not the only book we referred to, but it was the most useful for me in terms of grasping not only a visual sense of buildings, but also geographic locations and distances. Some of the most disturbing photos still haunt me with their sterile, black-and-white, graphic honesty. The book is no longer available through the Phoenix Public Library. I have to assume I inadvertently damaged it beyond acceptable circulation conditions. The book soon disappeared from the library catalog and was never replaced.

When I visited the archives of the Auschwitz-Birkenau State Museum in 2013, the book was one of the primary sources laid out for me in advance as a key reference tool.

The hanging pole outside the back of the kitchen, as recreated. October 2013. *Photo by author.*

POLAND WILL NEVER DIE

HENRY CONTINUES HIS STORY:

I saw my first hanging when I worked in the kitchen. Opposite my kettle of soup, there was a wall in the kitchen with windows that looked out the front and the back of the kitchen. Behind the kitchen, across from my old barracks, Block 16, there was the hanging pole. The kitchen was near the main gate, so work details had to walk past the kitchen area and hanging pole on the way to and back from their work. It was meant to be in a place that can be seen.

One day, I looked out and I see ten guys, prisoners, standing there on chairs, with the ropes already around their necks. I recognized them as Poles. Some of the guys had signs around their neck that read, "Hurrah, Hurrah, I'm Here Again." Anyone caught trying to escape had one of those signs hung on them before they were hung, just to remind us of the penalty for trying to escape.

While I was watching, along comes Aumeier [Deputy Camp Kommandant Hans Aumeier]. He was a short man, not too smart. He never really talked, he just sort of barked at you. He walked past these guys with nooses around their necks, in a formal review. I heard him say something, but couldn't hear it through the window. Then, I heard the Poles start singing the first lines of the Polish national anthem.

As with other musical memories, Henry started singing the tune, but stopped after about six words. He told me the song began with "Poland will never die."

As Aumeier passed by, one of the Poles leaned over and spat on him. I knew the guy from Kraków, I just can't remember his damn name. Aumeier was furious and he just kicked all the chairs right there. The Germans left the bodies there for two or three days so all the prisoners could see them.

THE BEGINNING OF BIRKENAU, OR AUSCHWITZ II

T he Nazis began building a second, larger prisoner complex designed to hold up to 125,000 prisoners, not far from the main Auschwitz camp. The Germans chose the small village of Brzezinka, a bucolic area surrounded by farmsteads, then proceeded to evict more than a thousand Polish families. The Germans reserved the better homes for themselves to occupy. They plowed under the verdant fields, destroyed the remaining homes and buildings, and harvested the bricks for construction of a new camp. Unlike adapting an existing military camp, the Germans could design the massive camp to suit SS needs. They labeled the new sub-camp "Auschwitz II" but referred to it as "Birkenau," the Germanized variant of "Brzezinka."

In June 1941, Hitler reneged on the German-Soviet Non-Aggression Pact of 1939 and invaded Russia, savagely murdering thousands of Russian soldiers, and taking thousands of Soviet prisoners of war. Some historians attribute Hitler's savagery towards the Soviets to his belief that most Russians were Bolsheviks and communists comprised of many Jews. That gave him all the more reason to invade and kill the "communist Jews." Regardless of the rationale, the effect was lethal. In all camps, the Soviet prisoners of war shared the lowest status in camps along with the Jews.

On October 7, 1941, the first major transport of Soviet prisoners of war arrived at Auschwitz, and more transports of Soviet POWs came shortly thereafter. Construction on Birkenau began the next day. All in all, 13,775 Soviets were brought to camp and immediately put to work building Birkenau. They lived without shelter, in the cold and mud. Nearly all perished. Only ninety-two of the prisoners survived to the liberation of Auschwitz on January 27, 1945.

The original camp became labeled "Auschwitz I" and continued to house primarily Polish political prisoners and Soviet POWs. Once construction was complete in March 1942, Birkenau, with its new gas chambers, became the destination for almost all the incoming Jews. Birkenau became designated a *vernichtungslager*, or extermination camp, for incoming Jews. The entire area of Auschwitz is some forty square kilometers, of which Birkenau occupies four hundred twenty-five acres. On one side, the boundary stretches for a mile. In the other direction, it extends for a mile and a half.

The same month that Auschwitz II was completed, the Germans opened Auschwitz III in a synthetic petrol and synthetic rubber factory owned by I. G. Farben. Germans there used the same "evict, clear, and destroy" method as Birkenau to clear the land of Polish farmers. Named Monowitz, and built entirely by slave labor, the factory employed brutal methods to extract as much labor from ill prisoners as possible before they perished.

Eventually, forty other sub-camps of the main camp were established between 1943 and 1944 as companies took advantage of free slave labor for their operations. The most brutal became the Buna factory at Monowitz. Collectively, more Jews died in Auschwitz and its sub-camps than in any other concentration camp or ghetto. It has become one of the most well-known symbols and sites of Nazi genocide.

Today, the offices and displays of the Auschwitz-Birkenau State Museum are housed on the site of the original Auschwitz I. Auschwitz II, or Birkenau, still stands, though few buildings remain on the vast property beyond the arched entryway over the train tracks.

In January 1942, a month after the United States entered the war—following the December 7, 1941, attack on Pearl Harbor—a group of fifteen high-ranking German officials convened at a villa located in Wansee, a suburb of Berlin. The agenda for the meeting listed one priority: develop an organized, efficient plan for eliminating an estimated eleven million European Jews. The Germans even laid out specific death estimates by country, chillingly mapped out with coffins in each country imprinted with an estimated death count. The final report, in essence, sanctioned and organized the industrialization of death and outlined a coordinated plan.

The number of Polish Jews was estimated at 2,284,000. Only Russia, where mass executions of Jews were already taking place, had a higher Jewish population. Auschwitz-Birkenau became designated as the primary and largest extermination camp for Jews. With the construction of a complex of four gigantic gas chambers and crematoria begun in mid-1942, the Germans estimated 1.6 million people a year could be killed and burned there. Initial testing of Zyklon B, a cyanide-based pesticide, had already been performed on 600 Soviet POWs and sick Poles in September 1941, in the basement of Block 11. All perished.

On July 17, 1942, SS Chief Heinrich Himmler inspected Auschwitz. Henry remembered being lined up at roll call when he came to camp, but had few comments about it. I remember one day, he sat there looking in a book. Henry said only, "There's Himmler, that son-of-a-gun. I saw him personally, you know. He visited Auschwitz, and we had to wash, and stand at attention very still, and he walked just like this . . ."

Henry rose and imitated strutting at attention, expressionless.

"He was so shiny, so clean," Henry stressed. "They were so clean, the Germans. But, here, we people can do nothing to clean. We can only stand there. We were suffering like crazy."

Two days later, Himmler ordered the "resettlement of the entire Jewish population of the *General Gouvernement*," essentially the sanctioned murder of every remaining Jew in what used to be Poland.

As I type these words, the sheer enormity of scale of planned industrialized murder is simply beyond comprehension. I think it's easier to acknowledge events that have already happened. But I think I understand those original doubters of early reports about the real scale of organized murder, or those Jews who refused to believe where they were being sent. Many people questioned early reports of killings and gas chambers. *Women? Children? Why would they kill skilled workers? What rational person could really believe it? Surely the reports must be exaggerated, right?*

Reichsführer Heinrich Himmler visits and inspects Auschwitz in July 1942. Himmler was the head of the dreaded SS and was the senior Nazi official in charge of implementing the "Final Solution" to eliminate and murder all Jews. Himmler is second from the left. Kommandant Rudolf Höss is in the foreground to the right. *Used with permission of the Auschwitz-Birkenau State Museum, Oświęcim, Poland.*

AN INCOMING TRAIN OF JEWS

Starting in 1942, the killings increased. You heard the whistle from the transports all day, and the smoke from the crematoriums hung thick in the air. Every day, every day, I saw the train; you hear the toot, toot, toot of the train whistle, coming in with Jews. The cars, two or three cars, would be full of entire Polish villages. The whole village went to the gas chambers, children and mothers.

I saw this from the kitchen because from this window, you can see incoming prisoners. I heard them cry. The hardest was to hear the children scream for their mommies and grandmothers. There were so many coming in, you got used to looking for who you know, friends and family. There were just too many coming in.

One day Kazio asked me if I would deliver bread to the ladies' camp at Birkenau. So, I say to myself, Why not? It's not dangerous. It would be a nice break.

The women were only at the main Auschwitz for a short time. As soon as Birkenau was built, the Germans moved the women there in August 1942. Maybe the kitchen wasn't ready, I don't know. But Kazio send me with bread. Under the bread I have plenty of silk stockings Kazio gave me to give to the girls there.

My friend Wilik Tomaszczyk and I went together. We had the big wagon with two wheels. One of us pushed and the other one pulled. It was heavy and awkward. We were just going, moving slowly, because it killed me the first time I went that way, walking so far in camp shoes. You walk to the field, then to the road, and Birkenau is about two miles away. Halfway there, we see a railroad ramp.

"Wait. So, you went outside the gates of Auschwitz to go to Birkenau? Were there guards with you?"

No.

"Then why didn't you run away if you're outside the gates of Auschwitz?"

Henry stopped and stared at me as if to say, *Did you really just ask that?* He rolled his eyes, held up both hands in the air, and lifted his shoulders. His next words came out angry and loud, almost condescending at my ignorance.

Where!? Where you gonna go? Tell me, where you gonna go?

Henry waved both hands away from his chest, caught his breath, and continued.

You can see for miles! There was nothing. Just the tower and machine guns there. No way. No way. The guys who escaped successfully stole the German uniforms and left in disguise.

So, the two of us are walking slowly and, not too far from us, we see a loading ramp by the train tracks. Then, we hear the toot, toot and, okay, the train is coming. So, we stop, and as we're standing there the train comes to a stop near the loading ramp, like one hundred yards from us. It stopped right there and no one even noticed us.

Right after it stopped, here comes the car full of SS and they jumped out with the dogs. The officers had white gloves and pressed uniforms, so clean. Everyone was standing there in front of the train cars. The wagons looked like what they transport, you know, cattle or animals in. Once the Germans were standing in place in front of the train, they opened the cars one at a time.

Henry imitated the screeching, groaning sound of a heavy door slowly sliding open.

These people were practically falling out of the cars, they were packed in so tight. Those poor Jews kept stumbling and falling on the ground. As soon as the doors opened I see them gasping for fresh air, like coming up from swimming underwater. All around them the Germans were yelling, "*Raus, raus, raus, raus.*" The dogs were barking. It was loud—noisy as hell.

I heard the Germans tell them to take their things with them from the train. Then, they get to a place and the Germans order them to write their names on the luggage. Then, they are ordered to stand in rows. I heard the guards order them, "Women and children to the left. Men to the right."

And they started to form two lines. I was closest to the men, so I heard the guards order the men, "Show the hands. Hold them out. Show us your legs."

Maybe they look to see if the legs were swollen, or the hands didn't look good enough. I don't know what they were looking for. Then, they'd point to the ones they liked.

Then, Wilik and I, we see a big truck, auto truck, like maybe a ton, and it stopped right behind this line of women. The guards put a staircase on it like, like a stepladder unfolding. We can hear the guards shouting orders from where we are standing.

"Please come with us. You going to take a shower. Leave the luggage here, it will be delivered to you afterward."

All the luggage was stacked in a pile. Then, the guards started kicking and pushing the men, the elderly men. They weren't too rough, but rough. It was all part of the ruse to not alarm the people.

I could see one mother standing there with one child. Two of her children were in another line yelling, "Mama! Mama!" The German guard said something I couldn't hear, but she calmed down a little, and she and the one child got in one of the trucks to Birkenau.

We knew what happened next. They would have to stop in front of the gas chamber and be ordered to take off all their clothes. They had to go in nude, and the SS *kommando*, like thirty of them, just stood around taking pleasure for what they saw. I don't know how the SS don't go crazy doing that work, except I think they were drunk. Mostly drunk. After a big heavy job like a transport of 2,000 people, they were always given extra alcohol.

Again, Henry stopped, unusually quiet, and chose his next words carefully.

I stopped believing in God in Auschwitz. If he is so good, so omnipotent . . . so, just send a, ah . . . ah . . . I don't know, hurricane or tornado and break loose all the doors. If I was a god I'd do that. And I figure it out I think. I figure it out who is the worst human enemy, the worst, the cruel human enemy of human body, of human body.

"What is the worst?"

Another human body. That's what we find out. You cannot find another animal more cruel to you like they can do like the Germans did it. Human to human. The worst enemy. Worst.

DEATH BY GUNSHOT

When Henry shared the following story, he described it as if he'd actually witnessed the event. He had not seen it firsthand, and in fact was no longer in the camp, but the story became a well-known and celebrated story among prisoners in Birkenau and other camps as word spread. When prisoners were transferred between camps, gossip traveled with them. I include this as an important story of rebellion worth remembering. The episode is compiled from Henry's words, and from multiple references in several memoirs. The incident is also included in a timeline of Auschwitz that is included as an appendix to *Death Dealer: The Memoirs of the SS Kommandant at Auschwitz,* by Rudolf Höss. The Jewish men forced to work in the *sonderkommando*, the *kommando* assigned to help dispose of gas chamber victims, stood by helplessly as they witnessed the events.

On October 23, 1943, a transport of 1,700 Jews arrived from Bergen-Belsen, in a regular train car, not a crowded cattle car. This particular group had paid the Gestapo a large amount of money for visas to South America, by way of Switzerland. On arrival, an SS officer played the part of a representative of the Foreign Ministry and gave the arrivals a polite speech welcoming them and explaining the disinfection process required before departing for Switzerland. He explained their train was scheduled to leave at 7 a.m.

The new arrivals apparently believed the disinfection and shower process was part of the normal immigration process. They were then escorted to the underground changing room leading to the gas chamber, which was of course disguised as a large shower room. Some of the people undressed and left for the large shower room. Others became hesitant, stopped undressing, and grew alarmed.

The SS grew impatient, unsnapping the covers on their gun holsters. Swinging at the crowd with their sticks, they began pushing stragglers roughly, and shouting obscenities to undress quickly.

Now truly scared, people reluctantly started undressing and the guards quieted down and stood nearby to leer at the women as they undressed. Two SS officers, Josef Schillinger and Walter Quackernack, became distracted when a beautiful, black-haired woman began a slow, seductive strip-tease act. As she lifted her skirt and exposed her thigh to them she glanced around to make sure she had their attention. As they stared at her, she looked straight at them and slowly shed her blouse.

Then, she casually leaned against a pillar and slowly bent down to remove her high-heeled shoes. In a flash, she had her shoe off and struck Quackernack on the forehead with the heel of it. She leapt toward his falling body and snatched his pistol from its opened holster and shot the nearest SS officer twice—Schillinger—who fell on the cement floor. As the other guards went to grab Schillinger and pull him out, Quackernack lay there moaning and holding his bleeding face in his hands. The quick-thinking woman got off a third shot, but missed Quackernack and wounded SS Sergeant Emmerich in the leg.

By then, the total scene was chaos and shouting, as the crowd pushed against the wall to get out. As soon as the SS got their three men out, they slammed the doors shut on the changing room, bolted them, and turned the lights off, leaving everyone in complete darkness. Kommandant Höss arrived, and immediately ordered his men to shoot everyone left in the changing room. Members of the transport already in the showers were immediately treated with the usual portion of Zyklon B and died. The Germans then opened up the doors, turned on bright spotlights, and machine-gunned the crowd. All the Jews died in minutes.

Schillinger died on the way to the hospital. Emmerich lived, but his leg was crippled the rest of his life. Schillinger had been in charge of the men's kitchen in Birkenau where he was known for being mean and tough. Later in his career, he played a key role in leading Jewish transports from the railroad ramp to the crematoria.

When Henry completed telling the story, he smirked sarcastically.

"It couldn't have happened to a nicer guy."

The incident was one of the few where a prisoner was able to shoot guards. The only other documented incident where a prisoner legitimately killed a German at Auschwitz was Prisoner No. 77, Teddy Pietrzykowski.

TEDDY PIETRZYKOWSKI

A lthough Henry spoke of Kazio as a champion boxer, multiple prisoners were engaged or forced to participate in boxing matches. Another friend of Henry's, Tadeusz Pietrzykowski, was a better-known boxer. Henry always called him Teddy, and they were only a month apart in age.

I remember Henry laughed when he first gave me Teddy's full name, as he had to repeat the Polish spelling three times for me, because there were so many consonants. Three other unrelated memoirs from the time mentioned admiration for Prisoner 77 as a boxer, long before I realized any connection. I just knew Teddy as Henry's friend; Henry never mentioned his number.

When I visited the archives at the Auschwitz-Birkenau State Museum in 2013, I had requested information in advance on three specific names: Henry, Kazio, and Teddy. It surprised me to find more information on Teddy than anyone. There was a documented record of Teddy killing a German in the ring— and being rewarded for being a good boxer—which makes him a very interesting person of the time. I also discovered his job responsibilities at the camp. Partly because of his skill at boxing, he got a choice job . . . working in the barn taking care of the cows.

Through the documents, I was able to corroborate a few other key stories, not yet told here. Teddy served as a key witness at the trial against Rudolf Höss, a testimony that amounted to thirty-nine pages of transcription. Later, in the 1980s, he made a thirty-plus-page sworn statement of his experiences in camp. These stories were previously undocumented anywhere else, including stories he never publicly revealed at trial. He had no desire to reveal everything to the Germans, even after the war. In 2012, a graduate student at a Polish university focused her doctoral dissertation exclusively on Teddy Pietrzykowski, and donated it to the museum.

Both Teddy and Kazio had been at Auschwitz from the near beginning and were well-connected in the underground, which is pertinent to Henry's next story.

BOXING MATCHES

On Sunday afternoons, the Germans liked to have boxing matches for sport. They gathered around in a big crowd. Kazio was one of their favorites. I tell you it was like gladiators entering the Colosseum in Rome. *Ave Caesar, morituri te salutant!*

Henry clapped his hands in imitation of an audience welcoming gladiators into the ring.

"Hail Caesar, we who are about to die, salute you." The Germans just loved Kazio. Bravo Kazio, Bravo! They'd clap and cheer, and place bets.

Kazio started boxing early in the camp. He'd get extra sausage and bread for fighting bravely. The Germans wanted to keep him strong for the boxing ring. The Germans let Kazio choose who he'd like to fight. In our underground, we would find out which kapo had been really, really bad. They were all bad, but some were really cruel. We'd feed the names of especially cruel kapos to Kazio before Sundays. Kazio had killed two Germans in the boxing ring, so no more Germans were willing to fight him. So, they made Kazio fight other kapos.

"Kapo Michael, come out and fight." No one could refuse an invitation to box. Not even Kapo Jakub, the Jewish fellow in charge of Block 11. Kazio would take on the kapo in the boxing ring. Sometimes he'd box so hard the other kapo would be unable to walk, and they'd send him to the hospital. Then, we'd make sure the Polish doctor knew which kapo was really bad. The doctor could give the German kapo an injection and end it. So, in some ways, there was small justice. But only because Kazio was a big shot, powerful and connected.

"Wait, Henry. Did you say Kapo Jakub was Jewish?"

Sure, sure. I hear later he survived and moved to Israel. You don't ask questions in the camp. I don't know how he did what he did. When they're shooting the men at Block 11 in the back of the head and he was the one who lead the men out and tie their hands with wire before the Germans shoot them in the head.

••

I never did verify a record of Kazio killing a German but, if it happened, it would have been in the boxing ring. I don't know if he exaggerated a story about this for Henry—relating events that occurred before Henry got there—or if simply no one recorded it. Since Kazio and Henry both worked in the kitchen, Henry did have more opportunity to talk with Kazio than other prisoners. At another point, Kazio worked in the infirmary, perhaps after Henry was transferred. This, too, would have been a powerful position if he had the ability to save people, or reject admission to the infirmary. I have no doubt Kazio was a fierce competitor, given his athletic background and physical strength prior to the war. He'd led Henry and four other athletes from the YMCA on the mission to pummel the Jew-beaters in Jordana Park in the summer of 1939. The fact that Bloody Michael, one of the most feared and vicious kapos, had responded to Henry with, "Kaz? Sure, Kaz, sure," confirms for me that other boxers had suffered enough injuries they did not want Kazio to call them into the boxing ring. Henry specifically mentioned two kapos his friend would often call into the boxing ring: Kapo Bruno and Bloody Michael.

A SECRET MURDER PLOT

Kommandant Höss loved horses. He kept very nice horses at Auschwitz and he loved to ride them. Teddy Pietrzykowski was living on these horses beautifully. The horses had carrots and vegetables to eat, so Teddy had plenty to eat, too, and would share with his friends. Sometimes he'd bring me some carrots. Pietrzykowski was one of the good guys.

Teddy told me a funny story. He was trying to get even with the Germans, and he figured out a way to kill the kommandant. He acquired an SS button, you know, one of the heavy metal buttons with the long shank to fit through coats. One day as he saddled the horse for Mr. Höss, he put the button under the saddle, with the sharp point under, against the horse. When Mr. Höss went out riding and went to jump over something, that button pressed into the horse and the horse threw him off into the bushes.

So, right away someone saw him fall, and the prisoners were hoping Mr. Höss had landed on his head, or broken his neck or something bad. The SS ran to help him, and they had to call for a stretcher to pick him up. But nothing happened to him except for a few broken ribs, not even a broken leg. He forgave everyone because he loved his horses. But he almost got it.

While everyone was running to help Mr. Höss, another friend of Teddy's, Władek Rzętkowski, who knew about the button, quickly went and pulled it out from the saddle. Mr. Höss never knew why his horse threw him that day.

"Wait. How did Teddy get an SS button?"

You don't think the SS cleaned their own barracks do you? No, that's prisoner work. Prisoners were assigned to clean the SS barracks, so someone just took a button from a uniform. After the incident, the button was quietly returned to the SS quarters so they wouldn't notice it was missing.

• •

To my knowledge, this story has not been published anywhere before. When I retold the story to Piotr, our Polish translator, who takes visitors to Auschwitz for a living, he looked at me skeptically as he'd never heard it. However, because I had requested information on Teddy Pietrzykowski, the museum had produced for my review the notarized statement made by Teddy in 1976 about his activities in the camp. The document completely corroborated Henry's story, and added more details. Our translator helped read it for me and, while I have a complete photocopy, it is written in Polish.

The document verified that Teddy worked in the barn with the cows—not horses as Henry had said—along with his friend Władek Rzetkowski, number 558, who did take care of Höss's horses. Together, the two of them began to hatch a plan to use the horse to kill him. At one point, Höss had been called away to Berlin for about four weeks. Władek was supposed to exercise the horse twice a day in Höss's absence. He tried walking her only once a day to make her more aggressive. It didn't work.

Next, they conceived the idea to use a long-shanked button between the saddle and the horse to make the horse throw him. Teddy "organized"—a common term among prisoners to acquire something by any means—the button from the SS quarters, and gave it to Władek to use. After a couple of tries, they decided to place the shank right next to the horse in such a way that when Höss jumped and came down on the saddle the horse would throw him off. Teddy wasn't present, but as caretaker of the horses, Władek made sure the button was placed, and also hidden away right after the accident. The SS never questioned that he would run to get the fallen horse—that was his job.

In Höss's own written words, neither he nor the SS ever suspected any wrongdoing other than a spirited horse. In his memoirs, penned after the war while in prison, he referenced the riding accident couched in his arrogant belief that nothing could happen to him.

"How many times did I miss death by a hair? I . . . in 1942, I had a riding accident where I wound up lying next to a stone just as the heavy stallion crashed down onto me, and came away with only broken ribs."

THE *STEHEBUNKER* IN BLOCK 11

HENRY CONTINUES:

Outside the kitchen, guys would lurk around the potato-peeling *kommando*, in case we opened the door and threw potatoes outside for the guys. Of course, if you got caught you were dead. But, when we could, we'd sneak extra food for friends. For a cigarette, a guy could get a handful of potato skins. But people ate them, then got bloody diarrhea and died. I don't know why. Maybe someone licked them before you do. It was very hard to stay clean, and typhus was a big problem. Since Auschwitz, I never eat potato skins or unpeeled potatoes. Never.

As cooks, we had cigarettes, so we smoked. We weren't supposed to, but we did. One day I was standing outside, leaning against the kitchen wall smoking. Usually we'd stand and blow the smoke down our sleeves. The smoke would keep us warm and the SS didn't see the smoke. But, one day, I was tired and just slowly exhaled and forgot to blow in the sleeve. At the same time, along came Baron Newton. We called him Newton because he was a stupid German kapo meat cutter.

"You," he pointed right at me. "Come here. What's your number?"

39551 Kapo, sir.

I don't know what would happen, but I knew I would get a strong punishment. I went to Kazio.

Kazio, what do I do? The Baron asked for my number.

"Don't worry, Henyu," he said. "I'll take care of it for you."

The next evening roll call I heard "Block 11, Number 39551." Block 11 was the dead block. There were jail cells and torture places in the basement. The dead wall was right outside Block 11. So, I know I'm going to get something bad, but I didn't know what.

So, after roll call, I walked to Block 11. Kazio was standing there waiting for me.

"Tell Kapo Jakub that I take care of you."

I followed Kapo Jakub down the stairs into the cold basement. He led me to the *stehebunker* [standing bunker], a cement wall with several small, square doors low to the floor. I had to get down and crawl naked through an opening near the floor level just like in a dog's kennel. It was cold, dark, and stuffy inside. I'm not sure. I could reach up and touch the ceiling. Kapo Jakub said not to worry.

Usually they put four guys at a time in this tiny space. You can't sit, you can't move, you have to stand all night. When guys were condemned to die they'd put them in there, and throw cold water on them.

There was only one other guy and me, and Jakub didn't throw any water on us. Sometimes he'd talk to us through the window. You had to stand the whole time, so I didn't sleep all night. The next morning, I crawled out and Kapo Jakub stood there waiting. He said only, "Say hello to Kazio for me."

I went to the kitchen. My eyes were red, my muscles stiff and sore, and I hadn't slept all night. But you have to work. Again, I was lucky. Because of Kazio I was only there one night.

The remains of a row of *stehebunkers* [standing bunkers] in the basement of Block 11, the punishment block. The original walls reached the ceiling. October 2013. *Photo by author.*

A NIGHT OF SWIMMING

T he other day, I was watching TV and I saw an ad for an endless swimming pool. The commercial showed a guy swimming in place. The swimmer was in a very short pool, and he swam against a water jet. But you know what? I had the same idea many years ago in Auschwitz.

Did I hear Henry right? Swimming? I sat there in puzzled silence waiting for the connection between a modern swimming pool and Auschwitz. No way was I interrupting this story. A big smile spread across Henry's face and he began to laugh.

One day I figured it out. I went to Kazio. "Kazio, how about we go swimming?"

He looked at me surprised. "Henry, how you gonna do that?"

You see, when we peeled potatoes, they went into a cement vat that held water. It was about one meter wide and about three to four meters long.

"Kazio, you know the potato vat? You heat the water and fill the vat enough. Then, I'll put my belt on and tie a rope. You hold me, and I'll swim. Then, I'll hold you, and you swim."

"Ah, Henry, that's a great idea." Kazio gave me a slap on the back and left. He was so strong he almost broke a rib every time he did that. I thought that was the end of it, and never mentioned it again.

Two weeks later, Kazio found me, and said in a low voice, "Tonight, we swim. Meet me here tonight after dinner."

I met Kazio at the kitchen. Kapo Warshawsky was there, but he liked me. He was big in the Polish underground. He was also the kapo of the potato-peeling *kommando*. No one else in the kitchen but us.

Kapo Warshawsky heated 800 liters of hot water. We each took turns swimming, holding each other's belts. We swam a little in the warm water. It was November, and cold like hell outside. When we got out of the warm water, the steam kept rising from our skin and the windows were all steamed up. If anyone bothered to look in the windows we must have looked like white, steamy, skinny ghosts inside.

Henry grinned.

That was the first and only time of swimming in Auschwitz I know of.

●●

When I visited Auschwitz, I asked our tour guide if such a potato vat would have existed. I told her only that I had a story related to a potato vat when Henry peeled potatoes.

She thought for a moment and said she had seen such a thing in the kitchen at Gross-Rosen concentration camp, now situated near the town of Rogożnica, where you can go in the kitchen.

Can I prove it happened? No. There were only three people there that evening, two of whom were champion swimmers before the war. But I could not have imagined this story in a thousand years—and, well, Henry was one of the two champion swimmers there. Why wouldn't I believe him?

Henry said more than once that Auschwitz was just a crazy, bizarre place. Amidst such suffering there were lighter diversions. On Sunday evenings, prisoners could attend orchestra rehearsals and hear a concert of sorts. Sunday afternoons allowed more "free time" for prisoners because many of the SS had Sunday afternoons off and work crews were shortened. Kapos might deliver mail to prisoners in their block—if they liked them. Prisoners had to occupy their time somehow while the Germans enjoyed their boxing matches, picnics with their families, or time off at the officers' resort built not too far from the main camp.

Sunday afternoons offered extra time to pick lice and fleas from clothes, play chess, play soccer, or sleep.

The director of the Birkenau orchestra, Syzmon Laks, penned his memoir, *Music of Another World,* describing his experiences. Prisoners fortunate enough to be chosen for a camp orchestra, through their musical talent, had a chance of survival not otherwise available to the average prisoner. Laks's book was later banned by communist censors who felt his reality painted the Germans in too kind a light.

Hermann Langbein, in his book *People of Auschwitz*, also wrote about soccer, boxing, movies, and occasional concerts by the inmate orchestra for other inmates. Most of these took place in Auschwitz I, rather than Birkenau. However, that, too, had its own orchestra, and a soccer field not far from the crematorium.

While it seems completely incongruous to the standard images of concentration camps, can we really fault anyone for seeking a temporary break from surrounding misery? In such an atmosphere of imprisonment and death, the instinct of survival meant people sought diversion wherever possible, if only to feel human for a short time and retain some sense of sanity.

I tell these stories because they happened and are part of the whole picture. There is no question Auschwitz was and is a place of huge, unspeakable tragedy, and the few light moments should not denigrate from that. Truly, those of us who haven't endured Auschwitz don't really know what it means to survive.

PART 4

KL BUCHENWALD, WEIMAR, GERMANY

MARCH 1943–AUGUST 1944

GÖRLITZ TRAIN STATION

HENRY CONTINUES:

Early in 1943, a general order came down for Auschwitz to transfer most Polish prisoners to other concentration camps in Germany proper. Space was needed for more Jews and, secondarily, it had a disastrous effect on a well-organized underground of Poles and other politicals. On March 12, 1943, a trainload of one thousand Poles left Auschwitz for Buchenwald. Henry was on that train.

"Henry, did you ever find out why you were transferred to Buchenwald from Auschwitz?"

They knew my name. The *schreibstuber* [clerk] was a friend of Kazio. Kazimierz told me not to worry. He had information that they were gearing up Auschwitz for more killing. He made sure I wouldn't go on the transport to Mauthausen. He said Buchenwald was much better.

Kazio went to the shoemaker and had them make a new belt for me. It was a wide belt, and Kazio showed me there was a small space inside the belt to put stuff into. We were experienced—we knew the only thing you kept was your belt. Remember the CYMA gold watch that showed up in my soup? Kazio gave it to me to take to Buchenwald. It fit into the hidden space in the belt.

"It still worked after being in the soup?"

It still worked, sure. CYMA is the best watch in the world.

I don't know if it was working, but I think it was working. It's gold anyway.

They give us a new prisoner's outfit, like you see the blue and white stripes, and I had my belt. One day they called my number, and [I] left the next morning. Finally I leave this typhoid fever camp.

So, I was in the train, loaded with fifty guys. The train stinks because in the corner of the wagon was the bucket, where you do these physiological things, and you had no choice but to breathe it in. We kept looking out the holes in the wagon to see if we were going west, which meant Buchenwald, or south to Mauthausen. Mauthausen was the worst camp of all.

The train stopped in Görlitz, a small German town, a train stop on the way to Buchenwald. The town had a wonderful train station. The SS opened the door and we all are like drunk for a moment as our eyes adjusted to the light.

We saw the water pump there for the train and we were so thirsty. Everyone started asking, "Come on, give us the *wasser*. Give us the *wasser*." So, what does the SS do? They just yell, "Shut up. Just shut up. Get back. No water for you."

A crowd of people stood there staring at us. Then, something so beautiful happened. My friend Witold "Witek" Myszkowski, he was a very good singer, started singing in this beautiful voice. Witek sang the song "Mamatschi! Schenk mir ein Pferdchen!" in German, to the people standing there waiting for the train, on the station in Görlitz. The people were standing there staring at us, then it got quiet as everyone listened. It's very well known, this song.

Henry sang the first two stanzas of the song in what sounded to me like perfect German.

It was a very touching song about a boy who asks his mother to give him a little horse, a horse that he sells in paradise, and so on.

Witek's voice was so beautiful, even the SS stopped what they were doing to listen. They just stood there, staring and listening. Then, some of the crowd started saying to the guards, "Give them the water. Go on, go ahead. Give them water."

You know, there were good people in Germany. Not everyone was bad.

So, the guards slide open the doors, and come with the pail and brought us water, again and again. Witek kept singing "Ein Pferdchen, Ein Pferdchen," such a very nice song.

Again, Henry sang the first two stanzas for me.

There were people with tears rolling down their cheeks as he sang that song, it was so beautiful.

But then, some of the women at the stations started to toss food items to us. The SS guards got angry, slammed the train door shut, and the women ran away.

Photo of entry gate to Buchenwald. The words *Jedem Das Seine* [To Each What They Deserve] were intentionally placed at eye level, and faced the prisoner *appellplatz* or roll call area. Photo taken April 1945 after liberation. *US Holocaust Memorial Museum, gift of David Cohen.*

Photo of main entrance to the prisoner compound of Buchenwald. The open gate in the middle with the words *Jedem Das Seine* is the main entrance to the prisoner compound, and was the only permissible prisoner entry and exit to the camp. The wing to the right housed offices of the SS. The wing to the left housed the camp prison and torture cells. The clock at the top remains set at 3:15, to commemorate the exact time on the afternoon of April 11, 1945 that American troops liberated Buchenwald. October 2013. *Photo by author.*

PRISONER 10948

As we entered through the Buchenwald gates, we passed through the main gate with the sign *Jedem Das Seine,* or "Everyone Gets What They Deserve." In Auschwitz, you marched under the sign. Here it was eye level to make sure you see it. I like this saying better than "Work Shall Set You Free" [over the entrance to Auschwitz]. The words faced the camp so, when prisoners stand in roll call, everyone can see the words.

I remember a barrel of this black disinfectant that stunk like hell. The barrel was about the size of a barrel of wine. Three hundred of us, and everyone has to go in the barrel and dunk in. The black powder was there to get rid of lice and typhoid.

Henry said powder, but I am not sure whether he meant powder or liquid.

They knew that there was a lot of disease and typhoid in Auschwitz, and the Germans were scared like hell of the disease coming to Buchenwald. After the barrel, you take a shower right away, put on your old clothes, and they send you to quarantine. They give me number 10948.

We were experienced, so we knew how this worked. That is why Kazio had the leather shop make me that belt. When I go to dunk in the barrel, we have to take everything off and dunk while we hold our belts above our head.

At the end of the camp there was an area surrounded by barbed wire, and they put about a thousand people there for quarantine. If somebody got sick we would have to stay longer, but no one got sick. I think we stayed there two weeks, then I was transferred to Block 51 on April 1.

So, we're trying to figure out what to do. They gave us food, and we started walking around trying to learn about this camp. After work, the older prisoners, the Poles, came to check us out, and then stood there and spoke to us through the wire fence.

"Ah, so you're from Auschwitz. You're from Auschwitz, you're from there." They talked about families and asked about news. Many had been there a very long time. There were plenty of German politicals, and plenty of nationalities: Polish, Czech, Holland, Russkie [Henry's slang for Russian], and so forth.

Buchenwald was a better place than Auschwitz because the prisoners were organized as communists. The prisoners, the kapos, and foremen were all old communist party members and they were decent people. From top positions, the camp elderly, to the police, to the kapos, to the clerks, everybody they were communist party members.

Many had been in Buchenwald since 1937. Some had been in the camps since 1933. Later in the war, the Germans sent many more guards to the front lines, so the communists were even more in charge.

The criminals, the bandits and thieves—green triangles—and the politicals—red triangles—fought for power in the camp, but the red triangles finally took over and made the camp very strict. The Germans mostly let the communists run the camp because they kept strict order. I was benign. I was not a communist party member, but I made sure I stayed on good terms with the communists.

Somehow, my knowledge of concentration camps began with World War II, especially knowing that Auschwitz opened in 1940.

"Wait, did you really mean 1933?"

Yeah, sure. When Hitler came to power, he arrested every Communist Party member and sent them to Dachau and Buchenwald. Buchenwald was one of the first camps. The first concentration camps were for communists and others who disagreed with Hitler, including *Bibelforschers*.

"Who were the *Bibelforschers*?"

Oh, you know. I don't know the English name, but they didn't believe in Catholic or Presbyterian.

No, I didn't know. However after some odd guesses, we eventually figured out the English translation is Jehovah's Witnesses. *Bibelforschers* translated literally is "Bible researchers."

Later, I researched Hitler's early persecution of Jehovah's Witnesses in Germany, a lesser-known facet of World War II. Hitler arrested them for one reason: by exercising their faith, they would not swear allegiance to Hitler above God, nor would they permit their children to enroll in Hitler youth programs or be drafted into the army. Had they signed a paper declaring God didn't exist, or that Hitler came first, they would have been released. I'm not aware of any Jehovah's Witness who swore allegiance to Hitler. By 1939, approximately six thousand of them were incarcerated in concentration camps. Henry explained how it was done.

Then, when the war began everything changed. They arrested the Jews, and the Slavs and Poles. Buchenwald was a men's-only camp. Sometimes there was a German or SS guard guarding his own father.

"What do you mean guarding his father?"

The fathers were arrested as communists many years ago, leaving their families behind in Germany. When their sons got older, they had no choice but to join the German army. Not everyone in the German army believed in Hitler; some joined because they had no other choice. What guard is going to shoot his own father, or others in front of his father? Also, if the father was communist, he was in power. These guards won't kill their parents, so they, overall, weren't as brutal.

"You said Buchenwald was better. Did you get more food in Buchenwald?"

No, no, there was no more food. But the kapos didn't steal from you, so you got more food. You can leave the bread on the table and nobody take it. Because, if you take it and somebody sees you, you're dead the next day. Stealing bread was the highest, worst crime in Buchenwald. Why? Because, if you steal someone's food you kill them.

See, if some guy have a problem, you know, someone hit

him or steal his bread, all he had to do was tell the foreman, "Heh, this number is stealing my bread." Then you don't see that number [prisoner] anymore. The next day that number goes in transport to Dora, to work underground on the atomic bomb or something. Dora was the worst command, the punishment *kommando*. No one ever returned from Dora.

Dora was a *kommando* village, where they have the digging of the cave, for the bomb production. They dig in the rocks, and they carried the rocks out, and they died like everything. Everybody who did something wrong in Buchenwald, everybody who steal the bread, everybody who come to *puff* was sent to the Dora *kommando*.

"What do you mean 'come to puff?' Everyone who smoked?"

No. No. The *puffhaus*. I'll tell you about the *puff* later.

As Henry smiled broadly, I had no idea what he was talking about, but I knew it must be good. My curiosity had to wait until Henry was ready.

AN OVERVIEW OF BUCHENWALD

A s a smaller and lesser-known camp, Buchenwald begs more explanation than Auschwitz to better understand the context of Henry's experience there. From the time it opened in 1937, Buchenwald existed in purpose, location, and design as a very different kind of hell than Auschwitz. The different framework, history, and power structure included a different composition of prisoners than concentration camps built in a conquered Poland after the start of World War II. The official death count at Buchenwald stands around 56,000, of which twenty percent, or approximately 11,000 were Jewish prisoners. Yet, between 1937 and 1945, the SS imprisoned some 250,000 prisoners there. For *some* prisoners, the camp represented a much better and safer place than other camps, though every prisoner risked a truly different and sinister brand of evil not repeated elsewhere. This narrative does not include most of those. The details of some of the tortures in the prison block, medical experiments, use of human skin, and certain methods of killing devised and used only in this camp, belong solely in the worst nightmares.

The origins of Buchenwald, located five kilometers outside the town of Weimar, Germany, date back to the late eighteenth century. The camp was strategically located on the same site of the historical hunting lodge of the duchess Anna Amalia, a patron of the arts and literature in the 1700s. She encouraged some of the artistic greats of Germany to visit frequently as a sort of artists' retreat. The young Johann Wolfgang von Goethe and Friedrich von Schiller composed their poetry and penned their writings there. Johann Sebastian Bach played the organ in Weimar, and Franz Liszt served as music director. The philosopher Friedrich Nietzsche wrote there as well. In many ways, Weimar, and the nearby Ettersburg Mountain on which the lodge was located, became the cultural capital of Germany.

Following World War I, leaders chose Weimar as the symbolic location to assemble and draft a new constitution for the newly independent country. Based on the constitutional assembly, from 1919–1933 the official name for the new Germany would be the German Reich. Most people just referred to the new country as the Weimar Republic. As early as 1926, Weimar became the setting for many fervent pro-Hitler rallies, and for the entire life of Buchenwald, townspeople were aware and complicit with the camp's purpose, if not fully knowledgeable on all the sordid details.

In April 1932, three men ran for president of Germany. An aging Paul von Hindenburg won with 53 percent, or 19 million votes. Adolf Hitler, as head of the National Socialist German Worker Party—in German, *Nationalsozialistische Deutsche Arbeiterpartei,* abbreviated as NSDAP—received 36.8 percent, or more than thirteen million votes. Ernst Thälman, head of the German communist party, came in third with more than three million votes, or 10.2 percent. When Hindenburg appointed Adolf Hitler Chancellor of Germany on January 30, 1933, Hitler legally maneuvered into near total power and authority. By then, the lengthy phrase "***Nationalsozialistisch***" became shortened to the simpler acronym "Nazi," based on its pronunciation in German.

In February 1933, Hitler signed a decree that enabled him to quash all political opposition. Members of the German communist party, as Hitler's key political opponents, became subjected to persecution from the very beginning. He immediately began construction of a detention camp on the grounds of a former munitions factory twelve miles northwest of Munich. The Germans named the camp Dachau. On March 22, 1933, only two months after rising to power, he ordered the arrest of his political opponents, specifically the communists and social democrats, including Ernst Thälman. None of those arrested were ever given trials or legal court sentences.

Dachau became the flagship and role model for a quickly growing network of similar camps. Ernst Thälman would be imprisoned under harsh conditions for more than eleven years until the Nazis executed him at Buchenwald in 1944. He is considered one of Buchenwald's most famous prisoners.

Throughout Germany, more than 150 provisional concentration camps for preventive custody were set up in 1933. With the exception of Dachau, most camps were temporary and only existed for a short time. Eighty thousand Nazi political adversaries—communists, and members of both the union and labor parties—were arrested in 1933. The communist party became subjected to the most brutal persecution from the very beginning.

Even though the first major provocation of Germany's 600,000 Jews began in April 1933 with an organized boycott of Jewish-owned shops and businesses, the intentional, calculated arrest and murder of Jews came much later. Thus, the legacy and culture of communists as the earliest concentration camp prisoners played a significant role in the social and power structure of Buchenwald. The German communists formed the largest communist underground in the entire SS concentration camp system. They held a monopoly on jobs and maintained a strict order among their ranks. As long as order was in place, the Germans backed off and allowed them greater control than at any other camp, devoting more guards and enforcement to other prisoner groups.

In 1936, Inspector of the Concentration Camps and Chief of the SS Totenkopf Squadrons Theodor Eicke became interested in establishing a permanent camp near Weimar. The citizens of Weimar considered a prison camp a stain on their cultural heritage, and protested vehemently. The German high command built the camp there anyway, but made a small concession by naming it Buchenwald—literally "Beech Tree Forest"—rather than KL Weimar.

Besides holding three to six thousand prisoners, the future facility was envisioned as a full community and military garrison, complete with civilian quarters for the personnel and their families. In many ways, it functioned as a veritable suburb of Weimar. Townspeople were invited to visit and enjoy the falconry as entertainment. In the first two years, the registrar's office recorded forty-eight marriages and twelve births in the SS community.

By design, the camp was built on the side of the hill. The SS community and barracks sat on the more sheltered and warmer side of the hill, while prisoner barracks eventually comprised straight rows of terraced levels down the colder, northern slope. Trees on the prisoner side were cleared for two reasons: one practical and one cruel. Guard towers built at the entrance and along the front fence at the top of the slope had an unobstructed view of the prisoner camp sloping down and, subsequently, prisoners had little buffer or protection from the frigid, cold winds of a German winter.

The first prisoners arrived at Buchenwald on July 15, 1937. Most were political prisoners moved from other camps about to close. Based on the color of identity triangle assigned to each prisoner class, half were the "greens [triangles]," persons with multiple criminal records, prone to blackmail, brutal physical abuse, and willing to carry out the first public executions in the camp on behalf of the SS. The second half, the "reds [triangles]," included primarily German communists and other "politicals," in essence anyone opposed to Hitler. Jews were primarily sent to Dachau.

In November 1938, *Kristallnacht* happened, an event that permanently accelerated the violence against Jews across Germany and Austria.

That November, Germany tried to evict approximately 17,000 Jews of Polish origins from the country and send them back to Poland. However, Polish authorities refused to accept them, and most were stranded in refugee camps. Herschel Grynszpan, a young Polish Jew, became angry that his parents were deported and stranded in a camp. When he assassinated a German diplomat, the reaction was swift and brutal. The German propaganda minister announced that all of "World Jewry" was responsible. In two days, more than two hundred synagogues were destroyed and an estimated seven thousand Jewish businesses looted, as police stood by with full assent.

Authorities arrested thirty thousand young Jewish men age fourteen and older, and sent them primarily to Dachau, Buchenwald, and Sachsenhausen, a concentration camp especially known for its brutality throughout the war. Hundreds died in the violence. The night of violence became known as *Kristallnacht* or "Night of Glass" due to the shards of shattered glass from the windows of synagogues, homes, and Jewish-owned businesses plundered and destroyed in the violence. *Kristallnacht* became the turning point and excuse for aggressive anti-Jewish policies. Even worse, the German government blamed the Jews for the violence, and assessed Jews a huge fine roughly equivalent to four hundred million dollars in reparations for the damage inflicted against them.

The arrested Jews were pressured to sign over all their property. In exchange, they were given an exit visa to leave Germany. Of the 17,000 Jews committed to Buchenwald from 1937 to 1941, more than 11,000 were released. But, while in Buchenwald, Jews suffered some of the harshest treatment and the highest proportion of deaths of all prisoners. Among many humiliations, Jewish prisoners were sometimes forced to stand for hours and sing the *"Judenlied."* This song, unique to Buchenwald, was comprised completely of anti-Semitic phrases, such as "All we did was profiteer, profiteer and lie." The reason the song originated in Buchenwald can be summed up by one name: Karl Otto Koch.

The Buchenwald camp kommandant Karl Koch with his wife Ilse. On the left is SS Main Leader Bruno Michael, head of the *effektenkammer* [storage building for inmates' personal belongings] and brother-in-law of Karl Koch. 1938. *Collection of the Buchenwald Memorial.*

Prisoners forced to build the house of the camp commander Karl Koch in the SS settlement. November 1937. *Collection of the Buchenwald Memorial.*

View of the Koch family villa sometime between 1938 and 1941. To the left stretches a street of more SS housing, though none are as large as the Koch villa. This is from a page of a family photo album Ilse prepared for her son. The entire photo album was used as evidence against her at trial, as but one example of their extravagant living. *Mein Geburtshaus* translates as "My birth home." *National Archives at College Park, College Park, MD.*

Koch was the first commander of the camp from 1937–1941, and is widely considered to be the most corrupt, fanatical Jew hater of all the German camp commandants, even according to the Germans. He encouraged rabid anti-Semitism in his staff, guards, and the guards' wives and families. Many concentration camp guards at other camps were trained first at Buchenwald under Koch's tutelage, and he encouraged one of the most sadistic jailers in all the camps' ranks, who cruelly tortured prisoners for the sheer pleasure of it. Ilse Koch, Karl's wife, justifiably ranks as one of the most evil women of all time for her many acts committed against prisoners in Buchenwald. At the same time, she and her husband lived in a luxurious villa, the closets filled with fur coats and fine clothes. Ilse's personal photo album, and photo album she assembled for her son, is currently housed in the National Archives in College Park, Maryland. It provides an incongruous contrast between a concentration camp, and the luxurious lifestyle they so clearly enjoyed. Even the Germans considered Karl Koch so corrupt they executed him by firing squad in 1945.

Häftlingskammer   K.L.Buchenwald, den 4. April 1943

144

Nachtrag zur Veränderungsmeldung vom 12. März 1943

Namentliche Aufstellung der 1000 Neuzugänge vom K.L.Auschwitz.

P o l e n :

10615	Adamczyk, Johann	11169	Bienkowski, Marceli
11408	Adamczyk, Stanislaw	11445	Biernacki, Zygfryd
10733	Albin, Mieczyslaw	11360	Biskiniewicz, Wenzel
10634	Ampulski, Mieczyslaw		-verstorben 26.3.43-
10685	Andrzejewski, Wieslaw	11550	Blady, Wladyslaw
10957	Babiarz, Stanislaw	11074	Blaszkiewicz, Josef
11409	Babuch, Michal	11007	Bobek, Josef
10900	Bachtig, Zbigniew	10670	Bodzek, Edzislaw
11233	Baczkowski, Wladyslaw	10977	Bogdan, Stefan
11130	Badynski, Tadeusz	10786	Bogdanski, Petr
10827	Baklarz, Franz	11270	Bogdaszewski, Czeslaw
11338	Balas, Mieczyslaw	11590	x Boelk, Marjan
11023	Balcerzak, Johann	11229	Boratyn, Roman
11402	Balmas, Blazej	11230	Borek, Boleslaw
10851	Bancerz, Wladyslaw	10961	Borek, Michael
11036	Bandelak, Adalbert	10966	Borowiak, Anton
11177	Barakonski, Boleslaus	11567	Borowiecki, Gerhard
11426	Barakowski, Wladyslaw		-entlassen 3.4.43-
11588	Baran, Antoni	10705	Borowski, Stefan
11064	Baran, Johann	11162	Borys, Mieczyslaw
11413	Baran, Josef	11531	Brodziak, Eduard
11178	Baran, Josef	11553	Broks, Josef
11296	Baran, Stanislaw	11584	Bronik, Stefan
10820	Baroikowski, Czeslaw	11341	Bros, Jan
10735	Bardo, Zbigniew	11561	Brozek, Jan
10973	Barewski, Dariusz	10814	Brylka, Waclaw
10265	Bartnik, Stanislaw	10907	Brzeczek, Franciszek
11266	Bartosik, Jan	10926	Brzezinski, Wladyslaw
10836	Bartusik, August	10933	Bubak, Roman
11410	Baryla, Josef	11082	Buczko, Jan
11591	Basta, Ladislaus	11040	Budniak, Wincenty
11234	Bamak, Lucjan	11479	Budweil, Wladyslaw
	-verstorben 1.4.43-	11470	Bulak, Josef
11578	Baselak, Boleslaw	11090	Burchacki, Wieslaw
10970	Bazyl, Waclaw	11500	Barianski, Josef
11348	Becker, Andrzej	11256	Burzynski, Stanislaw
11476	Bednarczyk, Zygmunt	11392	Byczkowski, Stanislaw
11298	Bednarek, Stanislaus	10974	Cebula, Antoni
10695	Bednarski, Kazimierz	10838	Cegielkowski, Stanislaw
10934	Beer, Johann	11223	Cekus, Marjan
11420	Bekalik, Bronislaw	11357	Centkowski, Henryk
11107	Bellach, Wladyslaw	11029	Cichocki, Aleksander
10826	Benda, Stanislaw	11014	Cichocki, Franciszek
11059	Berezka, Felika	11273	Cichoniec, Stanislaw
11267	Berg, Mieczyslaw	11166	Cichorski, Henryk
11538	Bernacik, Jan	10660	Ciekot, Zdsislaw
11524	Bernat, Johann	11148	Ciesla, Karl
11467	Betlej, Josef	11006	Cieslikowski, Tadeusz
11377	Bezprzywiska, Mikolaj	11176	Cislowski, Alfred
10734	Biedron, Josef	11159	Ciura, Stanislaw
10821	Bielanski, Jan	11454	Chlimon, Mikolaj
11217	Bielecki, Stanislaw	11207	Chlad, Marjan
10876	Bielski, Stanislaw	11375	Chlebny, Czeslaw
10995	Bielski, Edzislaw	11095	Chmielewski, Aleksander

Page one of alphabetical transport list of 1,000 Poles transferred from Auschwitz to Buchenwald on March 12, 1943. *Photo 52818653_0_1/ITS Digital Archive, USHMM.*

Last page of alphabetical transport list of 1,000 Poles transferred from Auschwitz to Buchenwald on March 12, 1943. Halfway down the page it shows 10948 Zguda, Henryk. *Photo 5281653_0_1 from the ITS Digital Archive, USHMM.*

Outside of Buchenwald Individual Documents envelope for Henry (Henryk) Zguda. The envelope included a prisoner registration card, a personal effects card, a postal control card, an office card, two prisoner questionnaires, a medical registration card, an employment card, and a prisoner number card. *Photo 7485572_0_1/ITS Digital Archive, USHMM.*

Buchenwald prisoner registration card for Henry (Henryk) Zguda included as part of his registration paperwork. *Photo 7485581_0_1/ITS Digital Archive, USHMM.*

A personal effects inventory card for Henry (Heinrich) Zguda included as part of Henry's registration paperwork. In the upper right corner it shows his new prisoner number, 10948, with his Auschwitz number 39551. *Photo 7485578_0_1/ITS Digital Archive, USHMM.*

General information card included as part of Henry's registration paperwork. *Photo 7485576_0_1/ITS Digital Archive, USHMM.*

Information card included as part of Henry's registration paperwork. *Photo 7485575_0_1/ITS Digital Archive, USHMM.*

Lfd.Nr.	H.Nr.	Name:		Lfd.Nr.	H.Nr.	Name:	Übertrag 145,-
1	1814	Kozlowski	5,--	61	10662	Szewczyk	20,--
2	10830	Nowakowski	5,--	2	10666	Wart	20,--
3	8044	Dreß	10,--	3	10673	Dworakowski	20,--
4	11345	Janik	10,--	4	10680	Zur	20,--
5	11323	Lipowski	10,--	5	10702	Nowakowski	20,--
6	11243	Kraeczyk	10,--	6	10702	Ders	20,--
7	11242	Kistela	10,--	7	10781	Swirat	20,--
8	11240	Sadok	10,--	8	10788	Murawski	20,--
9	11200	Giesohewski	10,--	9	10885	Piskorz	20,--
10	11188	Ptak	10,--	70	10908	Konklewski	20,--
1	11167	Musecki	10,--	1	11179	Jedlecki	20,--
2	11126	Czaja	10,--	2	10912	Strek	20,--
3	11106	Tonczak	10,--	3	10855	Müller	20,--
4	11090	Burchacki	10,--	4	10710	Polsakiewicz	20,--
5	10958	Kropinski	10,--	5	11044	Piorczynski	25,--
6	10820	Parcikowski	10,--	6	11044	Ders	25,--
7	10761	Foterek	10,--	7	11595	Patzer	30,--
8	10722	Gembka	10,--	8	11579	Piotrowski	30,--
9	10720	Sydor	10,--	9	11553	Halladin	30,--
20	10623	Skrypczak	10,--	80	11531	Brodzik	30,--
1	6412	Rieß	10,--	1	11522	Kleszcz	30,--
2	7730	Kubal	10,--	2	11488	Leszczynski	30,--
3	4960	Sobak	10,--	3	11486	Ziembicki	30,--
4	7978	Giese	10,--	4	11482	Pillich	30,--
5	7661	Ratz	10,--	5	11478	Mally	30,--
6	7433	Hühnal	10,--	6	11472	Faron	30,--
7	11585	Drachel	10,--	7	11477	Faron	30,--
8	11528	Filipek	10,--	8	10642	Chybinski	30,--
9	11387	Prewo	10,--	9	10693	Porwoll	30,--
30	11513	Lewandowaki	15.--15.	90	10822	Wegrzyn	30,--
1	11321	Kaczmarczyk	15,--	1	10957	Babiarz	30,--
2	11308	Roman	15,--	2	11191	Olszynski	30,--
3	11208	Soluk	15,--	3	11491	Jurkiewicz	30,--
4	11181	Hyra	15,--	4	11515	Pajak	30,--
5	11129	Sobczak	15,--	5	11544	Czermiewicz	30,--
6	10634	Ampulski	15,--	6	11570	Michalczy k	30,--
7	10946	Laskowski	15,--	7	11571	Stolarz	30,--
8	10948	Zguda	15,--	8	31	Mlak	30,--
9	11393	Wieczorek	15,--	9	10604	Dembinski	30,--
40	11249	Wypior	16,--	100	10611	Jamkowski	30,--
1	11434	Opara	19,--	1	10618	Sikorski	30,--
2	11055	Mazur	20,--	2	10632	Wiecka	30,--
3	11554	Kopczynski	20,--	3	10643	Glinski	30,--
4	11553	Braks	20,--	4	10637	Kopec	30,--
5	11547	Spichowicz	20,--	5	10644	Rodzewicz	30,--
6	11472	Pruski	20,--	6	10650	Kaplon	30,--
7	11437	Sikora	20,--	7	10682	Zygar	30,--
8	11429	Wojciechewski	20,--	8	10696	Konieczka	30,--
9	11419	Zdebik	20,--	9	10705	Borowsk	30,--
50	11408	Adamczyk	20,--	110	10728	Hyra	30,--
1	11392	Byczkowski	20,--	1	10742	Laszyk	30,--
2	11363	Kazmieczak	20,--	2	10746	Kucharski	30,--
3	11198	Miserski	20,--	3	10756	Oleniczak	30,--
4	11220	Przepiaur	20,--	4	10773	Malinowski	30,--
5	11231	Wazik	20,--	5	10774	Drecki	30,--
6	11294	Markowski	20,--	6	10803	Wachulski	30,--
7	11524	Madej	20,--	7	10723	Pokrzywnicki	30,--
8	7712	Goliasz	20,--	8	10832	Milewski	30,--
9	2778	Medwedew	20,--	9	10842	Wolnicki	30,--
60	10651	Moskaluk	20,--	120	10853	Treffenfeld	30,--
			845,--				2495,--

verkartet durch:

List of transferred funds from Auschwitz to Buchenwald for Polish prisoners on March 12, 1943. This record indicates 15 *reichsmarks* were transferred on Henry Zguda's behalf. *Photo 5307333_0_2/ITS Digital Archive, USHMM.*

```
                              - 3 -                                         625
                                                                      ┌──────┐
         Häftl.Nr.    N a m e :            Geb.Datum:     Zloty:      │  33  │
        ================================================================└──────┘==

                      Übertrag                            2.769.66
  10617  17398  —   Millak,Andreas j        18.12.19. ✓      26.—
  10685  18338  —   Andrzejewski,Wensel Wieslav13.3.11. ✓    10.—
  11075  19111  —   Krupa,Eduard            14.7.25. ✓       20.—
  11076  19113  —   Laszk,Eduard            18.3.24. ✓        7.—
  10826  26627  ~   Benda,Stanislaus w       4.6.12. ✓      127.75
         26628      Kielbasinski,Stanisl.   14.10.91.       100.25
  10883  27190  —   Krzeminski,Wladisl.     10.7.96. ✓       20.—
  10870  37258  ~   Czulak,Marian           25.3.25. { 19.I.25 ?  10.50
  11322  37648  —   Kierach,Heinry M        14.9.09. ✓       10.—
  11450  37693  —   Pabijan,Alexander        3.12.10. ✓      55.—
  11328  37700  —   Stachurski,Ceslaus       6.7.07. ✓      105.—
  11341  37714  ~   Bros,Johann Jan         22.2.06. ✓       30.—
  11342  37724  ~   Kupiec,Miecislaus w      3.6.03. ✓       30.—
  11191  39231  —   Obbzynski,Johann        24.1.21. ~       82.—
  11481  39434  —   Gaj,Georg Jerzy         30.9.13. ✓      221.—
  11518  39447  —   Krysiak,Kasimir         18.10.07. ✓     244.—
  11548  39490  —   Klehr,Marian            12.5.04. ✓       20.—
  11517  39538  —   Skoda,Theodor           12.6.10. ✓      350.—
  11457  39525  ~   Orlowski,Josef          18.5.00. ✓      165.—
  10949  39539  —   Stawasz,Johann          24.10.19. ✓     414.—
  10822  39544  —   Wegrzyn,Thadeusz         7.8.17. ✓       62.—
  10948  39551  —   Zguda,Heinrich          12.7.17. ✓      275.—
  11193  39552  —   Zulawski,Rafael         26.1.12. ✓      114.—
  10933  39553  —   Bubak,Roman             18.8.12. ✓       40.—
  11102  39595  —   Pszczelinski,Felix       3.11.04. ✓      60.—
  11587  59830 Ajll.Borowiecki,Gerhard       4.3.14.        125.—  Karte
  11768  39856 Jull.Golenski,Georg          31.1.17.        225.—  Karte
  11491  39839  —   Jurkiewicz,Stanislaw    14.4.20. ✓       98.—
  11487  39844  —   Kozlowski,Stanislaw     30.12.14. ✓     200.—
  11349  39849  —   Maciejasz,Josef          2.3.08. ✓       52.—
  11570  39851  —   Michalczyk,Marian        8.9.05. ✓     1.400.—
  11588  39859 Jull.Ponurkiewicz,Eduard     13.10.10.        50.—  Karte
  11515  39861  —   Pajak,Wladislaus         6.6.14. ✓       21.—
  11516  39866  —   Schmidt,Viktor          24.5.00. ✓       19.—
  11571  39867  ~   Stolarz,Stefan          24.7.11. ✓       80.—
  11519  39874      Wojdylo,Witold          29.1.10. ✓       82.—
                    Übertrag                 Zloty       7.720.16
```

Transfer list of prisoners' funds. This record indicated that 275 Polish *zloty* were transferred on March 12, 1943 on Henry Zguda's behalf. This list states Henry's assigned prisoner number from Auschwitz (39551) and Buchenwald (10948). *Photo 5307341_0_1/ ITS Digital Archive/USHMM.*

HENRY'S ARRIVAL AT
BUCHENWALD

I n March 1943, when Henry arrived at the camp, only one
   percent of the prisoners were Jewish, as most Jews were
   sent directly to their death at camps like Auschwitz. Even
after more Jews came to Buchenwald in 1944 for hard labor, they
were mostly sent to the harshest work *kommandos* in outlying
areas, and segregated from other prisoners. Once they were no
longer fit to work, selections were made and the weakest were
shipped east, doomed to immediate death in the gas chambers at
Auschwitz. At the time of Henry's arrival, twenty-two sub-camps
accounted for nearly fifty percent of the camp population. As a
political prisoner housed in the main camp, Henry had almost
no interaction with Jewish prisoners and never spoke of any.
His version of events can only be what he knew and saw, and
would not be duplicated in a Jewish memoir.

Henry never mentioned his arrival at the Weimar train
station; instead his story began with his entry through the main
camp gates. Though they left Auschwitz in a crowded cattle car,
the railway went only as far as the town of Weimar. There was
but one way to reach Buchenwald from Weimar: a five-kilometer
uphill trek to the top of Ettersburg Mountain. As the citizens
of Weimar watched indifferently, new arrivals were marched
through town, and either loaded onto buses, or forced to run
the entire distance uphill, through the dense forest, chased by

barking dogs and cruel guards shouting threats and swinging clubs. The initial road was built by forced labor, with stones from the quarry near Buchenwald.

Today, the road is known as *Blutstrasse*, or Blood Road, both for the number of prisoners who died building the road, and for the brutal trip up the hill. It is still the same and only road to the camp. Henry once described the camp as an ironic cruelty—so much evil in such a beautiful setting.

BUCHENWALD TODAY

D o you plan to visit Kraków, Poland? Auschwitz earned the designation of a UNESCO world heritage site, and landmark status in Poland. In 2015, more than 1.72 million people visited Auschwitz, guided by educators in almost twenty languages. As the best-known concentration camp, and largest Nazi death camp, it has become hugely symbolic of the entire Jewish Holocaust, and for many good reasons. The Auschwitz-Birkenau State Museum is one of the world's leading Holocaust institutions. However, many people mistakenly presume all camps were like Auschwitz, or that only Jews perished in the camps. They were not, especially concentration camps built in Germany, which were designed primarily for imprisonment and death of political prisoners by hard labor.

How about a visit to Weimar, Germany? There is but one small mention of Buchenwald on any travel website, none on any German tourist brochure I could locate, and only one single piece of information on the municipal website—if you knew where to look. I posted a Buchenwald question on the Weimar travel forum of Tripadvisor.com while planning my trip there. For days, no one responded. I eventually got a single restaurant recommendation. Conversely, "Classical Weimar" is listed as a UNESCO world heritage site for its ties to past German cultural icons such as Schiller, Bach, Liszt, Goethe, and Nietzsche.

Today, as in 1943, Buchenwald lies quietly hidden in the heart of Germany. Concentration camps and the Nazi heritage of three generations ago remain the dark history of Germany that is simultaneously mandatory teaching in all schools, and a painful national legacy.

••

Riding down in the hotel elevator the morning after we arrived in Weimar, I realized how much I look like my German heritage. On this, my first trip ever to Germany, I stood next to equally tall redheads, including one man who could have been my father's twin brother. Everyone presumed I was German, greeting us with a polite *Guten Morgen* as we headed for the breakfast buffet.

My German great-grandmother came to the United States a century earlier from the northern seaport of Hamburg. My father was one hundred percent German and taught me a few words in German when I was little. Even my married name, Shawver, was originally the German "Schauber," before it was "Americanized." For a brief moment, I wondered if I could have had distant relatives in my family tree who fought in the German army . . . or joined the SS. I didn't want to know, and chased the thought from my brain as completely irrelevant.

Still curious, though, years later I did look up an index of known SS guards. Two carried my very unique maiden name. It's not a certain connection, and I resolved my possible lineage as unknown and far too distant to be relevant.

When my husband and I visited Weimar that October, the city bus ride up the narrow road to Buchenwald wound through lush trees adorned in the warm reds and oranges of a brilliant German autumn. Upon arrival, I was immediately struck by the small, empty parking lot, void of tour buses and filled with only a few cars that, I would learn, mostly belonged to museum staff.

We walked the grounds for four hours in a cold autumn drizzle, accompanied by our private guide. Lulled by a warm hotel room, we had left our warmer clothes behind. Consequently, we spent most of the morning shivering, but determined to see what we had come so far to see. There were few other visitors to disturb us as we walked the wet grounds retracing Henry's steps and stories. At first glance, I found the camp far more oriented to German visitors than an international crowd, something I interpret as an indicator of a far smaller worldwide visitor base and interest. The books in the small visitor information center were primarily in German, save for a couple dozen in English. You can, however, request tour guides in advance who are well-versed in multiple languages, and the Memorial has developed a very useful tool for visitors and researchers—an interactive phone app in English, filled with solid information. The German government continues to invest funds in putting more information online in German, French, and English. I recommend the free iPhone app for anyone interested in a good overview of the camp.

I remain indebted to Torsten Jugl of the Buchenwald Memorial, who so graciously met with me for the entire afternoon and answered my many questions. He sent me additional information in English after I returned to the United States, partly in appreciation for my traveling such a great distance.

After visiting Buchenwald, the concept of "zoo" took on a creepy and sick new meaning. In 1938, Karl Koch built a zoo with animals like bears, monkeys, and birds of prey for the entertainment of SS officers and their families. The main attraction was a bear pit with four large, brown bears. Families frequently visited the zoo on Sunday afternoons, inured to the electric prison fence just steps away.

In the Koch family photo album, three pictures feature Koch and his young son visiting the zoo and petting the deer. With intention, he strategically situated the zoo ten steps from the electric prisoner fence, and in clear view of the general roll call area. The position allowed miserable prisoners to see how well fed the animals were, especially the large bears, in comparison to the starvation portions allotted for the humans. A pathway, or wide promenade, ran along the outside of the fence. Ilse Koch often rode her horse along that path, surveying starving prisoners. After the crematorium was built in 1940, its roof and smoking chimney stood in full view of the zoo.

Page from the Koch family album. Three photos show a happy family visiting the Buchenwald zoo, just steps from the prisoner fence. In the fourth photo Ilse wears a long, expensive fur coat. The caption reads, "With Papa in the Buchenwald Zoo, October 1939." *National Archives at College Park, College Park, MD.*

All day, I strove to keep that clinical distance that archivists and tour guides develop when they work in such places. I failed the instant I stepped inside the cold crematorium. As soon as I entered, I encountered such a musty, awful smell I gagged and coughed non-stop the entire time I was inside. Henry had described the inside of this building in such accurate detail, and knowing he spent two years in this isolated, lesser-known, and smaller camp of death, caused a greater pain than I had felt at Auschwitz to wrap around my heart.

On the damp bus ride back to the hotel, we sat across from an attractive young woman the same age as my daughter. My eyes glanced down to the block letters printed clearly in black, on her large, white, canvas tote bag. They read, "Whitest Boy

Alive Rules." I must have stared, at what I considered overt racism, because I remember her shifting uncomfortably. I found out later it's the name of a European rock band, but it wouldn't have mattered.

Chilled to the core of my soul, as soon as we got back to the hotel room I threw my soaked shoes—that had touched the crematorium floor—in the trash. I quietly ran a hot bath, sank in, and cried until the water turned cold.

FROM THE STONE QUARRY TO THE STONEMASON *KOMMANDO*

HENRY CONTINUES:

After quarantine, I was assigned to the *steinbruch kommando*. The work in the stone quarry was backbreaking work of the worst kind. The quarry was a large, open place or field where people died all the time just digging rocks. We had to dig and split large rocks and carry them up a long set of stairs. It was a killer *kommando*.

One night, not too long after I'd been working in the quarry, I saw my friend Stanley Jonas from Kraków through the barbed wire. He was working there in camp as a carpenter. He'd been in the camp since 1941.

"Henry! How are you? You hungry?" he asked me. Somehow, he could deliver me soup. They had food.

No, I'm good, thanks.

Then, I quietly told Stanley I had a gold watch in my belt. He figured it out that if I gave him the watch, he would pass it on to his supervisor and he could get me a job in a good *kommando*. Stanley's words sounded like manna from heaven.

"Listen, I'll try to get you work in the *steinmetzin kommando*. That's good work every day. You'll have milk, and work inside the stonemason barrack."

Henry laughed as he remembered thinking about the irony of his good fortune, and leaned toward me.

Milk? I hadn't seen milk in three years. You gotta be kidding me. Why not?

The next day, I found a place behind the barrack where no one can see me. I ripped out the belt and take out the little gold watch for him. I gave the watch to Stanley, and he gave it to the foreman.

The stonemason barrack was a much better *kommando* than working in the quarry. There were four hundred people working in the quarry, dying like everything, and thirty working inside as stonemasons. I was very, very lucky. The stonemasons worked under a long flat roof with about thirty tables. The barrack was wood and the roof was tarpaper held in place with rocks. The tables were like a long picnic table, only the side was higher and filled with sand so you can turn the rocks. Steps, plates, whatever they needed we carved out of stone.

The *kommando* barrack was maybe a quarter mile outside of Buchenwald. Stones were delivered from the quarry on a cart. Very quickly, I became practiced with a two-pound chisel, ten to fifteen inches long, pointed. The two-pound hammer cut the rock the way you want it. There were different chisels in different sizes. We had two Czech stone masters; they carved statues, lamps, fences. The stone was sandstone, which sounds soft, but it wasn't. The rocks were very hard, but they cracked very easy. The Germans knew that the dust from cracking the stones gives you lung disease. That's why we got a little milk each day to help against that.

Then Henry holds out his hand and shows me his thumb.

See how my thumb is bent. I hammered my finger and broke it. It's still bent wrong today. Behind the mason barrack, beyond the trees, was the barrack of the SS kapo. We had a young boy in our barracks, Ivan, a Russian boy who was about thirteen years old. We always had him looking out the window for the SS. Ivan just had to look outside and tell us if someone is coming. He always makes time. The thirty of us were always pounding the rocks, making noise. There was only one SS guard assigned to our barracks, and one guard every fifty feet around the quarry in case someone tried to escape. The Germans were more concerned about our escaping than in making us work, especially later in the war when more guards were sent to the Russian front, and there were fewer guards in the camp.

We had a little freedom, not much, but we could walk outside the barracks. The Germans just watched as we gather a little wood, or catch a few frogs. I met my two good friends there, Yost Slagboom and Hubert Lapailles. We have the nice frog legs, we cooked them in a small iron oven, cooked with wood from the forest. We take the frog legs, put them in red-hot oven, they are very nice piece of meat. So, I survived the quarry; I was strong from the milk and frog legs and bread.

THE GOETHE OAK TREE

The Germans loved the writer Goethe. He was the most famous and likeable poet of Germany. Germans grew up reading Goethe. He lived in Weimar and would write poetry to his girlfriend, Charlotte von Stein, an older woman. I'm going to give you one of his poems—it's a favorite of mine. He wrote it on the wall of the hunting lodge. It was said he would also sit under this large oak tree to write poetry.

Not far from the entrance to Buchenwald, at the end of a row of barracks, there was a large oak tree. It was a tremendous tree, several hundred years old. Some people said Goethe would sit under the tree composing his poetry. The Germans would hang prisoners on a big heavy branch of this tree and leave them there for one or two days. One branch of this big tree hung over the roadway up to the bunker. When you went to work you had to walk past these men, so you tried not to look because it would remind you "don't do that again." But this heavy branch died out and the Germans stopped using it for hanging. They came up with more efficient ways to kill.

There was a legend among the prisoners. The legend went that when the oak tree died, that Germans would disappear, go down. So, we watched this oak tree at the first of every spring.

Towards the end of the war, there were fewer leaves on the tree than people that were hanged there. Only one leaf was green, the rest of the leaves never opened. That tree is no longer there; it was damaged when the Americans bombed Buchenwald in 1944. It died by the end of the war.

PRISONER MOVIES, THEATER, AND CONCERTS

My friend Edmund Polak was involved with the theatre at Buchenwald. He wrote about the theater and movies in his book, *Morituri*. A *morituri* is a gladiator as in *Morituri te salutant*—Caesar, we salute you. I read his book. It was a beautiful book. Edmund Polak was number 16713 in Auschwitz. I know him mostly from the transport from Auschwitz to Buchenwald. In Buchenwald Polak was 10918, I was 10948. I was only thirty people behind him to Buchenwald, in the same transport from the Auschwitz to Buchenwald. He was a very nice man, young. Or maybe he was not so young, dammit, when I think about it. But he was very intelligent. He was a poet, a writer, and what he writes in his book is exactly what I went through.

So, he was young looking, younger than me. He was always writing on scraps of paper, or writing plays. Later Edmund Polak became the editor of the Warsaw newspaper. He could speak five or six languages, and was connected with professional university there.

It took a minute to register the incongruous existence of theater in such a place.

Wait. Did you say there was theater in Buchenwald for prisoners?

Yeah, for prisoners. We have movies, too. The movie theater was for prisoners on Sunday afternoons when no one was there. There were still guards, but Sunday afternoon many guards had off. Koch figured out that if he showed the movies, he could charge the prisoners for seeing them. He'd get about two hundred to three hundred *marks* [German *reichsmarks*] every showing, and the money went straight to his own pocket. He even built a prisoner movie barracks, and we used it for theater as well. The Germans later arrested him for abuse of power, cheating, and embezzlement, because he was profiting from Germans and from prisoners. That's what the Germans did, they all tried to make money from us. I still remember watching the movie *Stern von Rio*. The movies were always in German, of course.

"You had to pay for the movies? How did prisoners pay?"

If we had money in our account we used that. We also got about one to two *marks* a week for labor. This camp was beautiful—we got money for work, we'd sit under the tree with friends. We are safe, we have friends, we survive—as long as you are with the communists that is. There was more freedom to move about here than in Auschwitz. And then you start thinking about the end of the war, and we knew they are going to kill us all so there are no witnesses.

"Wait, you got paid?"

Yeah, sure. Later in the war, the camp tried to motivate people to work harder. They printed up camp money—it was only good in the camp. There was a canteen where you could buy things, but it was mostly rotten food.

Canteen scrip or coupon that could be used only in the camp store. *Collection of the Buchenwald Memorial.*

PRISONER DIVERSIONS

With Henry's new revelations of a prison life beyond that of work crews and long roll calls, I began to understand why he frequently thanked family members for sending money for his account. As with Auschwitz, the Germans encouraged prisoners' families to send money for their "accounts" at camps. In this way, the Germans could devise schemes to "charge" prisoners, and retained all the money sent on prisoners' behalf. A long-term imprisonment of years meant prisoners developed a subculture of sorts. Lest the reader blame the prisoners for "getting off easy," most survivors wrote that these diversions were absolutely essential to maintaining the human spirit. Remnants of chess pieces have been found in many camps, and during one story Henry proclaimed proudly, "I was second best chess champion in all the camp." Sustaining one's psyche, the will to live, and a hope of life after camp was, in itself, a rebellion and a refusal to allow the Germans to completely obliterate one's human soul.

Henry only mentioned the music in Buchenwald once, in a comparison to the Auschwitz orchestra. However, according to records in the Buchenwald Museum, the Buchenwald band had two things the Auschwitz orchestra didn't: an identity as a brass band, and circus uniforms. Somehow Commandant Koch had commandeered a truckload of circus uniforms with magnificent red dolman sleeves, black jodhpurs, and shiny high boots. Camp band members enjoyed better food and good quarters, and spent whole days in rehearsal. With the uniforms, they looked *and* sounded good. Given the cultural heritage of Goethe and Weimar, it seemed appropriate, if not essential, for a Buchenwald band.

Buchenwald's camp brass band was founded in 1938 as a work *kommando*, and reported directly to the kommandant. It was initially comprised of ten to twelve musicians: Sinti—gypsies—and Jehovah's Witnesses, plus one Czech inmate. The band expanded to about thirty-two inmates by 1942. They were ordered to play while prisoners gathered for roll call, as *kommandos* left the gate for work, and during punishments. They also gave concerts for prisoners, usually on Sunday afternoons.

Henry's copy of Polak's *Morituri* was written in Polish, and the account never was translated into English, so I didn't pay much attention to it at the time. His copy disappeared after his death, along with so many other things. The book, published in 1968, remains a popular resale item on foreign used-book websites, and is included in the library collection of the US Holocaust Memorial Museum. Several other prisoner accounts mention Edmund Polak as a memorable, likeable, and popular prisoner. He is known to have written several hundred poems, plays, and songs while imprisoned in both Auschwitz and Buchenwald. In his little-known memoir, *To Calm My Dreams*, Polish political prisoner Kazimierz Tyminski relates that he survived Auschwitz and Buchenwald because of his ability to play piano and the accordion. The true coincidence is that he was imprisoned in Auschwitz at the same time as Henry. While Henry never mentioned Tyminski, they quite likely crossed paths. Tyminski worked near the Auschwitz kitchen and played piano in the SS dining room. He was on the same transport from Auschwitz to Buchenwald as Henry and Edmund Polak, and described in his memoir the exact same story of Witold Myszkowski who sang to the crowd in the Görlitz train station. I truly wish the two men could have met. Tyminski specifically remembered that on Sunday, August 1, 1943, the camp band was allowed to hold its first prisoners' concert in the large cinema barracks. He clearly remembered the band played compositions by Mozart and Smetana, presented a violin solo, and that he played Chopin's "Polonaise in A Major."

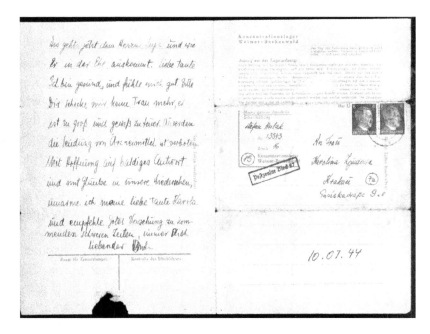

Front and back pages of letter on Buchenwald stationery
dated July 10, 1944. *US Holocaust Memorial Museum,
gift of Nancy Zguda.*

Inside pages of letter on Buchenwald stationery dated July 10, 1944. *US Holocaust Memorial Museum, gift of Nancy Zguda.*

Postal control card included as part of Henry's Buchenwald registration. The top line indicates two letters received on August 6 and September 29, unknown year. The bottom line indicates two letters mailed on August 15 and September 26, unknown year. These dates do not match to any known surviving letters. *Photo 7485573_0_I/ITS Digital Archive, USHMM.*

PRISONER MAIL, PACKAGES, AND MONEY IN BUCHENWALD

L ike other camps, Buchenwald had its own camp stationery for prisoner correspondence. Prisoners were encouraged to ask their families to send money to their "accounts." As described previously, receiving packages often constituted the difference between surviving and dying. Each translation of Henry's letters indicated different items sent, perhaps changing based on what was the most valuable commodity to trade. As with any prisoner letter, a literal translation might sound light and conversational but, again, prisoners were extremely restricted in what they could say to pass the camp censors. A man could be near death, but if he managed to pen a letter, his relatives would have no knowledge of his dire condition.

We have Henry's letters written home, because his mother saved every one. What mother wouldn't? A postal control card shows mail Henry sent on two dates that don't match to existing letters. His Buchenwald correspondence also includes two undated postcards. Records indicate that Henry sent more letters from Buchenwald than he still possessed at the time of our interviews. Buchenwald camp logged both incoming and outgoing mail for each prisoner. However, I did not discover a mail log for Henry until 2014, and the only month for which there was a record didn't match the dates of Henry's letters.

I'm left to wonder. Did Henry's mother receive every letter he wrote? Did she save every letter she received? I'd somehow assumed he had every letter he'd sent. It is another question I never thought to ask, and will never know. As to what Henry received, we have only his confirmation and thank yous back home. As in Auschwitz, all of Henry's letters began with *Liebe Mutti!* My dear mother!"

Auschwitz's rules for letters dictated that each letter begin with "I am alive and well." Per Buchenwald Kommandant Koch, the main rule was that no inmate could include any mention of hunger. As in Auschwitz, letters were written in German and stamped by a censor.

Even though Henry arrived in 1943, his letters from Buchenwald are all dated 1944 and 1945. I didn't notice this until much later, so I never had a chance to ask him. I observed that his handwriting was much more scrawled than earlier ones, perhaps indicating a harder time. It's solely conjecture, though. I don't know if he had to wait until 1944 to earn the privilege or other letters were lost in the mail.

Buchenwald's standard printed text of letter-writing instructions varied slightly from Auschwitz's, as per the translation below.

Concentration Camp Weimar-Buchenwald

The day of release cannot be determined yet. Visitations in the camp are not permitted. Requests are useless.

Excerpt from the camp regulation:

Each prison inmate is permitted to receive two letters or two postcards per month from his relatives, as well as send two letters or two cards. The writing must be clear and readable. Mail that does not follow these parameters will not be delivered. Packages may not be received. The sending of money is permitted, however money must be sent via postal order. The sending of money in letters is prohibited. Notes on the postal order section are prohibited, acceptance will be refused. All can be purchased in the camp. National-socialist newspapers are permitted, however, they must be ordered by the prison inmate at the postal location/office in the concentration camp. Letters that are unclear and not legible cannot be censored and will be destroyed. The sending of pictures and photos is prohibited.

When I borrowed Henry's letters to copy and scan, I looked at them carefully. One from Buchenwald in particular caught my eye. The handwriting was completely different and while it was addressed to Karolina Zguda, it was signed "Stefan Hulak, prisoner number 13543, Block 16." I asked Henry about this.

"Henry, I just noticed the return address on one of the letters identified a Stefan Hulak as the sender, and it was addressed to *Aunt* Karolina. Who was Stefan Hulak and why did he write your mother?"

13543 had no one to write to. So, Stefan wrote to his 'Dear Aunt' Karolina Zguda in Kraków for me. I tell him what to say.

July 10, 1944

Dear Aunt!

I thankfully received a letter from you. I am happy that all is in order with you [plural] and that Ryska wrote. I was worried that something may have happened. I am writing this letter with hope of a better future and that you are able to work through all hard things. July 9 I received two packages. From Wroblich and Roz [?]. From Wroblich, butter and cake. Write to Rosz [?] that I received the ten Marks. I ask of you to better package the products because they ran together. I thank you for all [whole] heartedly. Best thanks to Uncle Franz for the two packages and for Janka, 20 [currency?] were deposited in my account. All from you was received in an orderly fashion. I already drank the Trau [cod liver oil] and the marmalade ran out twice. Thank you for the socks, however, I do not need socks or underwear anymore. Do not oversend me anything. The slippers provide me great joy and they fit well. However, in the future, please do not buy me such expensive things. Thanks to Ms. Gena on my behalf and apologize for all the worries. How is Mr. Lupa and his marriage? Dear Aunt, I am healthy and feel well. Please don't send me any more Trau. It was large and certainly expensive. Also, sending First Aid/Medical items is prohibited. With hope of a quick response, and with the belief of seeing each other again, I hug you my dear Aunt Karola and commend God's providence to come in hard times.

Your forever loving [scribbled]."

THE *PUFFHAUS*

A s promised in a former interview, Henry finally described the "puff."

Every camp had a *puffhaus*, or bordello, by order of Himmler. We just called it the puff. You see, the Germans were so smart. By the end of the summer of 1943, the war was getting bad; the Russians were advancing on the eastern front, and squeezing the Germans back to the borders. The German command *decided to be nice* to the senior prisoners and guards. The prisoners worked hard so they needed some girls.

As Henry said "decided to be nice," his voice dripped with sarcasm. I paused in my note taking as my mouth dropped open in surprise. So *this* was the "puff " Henry referred to earlier? A bordello for prisoners? I clamped my mouth shut, as I let Henry continue uninterrupted. How many more surprise revelations would Henry share in this narrative?

In 1943, they built the *puff* at Buchenwald. There were bathtubs, towels, curtains, small rugs, and other little things. Kapo Arno was a *tischler,* or carpenter, and was kapo of the carpenters. They worked day and night building fourteen rooms of furniture, as they were ordered to finish quickly. The girls came from Ravensbrück, and were hand selected.

They made everything so nice for the *puff.* The flowers, carpets, everything was nice. There were only fourteen girls in all:

including Germans, four Poles, and two Russians. The prisoners see the faces with hair done, and make-up, and curtains on the windows. When comes the opening of the puff, the guys who want to visit the girls give their name to the *schreiber* [clerk] of the block and he sent that to the *schrieber* of the camp. There the *Blockführer* reviewed the qualifications of the guys who request it. Do they deserve it? Do they have a crime outstanding? Then, they send back the paper with the date and number when he can go to the *puff*.

There were so many guys ready to go, you usually had to wait several days for your turn. Every day, after roll call, there was a group waiting their turn. They stay in line on the steps going to the block. When the bell ring that labor is finished, everyone ran like hell to Block 24A.

"Did they get a chance to wash up first?"

No, over there they wash them. And the guys, they run like hell to steal the hearts of the girls. The regular prisoners don't even try for the puff cards. Only the prisoners in better positions, like the kapos and those in good standing with the Germans, could go. The regular prisoners didn't even try. Many men were shy, or were husbands, and didn't want someone else to see them go. They just didn't feel right. So, mostly, the bandits, the thieves, and *blockmeisters* [foremen] were the ones who went to the puff. The time to visit was only twelve minutes.

"Each man only got twelve minutes?"

Yes. That was the limit. Twelve minutes. Besides, we are all tired after work. In Buchenwald you don't "puff" too long.

Henry laughed at his own joke.

How was it, I continued to ask myself, that Henry was able to find a light side to such a dark place?

Not everyone screwed—there was no time. Sometimes they just stroke the girl's arm, give them a kiss, reassured them, then they're done. And then, afterwards, the guys have to line up for the injection. Along comes the *pfleger* and everyone has to stand in front of the sanitary man for the injection of disinfection. Then, they're out and back to the barracks. The injections were mostly to protect the girls.

"Did prisoners have to pay?"

Yes, two *marks*, I don't know, something like that. The

Germans don't do nothing for free.

Thinking back to Henry's younger days in Kraków, and his friendship with Blind Marie, I explored the topic further.

"Did you go to the *puff*?"

No, no. That's not something I do. Besides, the communists checked on you. They were very strict and they knew who went to the *puff*. If you're married and you go to the *puff*, the communists made sure you got sent to the Dora *kommando*. Stanley was also afraid to go. He knew going to the *puff* meant almost certain death in the Dora *kommando*. So, mostly the guards went, but we never did.

Late at night, between 24 and 24A block, mostly the greens, the bandits, and murderers, would whistle at the girls, and call out their favorite girl if she had been good to them. There were curtains on the windows, but you could see through them. Sometimes you'd see the girls just put their foreheads on the window and cry. You could see the face of Krystyna, the Polish girl, and the little German girl, I forget her name. She was waiting for her beloved kapo who came with gifts. Puff Mama Annie, she just stood by the window like a statue.

Many times prisoners would try climbing the fence to reach the girls. Sometimes a girl might throw a rope down to her friend, someone she likes. But Kaduc, the *rapportführer*, was waiting for just such an occasion. He'd come with other SS and kapos, and run into the fourteen rooms, and give a nasty beating to the girls. All night you heard the loud screaming and crying.

The men would try to get to girls privately, to avoid injections. They were the ones who climb walls and break legs falling down.

I felt sorry for the girls, even though they had everything they wanted. The girls were prisoners, too. Mostly those girls got mental shock for the rest of their life. They were called whores, or *szmata,* the rest of their life. *Szmata* is just a dirty floor rag.

••

Side view of the Buchenwald *puff* or bordello. Notice the curtains in each window. 1943. *Collection of the Buchenwald Memorial.*

There were *puffs* at both Auschwitz and Buchenwald, and in telling his story of the *puffhaus*, Henry mixed up the two camps. I chose, however, to relate the story as told to me. Though Henry related these details in the context of Buchenwald, Block 24A was in Auschwitz I, *Rapportführer* [Oswald] Kaduc was a mean German officer in Auschwitz, and Kapo Arno was indeed at Auschwitz. Also, the *puff* at Buchenwald was a single story structure.

In looking at a layout of Auschwitz, once Henry was promoted to the kitchen, he lived in Block 25, not far from Block 24, and would have been keenly aware of the activities there. Just by standing outside his block, he would have been able to look up at their windows, and hear their cries when they were beaten. By proximity, he witnessed the outside of the Auschwitz *puff* personally, but never mentioned that he saw the Buchenwald *puff* in person.

The story and circumstances surrounding the camp *puff* would be similar in both camps except that, within the power structure in Buchenwald, the communists controlled their people with their own moral standard with the very real threat of reassignment to the Dora *kommando.*

Henry never mentioned kapos at Buchenwald, perhaps because the communists served as their own block leaders. Henry instead referred mostly to the staff as guards or the SS. Evil indeed reigned at the camp, but just by another name. Henry seems to have intentionally stayed friends with the [Polish and German] communists and referred to them as decent men.

THE AMERICANS BOMB BUCHENWALD

HENRY CONTINUES:

On August 24, 1944, the Americans bombed Buchenwald. I was working in the stonemason barracks, and I still remember the sirens and alarms. All over the sky was the American supremacy in the air.

Lapaille, Slagboom, Stanley, and I went outside our barrack. We left Ivan posted at the window. There were maybe twenty-five of us in the barracks as we stood outside. So, whir, whir, and we look west. The sky from horizon to horizon was full of planes coming in our direction, like a *bomben teppich,* or bombing rug. There must have been six to eight waves of bombing. We said, Bravo, very nice. The Americans are here to save us! We start cheering and waving to the planes. Until the bombs started hitting. The rocks on our roof holding the tar paper started caving in.

I yelled at everyone to put a rock plate above their heads. I dove and saved my friend Lapaille's life by covering his head. We all got cuts and injuries from flying rocks, but not from the bombs. Lapaille and I stayed friends our entire lives; he never forgot I saved his life.

Stanley and I ran like hell out of there. First, we saw a bomb with "500 LBS" on it, stuck half in the ground. If it went off the whole barracks would be gone. I didn't know then what "LBS" meant, I just knew it was big. Geesh, the biggest bombs we'd seen before that, and what Germany used to attack Poland, had been twenty-five kilos at heaviest.

Suddenly coming from the quarry we see Hugo, one of our friends coming to us. He has a cut from his ear to the top of his head.

"What happened? What happened?" he kept saying as he walked around in a daze, holding his head while blood poured out. Stanley looked at him and we could see his brain. Hugo stood there, looked right at us, passed out, and dropped dead right there in front of us. We ran like hell past the quarry and towards the gates.

I think like maybe ten bombs fell into that quarry. On the way out of there we saw, coming from the quarry, hands and feet, body parts cut by bombs. We were heading for the main gates. The whole quarry was bombed in, so the bomb in the quarry cut the people in the pieces, and threw the body parts out in the forest. As one more bomb exploded, more body parts fly through the air. The SS rang alarms and ran and hid in the forest or ran to the prisoner barracks to hide.

The Americans bombed the SS housing and they hit the Koch villa. I don't know if Ilse Koch was still there. I know only that prisoners helped the children of [Kommandant Hermann] Pister get out of his burning house. Maybe he was grateful to the prisoners, I don't know, but he did leave the Buchenwald gates open.

We went through the gates and ran down the hill towards Weimar. We passed this one dead SS officer, so we took his gun and kept going. I took his watch, too. Weimar had civilian police. Some of the townspeople came to us with milk and bread.

But then we ask ourselves, Where can we go? Buchenwald was still in Germany. We hear shooting everywhere, and we think the end is close. So, we went back up the hill to the camp. Along the way we find one gun, then another and another. We brought these back to camp.

On the way back to camp, I found an SS man dying under the

tree. We are running away from the Americans because of the bombs, and we heard this man pointing at us and yelling at us, "*Kameraden*, help me. *Kameraden* help me."

We turned and got to the SS guy, and I said to one of my friends, Yeah, we'll help him. Just let me at him with this rock. Two years in camps and the Germans killed so many people. I picked up a big rock ready to drop it on him. But, something stopped me. I sure thought about it though. We didn't kill him, but I took his wallet. I was looking for papers, maybe money, I don't know, whatever I could find. I took a picture out of his wallet, then I left the wallet with the dying soldier.

On the way back to the camp, we found more hands and feet that had been cut off by bombs. When we passed any dead SS officers we grabbed their guns and brought those back to camp.

We got back to the camp, but it was very strange, almost quiet. We didn't see any guards because they run off to hide in the woods. We came into the barrack, and saw a friend with a wound here, a cut here. Luckily, the old Belgian guy and Czech guy were okay. So, I take my friends wounded bad, and loaded up with guns, and drag them to the hospital. Now, there was no one to tell you what to do. We gave them to Kowalski, also to the *Revier* [camp hospital] to hide. I think the Resistance used these guns later against the SS guards. After we gave the guns to Kowalski, Stanley and I just leaned against the wall of the *puff*, and slid down to the grass, and shook like hell. For about five minutes, I just shook like with tremors. I couldn't help it. My nerves were shot from being bombed and everything else that I saw and had happened. The fear struck me to the core.

During that attack, many SS and guards from Buchenwald died. But more prisoners than SS died. The US gave the Germans hell and we were very happy for that. The Americans bombed directly on the housing of the SS, and the arms factory. They worked in the factory or quarry.

During the bombing, one of the US bombs fall on the wood shop and started fire. The fire went to the Goethe oak tree and burned it down. The oak tree was gone. Then, we knew that everything is all right, that the end of the war is near.

Even with the casualties, the Germans cleaned everything up and kept the camp going for eight more months. After that bombing, there was an even more powerful communist underground in the camp. Remember, towards the end of the war there were fewer German guards—they kept getting pulled to fight at the front. The ones left behind were the older and younger ones. This underground helped us to survive and defend ourselves at the end of the war.

BOMBING AFTERMATH

The Americans strategically aimed their bombs at the armament factory and SS housing and garrison. While the Germans were never able to resume much functionality of arms production afterward, the freedom so many prisoners assumed would come with the bombing and the destruction of the Goethe oak tree would not come for another eight months. Prisoners continued to flood into the camp, mostly Jews destined for the many sub-camps, including the dreaded Dora *kommando*.

In late 1944, as the Russians began to advance into occupied Poland, the Germans evacuated prisoners of both Auschwitz and another camp, sending them on death marches toward Germany. More than 10,000 exhausted prisoners from Auschwitz arrived in Buchenwald. As the age of the guards grew younger, so did the prisoners. By December 1944, more than a third of the prisoners were under age twenty—the youngest was three years old. The communists played a key role in helping the children as much as possible.

Despite the aggressive bombing run of August, there would be no more contact with Americans until the following spring.

PART 5

KL BUCHENWALD, WEIMAR, GERMANY

JANUARY 1945–MAY 1945

Wallet-sized photo that Henry Zguda claimed to have taken from a dead German soldier in 1944. *US Holocaust Memorial Museum, gift of Nancy Zguda.*

THE BUCHENWALD CREMATORIUM

During one interview, Henry matter-of-factly pulled out a small, wallet-sized, black-and-white photo, taken inside a crematorium. That was the thing about talking with Henry—I didn't really know the extent of his stories until we talked. He kept bringing out surprising things I had never seen before, like his camp letters, and now this photo.

The photo showed four men standing in front of a crematorium oven, and was one I have never seen in a single Holocaust book or any reference material. There were two men, presumably prisoners, standing at the feet and head of a very skinny cadaver. The man on the left by the cadaver's feet wore a striped prisoner uniform. The man on the right appeared shirtless, and wore shorts. They appeared to be posed as if about to lift the body to the oven door with what looked like large metal forceps or tongs. In the back, a third prisoner stood next to a man meticulously dressed in a clean white shirt, fashionable haircut, and striped, but very clean, pants.

Clearly this was a staged photo, with all four men seemingly posed and facing the camera. The picture was obviously old, crinkled, and original. I was stunned that Germans would be so proud of the task of burning the camp dead that they would pose with a cadaver and body-sized forceps to memorialize the scene. With that photo, our interview took an even more chilling turn.

"Henry, where did you get this photo?"

From the German's wallet after the bombing. This is a picture of inside the Buchenwald crematorium where I worked once. My friend Mietek Kowalski worked in the hospital and so, one time, he made me a pass so I wouldn't have to go to work for a few days. I remember it was winter, because it was very cold outside. Kowalski was a captain in the Polish army, and he was smart like hell. I don't know if he was a spy for the Russians or the Polish, but he spoke perfect Russian and perfect Polish.

So, one day the following January, there's about five of us there in the barracks, and I'm sitting at the table playing chess with my friend. I remember the long icicles hanging from the roof. Then, all of a sudden, the SS comes in with the guns out.

"Everybody *raus! Raus*! Come on, get your asses out here. *Schnell*. Now."

They rounded up about twenty of us guys. "Stay in lines of five. Run, run, run!" They ordered us in the direction of the crematorium. They brought us across the whole Buchenwald to the crematorium place at the end of the *appellplatz* [roll call area].

The crematorium was surrounded by a tall concrete wall, about 400 meters square. You can't see the other side until you go in the gate. Passing this door to the crematorium, on the right side, we see a big pile of Jewish cadavers about one story high, brought from Budapest, and they were frozen to the transport. Over the fence, you can see the heads and hands, high, just like this. They were piled over one story high.

They were there in all different positions. We were told to take the cadavers from the transport and bring them to the ovens. There was tape that somehow held them together. But the tape was full of blood and pus from these bodies, some with gangrene. I didn't want to get any of it on me. That's what I hated mostly, but it was awful, I tell you. The look on their faces, you know, their mouths hanging open, their eyes looking at nothing . . . or at you.

Henry made a long twisted face between both his hands, not unlike the appearance of *The Scream* by Edvard Munch, in imitation of their faces. I've seen similar horrific photos, especially from camp liberation photos. But to sit across from someone who was there, and who described the scene in such a no-nonsense, factual manner, was akin to bringing a black-and-white photo into full living color.

I wanted to stop the story—I didn't want to know the rest. Yet, prisoners forced into such a horrific work detail did not have the luxury of turning their heads by quickly flipping the page in a Holocaust chronicle. They couldn't avoid the work, short of being shot on the spot. In a morbid reality, can you be grateful at such a time to still be among the living? No, I owed it to them, and to Henry, to get the story so they would not be forgotten, no matter how difficult this interview became. I sat still and silent as if frozen in place, fervently hoping the tape recorder did not run out.

He continued the story and brought my thoughts back front and center.

They were frozen together so you couldn't just pull them down. We had to break the legs and bones so we could get them to lie flat. I wasn't killing them, they were already dead, but *oh my God!*

As I continued to cringe inwardly, Henry continued his story, holding up the photo to show me the details, pointing to it.

You can't see it in this photo, but in the front of the ovens there were these carts on wheels on a small track. They called these the "tray on the track." They put the bodies on these carts, then put a little water on the carts to help the bodies slide easy. The guy at the oven just pushed with a jerk and closed the door. In the back of the ovens was where you put the coal in. The coal was these briquettes, you know, like for a barbecue. You shovel it in a door in the back of the ovens, and they heat the temperature to over one thousand degrees inside. The skinny guys burn in twenty to twenty-five minutes. If the bodies have some fat, they burn in forty-five minutes, but there weren't very many like that.

There were so many bodies to load we had to stay until all the cadavers were taken care of. I want to say there were four hundred or so. And they didn't burn more than six at a time per hour in the ovens, so it takes a while. Meanwhile we had to continuously transport the dead.

It was late in the day, so after only one hour, they sent me to a little wooden house in the back to spend the night. These barracks were close to the crematorium, separated completely from the rest of the camp. The crematorium workers were kept separate from other prisoners. They knew too many secrets of the dead, so the Germans were never going to let them go.

When I walked in, I saw my friend Zbigniew Fuchs, who was working there. I knew him from Kraków. I also saw my friend Marian Zguda. I was always worried they would mix us up, both being named Zguda. My friend Marian was one of the foremen at the crematorium.

Zbigniew was enrolled in Jagiellonian University studying law when he and his younger brother were arrested by the Gestapo in Kraków on January 13, 1941. His brother was sent to Auschwitz where he was murdered in 1943. Zbigniew was transported to Buchenwald. He was a prisoner there from April 1, 1941, until the camp liberation in April 1945. He was arrested for being a *deutschfeindlich*, or having a hostile attitude towards the Germans.

Fuchs greeted me, "Heh, Henry, how are you? Don't worry. You are safe here. They don't kill you, they don't take your food. You won't live to see the end of the war, but for now you are safe." Right away Fuchs gave me soup and beer.

They had everything they wanted because they worked in the crematorium *kommando*. They even had a radio there. All right, so I stayed and we listened to the radio. They had good soup, coffee, and chocolate. Fuchs and Marian Zguda were "dead people" and they knew it. They knew the SS would never let them live to see the end of the war because they were witness to all that happened in the crematorium. I thought it was funny in an odd way—the gate said *Jedem das Seine,* To Each What They Deserve. I don't think this is what Koch meant. No one deserves this *kommando*. That night I ate well and shared a bunk with Fuchs.

The next morning I woke up and had to use the bathroom. I asked Fuchs where it was.

So, Fuchs says, "Well, there is no bathroom. You go to the basement in the crematorium. Go down the staircase, and there is the cover on the hole in the ground. You open that, and you do what you have to do there."

"Henry, you seriously mean inside the crematorium building?"

Yes. In the crematorium itself, on the bottom. Ovens were on the main floor, and there was a basement below. I went to relieve myself. I found the covered hole and I opened it. I'm standing there in this big square room doing my business, and something caught my eye. I looked around and went whoa, and then *What the hell* . . . I found myself standing right in front of two dead guys hanging there.

Then I looked around and saw walls so smooth they looked like mirrors. On the wall, all around the room, near the ceiling there were large hooks, like they use for animals, you know, cows when they kill them. Hook, hook, hook, all around. Then, I see the window, up high on the wall, looking out at the main courtyard by the crematorium. It was made out of metal, and slanted like a sort of slide, like when a trap door opens. Whoosh, and down you go. And as I looked at the hooks under the entry to the outside, I saw what they did. You open the entry [window], lead a guy there in the night and 'whap' they slide down before they know it.

The Germans or foremen would wait for someone to come down the chute and land on the floor. They put the noose on the neck, and they hang him up on the hook. And the people as they were dying, they kept struggling, jerking as they die from the cord on the neck. That's what make the walls shine like mirrors . . . their struggling. I learned later that sometimes they have four or five guys hanging in the night. Then, the guys who sleep in the crematorium barrack sometimes have to get up early, say 5 or 6 a.m., and take these men upstairs to the oven.

In this corner of the room was the table for the doctor, and a pail of red fluid like iodine next to it, like a disinfectant for the SS. There were plenty of nooses on the table in the corner. On nails on the wall were the rubber gloves for the SS, and a whip. This was the space for the SS doctor who was always by the execution to sign the death certificate.

So, I start backing up and look to the corner to the right, and there is the elevator. In the elevator I see one woman, a beautiful girl, a major, a private, and a civilian. All dead. There were only two ways into that room—down the stairs, or through that window chute. There were only two ways out of that basement— up the stairs, or in the elevator for cadavers up to the ovens. I turned and got the hell out of there. I ran up the stairs two at a time and back to the barracks.

"Heh, Fuchs, you son of a bitch! Why'd you send me there? I almost dirtied my pants in that atmosphere."

I asked Henry, "Was Fuchs one of those helpers in the crematorium? Was he one of the ones who hit the guys on the head?"

No! Only the Germans and kapos hit the prisoners on the head. The prisoners are to handle the dead.

After that, we had to go to work. I took the position of delivering the coal briquettes to the back of the oven. Only, it had rained in the night and I didn't notice there was water in the coal bucket. When I opened the oven and threw in the bucket of coal—heat like hell, like a thousand degrees—and poof! It was like an explosion almost. This huge steam wave and fire instantly come out so hot and so fast it burned my eyebrows off and almost burned my eyes. I fell down hard. I was so surprised. It happened so fast I didn't know what happened, and I smell my own hair burning. In the camps they don't tell you how to do anything, they just tell you to work.

"Get outta here," the guards ordered me, swinging their rifles at me. They sent me back to carry the cadavers. We had to continuously transport the dead. At one point, I tripped and fell with these bodies on top of me. My knee rammed into the cement stairs. The SS saw me go down and came over waving at me.

"*Schnell! Schnell!* Hurry, hurry up." Because I was unable to get up quickly enough, I was beaten and kicked severely about my back and kidneys by the SS guards. Fuchs came over and intervened on my behalf. He got me back to the hospital to my friend Kowalski.

Kowalski told me, "Hi, Henyu. Here, you lie down here. You are a heavy patient for us."

My knee was all inflamed and hurt like hell. Kowalski found a bed for me to lie down on. My knee became very infected, but they can do nothing for me. No medicine, no nothing. But I could rest, and after about ten days, I went back to my stonemason *kommando*.

"So, Fuchs and Zguda did this every day?"

Yes, but Fuchs was not a killer. Fuchs survived the war and

we stay friends. He wasn't a communist during the war, but he became one later you see, to survive. I have pictures of him—and an article in Polish from after war, and again in 1985—when he was witness against Buchenwald and the kapos.

You know, in Buchenwald, there were two French generals and most of the communist party. After the war when the Russians took over Poland and everyone was communist, the communist party investigated the death of Mr. Ernst Thälmann, the head of the German communist party. Mr. Thälmann was killed in Buchenwald in August 1944 when I was there. Maybe he was killed in that basement, I don't know. I do know you could scream all you want down there and nobody would hear you. The communist government sent me letters in later years asking me to testify to what I saw, but I never responded.

I don't want to make Fuchs out as all bad. He and Marian Zguda worked constantly in the crematorium. Every day there are people to burn. That was a regular day in the Buchenwald crematorium. I am telling you these things because I was there. This is how it was.

Partial view of the basement of the Buchenwald crematorium in October 2013. The center of the photo shows the chute into the basement. Forty-eight hooks were placed high near the ceiling to hang prisoners in secrecy, often prisoners of war or condemned prisoners of importance. Public executions were mostly held in subcamps. Condemned Jews were sent directly to Auschwitz. *Photo by author.*

Photo of the trapdoor outside the crematorium that leads to the basement chute, and through which either prisoners or corpses were thrown. Photo taken June 6, 1945. *US Holocaust Memorial Museum, gift of Richard L. Rennert.*

View of the front of the Buchenwald crematorium ovens in October 2013. The tracks on the floor were used for the carts to slide the bodies in. The small doors below were used to empty the ashes. The large black square in the back right is the elevator used to transport bodies from the basement. *Photo by author.*

View of the back of the Buchenwald crematorium ovens in October 2013. Henry was stationed there to shovel coal into the back of the ovens. *Photo by author.*

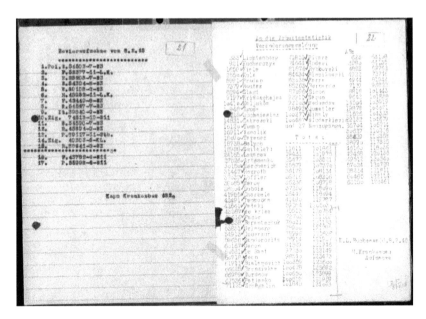

List of arrivals at the prisoners' infirmary of Buchenwald
Concentration Camp, indicating that 10948 Henry Zguda was
admitted on February 8, 1945 (document on the right side.) The
German word *tote* means "dead." *Photo 5339615_0_1/ITS Digital
Archive, USHMM.*

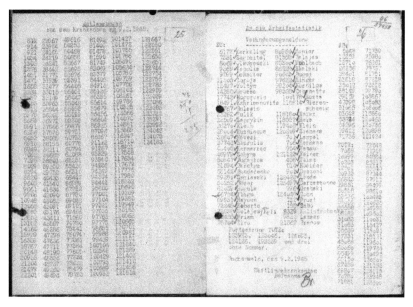

List of departures from the prisoners' infirmary of Buchenwald Concentration Camp, indicating that Henry Zguda was released on February 9, 1945 (document on the left side.) It lists only prisoner numbers. Henry's number, 10948, is in the first column on the left. *Photo 5339617_0_1/ITS Digital Archive, USHMM.*

PROVENANCE OF HENRY'S GRISLY PHOTO

The photo was donated to the United States Holocaust Memorial Museum after Henry's death. In 2013, I shared a digital copy of Henry's photo with the Buchenwald museum. They later contacted me to let me know that Henry's photo was taken in the crematorium of Dachau, not Buchenwald. Later that year, I borrowed a DVD from the library entitled *Swimming in Auschwitz*. Given Henry's unique story of swimming in a potato vat there, the title intrigued me to know if in fact there was actually swimming in Auschwitz.

The documentary, through a series of interviews conducted in 2006, followed the lives of six women who survived Auschwitz. The title came from the story of one woman who had been a lifelong swimmer, walked past the SS swimming pool and jumped in. Indeed, a small statement in the epilogue to Höss's memoir reported that Kommandant Liebchenschel, the kommandant after Höss was transferred to Berlin in November 1943, filled in the water trough near Blocks 7 and 8. The site became a swimming pool for kapos and prisoners who worked well. During a background segment on the history of Auschwitz, for just a second, Henry's crematorium photo flashed on the screen. I knew instantly it was Henry's photo because it creased in the exact same places I remembered.

In 2014, I visited the National Archives in College Park, Maryland. There, I donned protective white gloves, and sifted through dozens of original photos from both Dachau and Buchenwald. Because the Americans liberated these two camps, any original confiscated photos and documents went into the National Archives. Records from camps that were liberated by the Russians were shipped back to Russia. Only in recent years have many of those archives been opened up to researchers. Many of the pictures I held in the National Archives, I've seen featured in social studies texts, or used in other memoirs from the time. The fact that these were the *originals*, all nearly seventy years old, and I could turn them over and read the captions or comments on the back of each, held a certain reverence for me.

Incredibly, I found a photo in the Dachau collection that was clearly a sibling of Henry's photo. The image in that one was even more disturbing. It showed the same man-in-a-clean-white-shirt and man in striped prison garb loading a corpse into the oven, as one of them clearly pauses to look at the camera. This fact, along with the notion that an SS soldier considered the scene so worthy he carried an original photo of it in his wallet as a souvenir, will forever haunt me.

On the back of the photo in the National Archives, there was a crumbling strip of paper attached that read: "One of a set of seven pictures taken at Dachau Nazi concentration camp near Munich. They are copies of photos which are being sold by ambitious inmate to American soldiers visiting camp. Sent by H. R. Hollen to New York." At the end of the war, there is no way for a US soldier to know how the photo was acquired in 1944. Therefore, I wonder, could Henry have stumbled upon the man in the clean, white shirt? Did the Germans print up a series of copies, or did Henry accidentally discover a single original? Could the Germans have seriously printed a series of seven staged photos? Could a prisoner truly be so inured to the evil represented in those photos he would actually sell them to American troops? I will never know and I wish I could erase the images from my mind.

Clandestine photograph of prisoners marching to Dachau in the last weeks of the war. Photo was taken by Maria Seidenberger, who took the photo from the second story window of her family's home while her mother stood outside and gave potatoes to the prisoners. Her house was only three miles from the entrance to Dachau. *US Holocaust Memorial Museum, gift of Maria Seidenberger.*

Henry's Death March

■ Concentration
  Camp

● City

- - - Henry's March

0   100
|_____|
       MILES

EVACUATION OF BUCHENWALD AND THE DEAD MARCH

HENRY CONTINUES:

On April 8, 1945, we were called to roll call. We heard the artillery near Weimar and knew there would be no work today. There were about five thousand of us left in the camp that I know of, and fewer guards than ever. The ones left were mostly young and very old. When the Germans began losing the war, they kept sending more men to the frontlines. I could have stayed in Buchenwald; Kowalski would have given me his police armband. But I had friends who were going someplace and get liberated by the American Army. So, Edmund Polak and I left together. The first thousand men left. I was in the second group of thousand men to go. Out the gates, down to Weimar, on the train, and we left. We traveled through the night. I remember going through Zeitz, fifty-five miles from Weimar. I remember plants burning, smoke, airplanes over our train. If they got close, the SS guards would just hide in with us.

Right there in Zeitz, we stopped on the station and see trains full of cadavers coming from the Czech border. So, what do we do? We get out of the train, and start walking. The dead march began. We don't know where we are going. We head south towards Weiden, a town near KL Flossenbürg [another concentration camp]. We walked through the beautiful forest. But we have nothing to eat and one hundred eighty miles to Flossenbürg. Out of this group of a thousand guys, maybe four hundred of us survived as far as Flossenbürg. You walk with no food. You have no strength. When you fall to the end of the column, the SS guards shoot you. We walked, and heard shots behind us. That way we walk very fast, so we don't get shot. I didn't look back.

After seven days, we finally reached Flossenbürg late on April 15. They put us in a big empty building in the camp like an airplane hangar. We made sure the windows weren't sealed and it wasn't a gas chamber. We slept on the concrete floor right there. Still, we had nothing to eat or drink.

KL Flossenbürg opened a year after Buchenwald and was mostly the criminals and politicals, not Jews. The Jews come there later in the war. It was smaller, but by the time we get to the camp there's only a few thousand prisoners left.

One of the better fun the Germans would do, just like in Mauthausen, the other *good* [concentration] camp, was in this big quarry, and they make the guys carry rocks from the bottom of the quarry up to build the rooms and walls. They built the barracks for prisoners on top. There were maybe one hundred steps of rock cut by prisoners. They were very high steps, one hundred eighty of them . . . wide, maybe ten feet. But, while carrying these rocks, when you have no strength, the SS would push one man back and, like dominoes, the prisoners behind him would all fall down one hundred and eighty steps. The more they push down and kill, the more the SS laughed. They didn't do that when we were there, but those were the stories of that camp.

After this "sidebar" account, Henry returned to his own experience.

Next morning, we get up, walk outside and see we are in the camp with other prisoners. We get coffee and we see every barrack at the camp has a white sheet for surrender. We knew the Americans must be very close by. The Germans could hear the American tanks and shouting, so they told us, "We have to surrender the camp nice, boys. Be nice." The soldiers went and hid in the hills and left the kapos in charge. The kapos were very nice to us, I think so we wouldn't tell the Germans their crimes. They give us cigarettes, food . . . so nice all day. For four days we were pseudo-free. What happens? The noon comes, and here come the German soldiers back from the little hills. At first we were so happy and began to cheer because we thought it was the Americans. It was just the SS coming back. We were very disappointed.

The next morning at 4 a.m. they wake everybody and order us to march again. They ordered thousands to leave the camp. Edmund and I were in the second group of a thousand men. As we marched down the road, we saw so many dead people by the side of the road, shot from the first thousand.

The beatings continued like always, and we start hustling towards Dachau [concentration camp, ten miles northwest of Munich], a distance of one hundred fifty kilometers. We walked and walked. There was always shooting at the back of the line, so there's less and less of us all the time. The old and exhausted were unable to run, so they were shot on the spot and left by the side of the road. There was a special group of prisoners assigned to bury the dead. But, with everyone running, they only had time to throw three or four shovels of earth so they could keep up with the main group. Shouting was constant, loud like hell.

At dusk, everyone rushed to a big field of grass. Right turn, down, and sleep. You slept wherever you were. Water, mud, whatever, you sleep in it. Some prisoners crawled to find some grass . . . something edible or water. I just slept right there in the mud and water, too exhausted to move. The guards were right there ready to shoot at any heads if they saw movement.

From there, we left and kept marching to Dachau. The Germans had no bread, but they had sacks full of grain, so everyone got one or two handfuls of grain, about a pint's worth, before we leave.

You can't eat that dry. On the way to Regensburg [halfway between Flossenbürg and Dachau] I figure out how to cook the corn. I took two cans, one in the bottom of other, made holes and stick wood there, dry grass, paper, whatever can burn in the bottom. In the smaller one you put a little water with the corn, and make a fire in the bottom, and heat up and you have hot water and put grain in so you have a little soup. Somehow I found a chain or string or something to carry it with.

"Wait, Henry. Where did you get the cans? Did anyone else do this?"

I think I was the only one who do this. You always have to think to survive. The SS had cans of food in their rucksacks. When they finished eating their rations we picked up their cans and trash. They had cans of beef, plenty of rations for whole week . . . at least ten cans of food per soldier. That's also why their rucksacks were so heavy. The guards couldn't afford to lose their rucksacks. The rucksacks were so heavy they still made prisoners carry them.

The next day, I'm done. I decided to escape. All around us was very dense forest like the Bavarian mountains. The SS guard was way behind in the line, so I took off and ran through the trees, protecting my eyes, going, going, going. I'm exhausted, but I go as fast as I can. Only, I didn't know the road curved, and when I came out of the trees, there was the head of the prisoner column. The first SS guard in front of the line was so tired he just laughed when he saw me and waved me back in line.

There were about seven more days of marching. Regensburg was a nice town near the river, halfway to Dachau. Narrow streets, old town. But, as we walked through the town, the people there screamed at us, "*Raus, banditen.*" You bandits get out of Germany! Only one lady opened the window and threw bread to us. She was afraid to be nice I think. Just think, only one person in the whole town was nice to us. Even boys age fourteen or fifteen, like Hitler youth, yelled at us and threw rocks at us as we went through the town.

My souvenir from Regensburg was illness. Everybody was getting sick. We were all sick with edema and swollen legs from hunger. Everybody around me had the diarrhea like hell, bloody diarrhea like with the typhoid. If it wasn't typhoid, then it was something like that. It stunk like hell.

On April 27, 1945, we arrived at Dachau, which was full of other Czech prisoners ready to march to the mountains. By now, there were maybe only a hundred prisoners left behind me, out of the thousand we started with. It was a rainy day, and I remember being very exhausted and ill. I fell down and crawled to the street gutter to get some water. I think I passed out because the stronger friends took me, and others, to the barracks and left me in the corner to die. I remember it was very cold and the window was broken. Somehow I found an old blanket and fell to sleep.

At this point I don't care where I have been or where I am. I was very sick. One sip of water and I go to the bathroom. I was completely dehydrated. For three days, we are very nervous because we know the Germans were ordered to destroy the camp before the Americans got there.

On April 28, I'm on the block. On April 29, they moved me to another block. I could not eat. I gave my soup to someone else. I didn't go to the hospital because I know from Auschwitz and Buchenwald they kill you in the hospital.

On April 29, I'm on the third floor of the barracks. The block was closest to the camp fences and guard towers. That's when I see the SS going down from the tower with their hands up. I called to my friends, "Look! Look!" And I saw American helmets in the distance . . . they were flatter and different. Then, a big siren announced the Americans were coming, and everyone rushed to the fence to see the Americans. There was no shooting, no nothing. The camp kommandant was ordered to shoot us all, but he didn't want to take the responsibility, even though he had ordered the camp be destroyed. And I see the SS standing there at gunpoint. The Czechs, the Americans, were saying and signaling, "Everything is all right, you're free! You're free!"

Then we see the last German coming slowly down from the guard tower, hands up. But we could see he had a revolver in his back, and we spot it and tell the Americans. "*Kameraden, kameraden!*" We pointed to him. The Americans shot him. Then, they pointed to him and told us, "Do what you will with him." Many prisoners jumped on him. In three minutes, they flattened him like a pancake, like less than ten inches.

Henry's letter written to his mother on May 3, 1945 while in
Dachau. For the first time in three years he can write home in
Polish. *US Holocaust Memorial Museum, gift of Nancy Zguda.*

BELOVED MOTHER, I AM ALIVE

So, now we're liberated by Patton's army. American medics, young boys, fresh out of medical school came to help us. First of all, beginning the next day they give us very good soup with beans and bacon. But, after several days, this soup made many of the prisoners even more ill; some even died from that soup. Because they were hungry like me, they eat it. But the stomach was no longer used to fat, and the food kills you. The grease chokes you because you cannot digest it. You are sick and with no help, and on empty stomach the grease kills you.

But they got smart. They changed to a watery soup with a little meat, a little margarine. I couldn't even think about food. I still had very strong diarrhea. Nothing I eat or drink I could hold in my stomach longer than five minutes. The hospital gave me some pills for stomach disorder, but they had no X-rays or anything to diagnose. The pills didn't help me at all. I had a problem with bacteria developing in the body, in my blood.

I'm done. I'm so sick, so skinny, so filthy from the constant diarrhea, I just wanted to die. I found a bathroom where they had a simple bathtub. I turn on the warm water, and get in. Ah-h-h. I hadn't experienced warm water for three years. I laid back. Now, I can die warm. I put my head under the water spigot and turned the cold water on. I decide to drown myself. I laid back with my mouth open under the water. I drank and drank this water until I see my stomach swell up like a balloon. I was sitting in hot water, so I didn't feel the cold water.

What I didn't know is the water was heavily chlorinated with disinfectant. I run to the toilet to empty myself and, after that bath, I was okay. The chlorine disinfected my entire system, and I am okay. The next morning I can swallow breakfast with no consequences. After that, I only had the paratyphoid fever, and I was alright.

"Wow. Did anyone else do this?"

No. You see I was trying to die. Instead, the water cured me. All my life water has been my friend, and I survived by the water. After that, I recovered in a week. Then, I was able to write to my mother in Polish so she would know I was alive.

Dachau, May 3, 1945

Beloved mother,

> *Finally the bell of freedom tolls for me. After sufferings that cannot be described, on April 29 at 5 o'clock we were liberated by the US Army. Our joy cannot be put into words.*
>
> *We marched by foot from Buchenwald to Flossenbürg near Weiden Bayerische Ostmark from April 10 to April 15. From there, after 5 days we kept walking farther, under the guns of bandits dressed as SS, till we reached Dachau. It was truly a march of death; thousands died. The rest of us got to Dachau, where after a couple of days of uncertainty the freedom had come.*
>
> *I am extremely exhausted and ill, but happy. My feet are completely swollen, but the life, which is coming back to normal in the camp, gives the hope for a happy ending. At this point, I am writing to you only that, to my surprise, I am alive and I am waiting to see what fate has reserved for me next.*
>
> *We will be staying here for the next 3–4 weeks, after that we will go either home or to France. Thus, don't worry about me, beloved mother, we should see each other soon. [You]*

may have already heard from the radio about Dachau and its liberation. There are thousands of us here, and the food is getting better and better. I am feeling terrible, exhausted, my stomach is sick with diarrhea from dirty water, but day after day I am doing better. I am so happy that it is over, if Doctor K or Gena could help through the Red Cross to pull me out of here earlier, I would be very grateful, maybe through someone from France or America.

Look up and down and ask people about this. Big hug, dearest mother,

Your son, Henryk

TWO NEAR MISSES

Henry never knew how close he came to liberation by the US Army . . . twice.

Between April 7 and April 10, 1945, as the US forces approached ever closer to Buchenwald, the Germans ordered nearly 28,000 prisoners from the main camp—and at least 10,000 from the subcamps—to evacuate in a series of what Henry accurately described as "dead marches." These prisoners were either driven out on foot, or were marched to enclosed train cars to be transported part of the way. Only an estimated 7,000 of those prisoners evacuated from Buchenwald reached the Flössenburg camp, though exact numbers will never be known.

US forces reached Buchenwald on April 11, a mere three days after Henry had left to seek freedom.

Again, after his group of weak and dying prisoners reached Flössenburg, they were held there for four days and then sent on a second forced march on April 20. This last evacuation toward Dachau included not only the incoming prisoners from

Buchenwald, but almost all of the remaining 9,300 prisoners in the camp, which included 1,700 Jews. US forces reached Flössenburg on April 24.

Against all odds, Henry survived the second death march and reached Dachau on April 27 near death from starvation, typhus, and pleurisy. Fewer than 3,000 prisoners—of the more than 16,000 who left Flössenburg with Henry—made it as far as Dachau. Estimates say a few hundred escaped through the forest, or gave up marching when the SS guards deserted the prisoners to run from the approaching Americans. But, for most of the prisoners, the march represented a final death sentence.

US troops liberated Dachau on April 29. Finally, nearly three years since his arrest on a dark street in Kraków, and after years of starvation, imprisonment, and witnessing so much death, Henry Zguda was a free man.

PART 6

POLAND UNDER COMMUNISM

1946–1956

After the liberation of Dachau, Henry remained in a US Army hospital for three months recovering from malnutrition, typhus, and serious pleurisy that made it extremely difficult to breathe. Among the fortunate to have survived years in concentration camps, like so many other survivors, his health was never quite the same. The main sports he continued included swimming, water polo, and, for recreation, tennis, because they were easier on his heart than running sports. In one of multiple failed attempts to obtain war reparations, he listed his war injuries as follows:

From frequent beating of the head, probable partial deafness, Meniere's Syndrome, lack of concentration, impairment of memory, constant buzzing in right ear (otosclerosis);

Typhoid fever with possible sequelae;

Pleuritis and pleurisy with possible respiratory complications, such as frequent bronchitis and sinusitis;

Varicose veins possibly requiring surgical intervention in the near future;

Genito-urinary complications due to prolonged exposure, general mistreatment including blows to the body and dietary insufficiency. These complications include frequent urination, high uric acid, and gout.

Additionally, Henry lost most of his teeth due to getting kicked in the face by the SS on multiple occasions and more than three years of malnutrition.

Kazio remained at Auschwitz for the duration of the war. Near the end of the war, one of the SS guards in the kitchen took a liking to Kazio and tried to convince him to marry his daughter. The guard was a butcher, and Kazio had learned to butcher meat and make sausage in the camp. Kazio followed that guard to

Germany. There was nothing left in the town they went to, and he didn't like the daughter, so he returned to Kraków. He and Henry worked as gas meter readers, and secretly delivered BBC news to the people. But Kazio was too well-known for helping other Poles. Like thousands of other loyal Poles, the communists arrested him for working for Poland, and sentenced him to two years in Montelupich prison. There, he became chief of the prison laundry. The communists rationalized that if people could organize for Poland against Germany, they could also organize for Poland against communists. Kazio was among the fortunate few loyal Poles not sentenced to execution by the Russians. Kazio and Henry remained friends for the rest of their lives, though there are no photos of an older Kazio.

The communists issued an arrest warrant for Henry as well. With the help of a former teammate at the YMCA, Henry escaped to the Tatra Mountains south of Kraków, where he spent a year as a caretaker for an isolated mountain lodge. In the clear mountain air, he slowly recovered his health, hiking long distances into Zakopane for groceries, and skiing to other remote chalets.

Jozef Cyrankiewicz, future prime minister of Poland and a former prisoner in Auschwitz, testifies at the trial of Rudolf Höss, former kommandant of the Auschwitz death camp. The trial of Rudolf Höss took place March 11-29, 1947 in Warsaw, Poland. The Tribunal found him guilty and sentenced him to death. He was hanged at Auschwitz on April 16, 1947, next to the Kommandant's office where he had worked. *Used with permission of the Auschwitz-Birkenau State Museum, Oświęcim, Poland.*

Jozef Cyrankiewicz (1911–1989) survived the war. He was a socialist before the war, and afterwards aligned himself with the communists, then became secretary-general of the Polish Socialist Party's central executive committee in 1946. In 1947, he was elected premier of Poland and served in that position from 1947–1952, and again in high government leadership from 1954–1972. His legacy remains mixed. He worked with the underground in Auschwitz but, as premier, he remained allied with the Russians against many of his countrymen, even as the Russians executed Poles loyal to their country.

Once Cyrankiewicz rose to power, he intervened on Kazio's behalf and freed him after only a year in Montelupich.

HENRY TELLS THE TALE:

So Cyrankiewicz, one time he sends the wife, and the friends with the agents surrounding the car to my tourist home in the high mountains. I see the cavalcade coming down from the road. Two cars in front, then the agents, then comes the wife of the premier. I go out to greet her.

"Ah, Henry. How are you? Oh, the view. The mountains. So beautiful. We love it. Do you have something to drink?"

I have vodka only, but I was stingy. I want that vodka for my boys I'm running from Poland through the mountains to Italy. But I give it to them.

"Ah, Henry. So nice. Do you have food too?"

I was saving my grain, too. You know, the store was ten kilometers away on skis. But what you gonna do? I share my grain too.

Undated photo of Henry and Zbigniew Fuchs in later years.
Henry Zguda's personal photo album.

Zbigniew Fuchs reluctantly joined the communist party and rose to a position in the Ministry of Finance. He and Henry remained friends throughout their lives.

Edmund Polak continued to write, and eventually rose to editor of the Warsaw newspaper. His book, *Morituri*, continues to be sold on foreign book-trading websites.

Henry's friend from Buchenwald, Mietek Kowalski, became a buyer for the Department of Agriculture in the Polish government. He often traveled to Berlin, purchasing dried pig intestines for Polish sausage makers. His brother was a director for the railroad station in Moscow. When the communists again issued a warrant for Henry's arrest, it was Mietek who secured a position for Henry with the Academy of Sports in Warsaw. Henry once described the move: "I escaped from the communists by hiding right in the middle of the wolf's lair." Henry mentioned two other Poles who were Russian prisoners of war that Mietek helped secure their release as well: Janusz Zarzycki and Teofil Witek.

The position came with status, free housing, and relative freedom. As a former prisoner of the Germans, he was respected as a former "Auschwitzer" who, as he put it, "was suffering in German concentration camps." Premier Cyrankiewicz, as a former "Auschwitzer" himself, remembered peeling potatoes with Henry. In a letter dated January 2003 written to a friend, Henry remembered that after four or five consecutive wins by the Polish water polo team, he was introduced to Marshall Rokossovsky, chief of the Polish army. In yet another recollection, he remembered in 1956 when his team was invited to compete in Leipzig, Germany. They were treated to an opera, and then the entire team was introduced to Walter Ulbricht, the [communist] leader of the D.D.R., or what Americans referred to as "East Germany" during the Cold War.

Two of Henry's cousins became professors, and one became a general in the Polish army. To the end of Henry's days, he remained upset that his cousins served a Polish regime that ultimately "destroyed the lives of two remarkable men."

Even with his powerful connections, Henry once confessed to me his biggest regret.

"In the end, I make a mistake. Instead of going back home to Poland, I should have gone to Switzerland, and then from Switzerland, right away I should have gone to the United States. I wouldn't have come back to Poland. I never liked communism. I don't like somebody who tells you what to do. They [communists] always dictate what you do, how you have to do it, and when to do it. But I didn't know that at the time, and I was very ill with pleurisy. I figure I go home to see my mother and then I can die."

Henry Zguda and the Polish army swim team. Henry is on the far left in the white collar shirt. Photo is undated but probably circa 1950s. *Henry Zguda's personal photo album.*

Henry Zguda and the Polish army swim team in 1956, Belgium. Henry is on the far left in the white bathing cap. *Henry Zguda's personal photo album.*

Henry and Polish water polo team. Photo is undated but probably circa 1950s. Henry is under the small arrow.
Henry Zguda's personal photo album.

Henry aims for the goal. Photo is undated but probably circa 1950s. *Henry Zguda's personal photo album.*

Henry diving off a highdive platform. Undated, but probably circa 1950s. *Henry Zguda's personal photo album.*

Henry diving off a highdive platform. Undated, but probably circa 1950s. *Henry Zguda's personal photo album.*

For ten years, he lived in Warsaw and coached the army swim and water polo teams. He enjoyed a relatively privileged lifestyle, especially for a communist country. He toured throughout Eastern Europe with his swim and water polo teams in the summer, and convinced party officials it would be good training to take his teams skiing in the Tatra Mountains in the winters. He also took them to the 1952 Helsinki Olympics as observers. On every trip, a party official accompanied the teams to spy on the athletes and make sure they weren't working against communism.

For many years, Henry was able to avoid joining the communist party. Did he maintain friendships with well-connected people? Of course. But would he join an ideology he didn't believe in? Never.

Fortune changed in 1956.

Władysław Gomułka became head of the communist party that year. He was a hard-line communist from the labor party. The new communist leadership specifically targeted Henry for detention.

"You are a teacher and a trainer for the Polish army and you're not a communist? It is time we send you for two months of reeducation on Marx and Lenin."

Henry began to plan his escape to the west. He penned a letter in German to Hubert Lapailles, his friend from the stonemason *kommando* in Buchenwald. He gave the letter to a friend traveling to the West to deliver to Yost Slagboom, then living in Holland. He and Lapailles, now a senator in Belgium, organized a special competition in Brussels. Lapailles issued a formal invitation to the Polish water polo team to visit Brussels. One evening, when Henry was supposed to attend an official party meeting, he and his friend and fellow coach, Leon Kraska, feigned headaches and stayed in their rooms. Once everyone had left, they hurried down the hallway, down a back stairwell and out to a waiting car, where Lapailles escorted them to a government office to seek asylum. There, they were heavily interrogated for a week. Officials doubted their sincerity to defect, given their high positions and Henry's many connections to high party officials in the communist party. Without the help of Lapailles and Slagboom, Henry could not have escaped. Quotas on immigrants were closed. Lapailles waived the quota and helped them obtain refugee status. Slagboom found them employment in Holland at a time when jobs were very difficult to find. Lapailles, Slagboom, and Henry remained good friends for the rest of their lives. Henry and Leon moved to Holland with Slagboom's assistance, and they made a life there for nearly two years, working odd jobs and traveling, never again to have a political officer supervise their every move. By now Henry was nearly forty years old. Neither he nor Leon had married or had children, and so were free to create new lives. Henry became a swim instructor and coach again. But, in his eyes, he still dreamed of seeing the United States before he died, the home of his favorite movie stars: Tom Mix and Elvis Presley. He and Leon applied for visas to go to the United States.

PART 7

THE UNITED STATES:
LAND OF THE FREE
AND HOME OF THE RICH

1958–1968

THE SS *AMERICA*

I n one of our later interviews, Henry brought out two documents I'd never seen. One was a ship's menu from January 1959, and the second was a printed passenger list from the same cruise. In contrast to modern-day concerns for privacy, in 1959, ships printed up passenger manifests as souvenirs for the passengers. I noticed there were autographs on the menu.

So, we are in Holland, and here comes the time to quit Holland. I was coaching swimming in Skarbek, but the Belgian coaches were giving me a hard time. They thought they were good, but were jealous of my success. I say forget it, and I get my favorite job. Leon and I work for the Polish nuns in a convent, sorting donations.

The donations of the American people were very nice. They send so many things to the Polish Relief Society. We go through shoes, hats, ties, shirts. The convent had so much stuff they didn't know where to give it. There was only one place for refugees. We pick out certain things for ourselves, including the best jacket, and shoes, and luggage. We know we are going to America. We knew we would be going to America by ocean liner, so we each picked out a tuxedo.

Leon and I have two big valises full of goods from this job. The day of departure comes, just two Polaks going to the United States. There at the train station were our two girlfriends, crying like babies. They cry so much we cry, too, but we go anyway. It was a very touching situation. But we went to the train, to go to Le Havre, from Brussels to Paris. We are going to America!

We spent a month in Paris. We stayed in a small place near the railway station, in a little hotel. We got it as cheap as possible—we didn't have much. The entire trip was paid for by the refugee society. Imagine, we have a month in Paris and someone else paid for us to be there.

So, now we start going around Paris, the Champs-Élysées, the Arc de Triomphe, the Eiffel Tower, we get to see everything. The month went by very fast. Then, Leon and I found ourselves on the train to Le Havre, and there was waiting for us the SS *America*. We walked the ramp onto the ship, each carrying our two valises. We still had a little money left. We never looked back.

We had been there on the ship for an hour or so. We get situated in the third class, the very bottom of the boat. Right away we figure out what to do. It was December 31, 1958, and there was a New Year's Eve party on the boat.

The steward came to fix the bed. Leon and I each have a liter of rectified alcohol, which we make vodka from. You take it, dilute it with water, and you have vodka. The proof is dependent on dilution. We make many friends that first day.

For fun, we give the French steward some Polish vodka. I was able to speak in broken French. He takes one drink, his eyes get big, and he says, "Ooh. *Oui, oui, monsieur!*"

But we did not tell him the secret of Polish vodka. You have to drink without smelling. The Polish secret is to exhale, pour down the shot, and let it take effect in the stomach.

That steward takes one drink, gasps, it burns like hell. "Ooh, ooh, delicious." He runs out, comes back with the cook and two helpers. They scream, "Ooh, ooh," and now Leon and I have friends. Now, my new ship friends invite us to the New Year's Eve dinner.

We get a small table overseeing the dance floor, and we got whatever we like. Certainly we liked the lobster. We got a nice full lobster, but I had to ask the steward to break it. We didn't know how to break it—Leon and I never had lobster before. There was crab in Poland, but very small, without much meat. I remember beautiful slices of lobster, wine for everyone, because it was the New Year's Eve party for the captain. Everything was free on the boat. We saw the American admiral officers, with white uniforms and epaulets, and I fit right in with my tuxedo. I never had a tuxedo in my life before this.

We're going to America and off to a good start. Lots of good food, everything was perfect. The cook and steward—one bottle of vodka went to the stewards. They love it. They gag, then, *ahh*, and drink it. They love our Polish vodka.

I decided to order vodka from the bar on the ship. I still remember the first time I changed the paper dollars in the bar for vodka; they give us twenty-five cents. I'd never seen such precious coins, the ten-cent coins, I'd never seen such shiny coins before, and now I had two, and a nickel. The dimes were shinier than the nickel. They looked like real silver.

They treat us so nice. We were invited to the captain's dinner because of the cook. The stewards never told the captain who we were. We were just two passengers dressed up in tuxedos going to the dinner. We had fun with this dinner, during the storm. The boat goes up twenty feet, then down, then up and down. The waves were very high all the way to New York. We enjoy like hell, who cared about danger?

After the first night we were always invited to the main dining room, such a nice event. The whole ship goes up, down, up, down. Big waves, stormy sea the entire trip. Everyone at our table was foreign: Indian, Arabs, Turks. But, most of the time, Leon and I had the table to ourselves—we never got seasick. There were so many people sick in their cabins, the dining room was mostly empty, and the ship had cooked so much food. Oh boy, oh boy. Two shrimps, two hams, two lobsters . . . everything as much as we could eat.

Then I see for the first time how rich America is. For two days, no one is at our table except Leon and me. I watch what the waiters do. After dinner, the waiters took the plates—whatever left over, meat, chicken, pork chops—they put on the tablecloth. They just turn over the plates, take the tablecloth to the kitchen. Leon and I follow them into the kitchen and watch them open the window and feed the fish. I see enough food to feed an entire village in Poland, and they just wasted it all and threw to the fish. I think to myself, America must be a very rich country to throw out this much food. They didn't save any leftovers; they had no storage space, and still had meat for next day. When they were tossing the food out the windows, Leon and I would grab food, oranges, fruit, anything to save for later. And they told us, "Take it, take it boys, we are just throwing it out." There was more than we could possibly eat.

I knew then I was going to a very rich country. I have two silver coins in my pocket. And they have so much food they feed pork chops to the fish.

The front of the dinner menu for January 5, 1959.
Henry Zguda's personal photo album.

Captain's Dinner

Baby Shrimp Cocktail   Iced Table Celery   Antipasto Italienne
Queen Olives   Eel in Jelly   Pâté de Foie Gras Sur Croute
Seelachs in Oil   Chilled California Fruit Cup aux Kirsch
Rose Radishes   Ochsen-Maul Salad   Spring Onions

Cream Champignon   Terrapin with Sherry

Broiled Filets of Gaspé Salmon au Citron (Seelachs)

Assorted Vegetable Dinner à la America (Gemüsseplatte)
Shirred Eggs Suisse (Sets Eier)

Roast Turkey, Dressing, Cranberry Sauce (Truthahn)
Grill: Choice Tenderloin Steak, Bordelaise Sauce, Mushrooms Sauté
(Lendenstück vom Rost)

Corn off the Cob, Melted Butter (Mais)
Garden Broccoli Hollandaise (Blumenkohl)   String Beans
Potatoes: Boiled, Mashed or Browned
Kartoffeln: Gekochter, Püree oder Braten

Mixed Fruit Salad (Gemischter Frucht Salat)

Compote: Preserved Royal Anne Cherries (Kirschen Kompott)

Mocha Layer Cake (Schokolade Kuchen)
French Ice Cream, Chocolate Sauce (Französische Eis, Schokoladen Sauce)

Roquefort Cheese and Toasted Crackers

Table Raisins (Tafel Rosinen)   After Dinner Mints (Pfefferminz)
Crystallized Ginger (Ingwer)   Table Dates (Dateln)

Fresh Fruit in Season (Frisches Obst)

Coffee   Tea   Fresh Milk
Kaffee   Tee   Frische Milch

WB-TC Capt. Din.-7   **Monday, January 5, 1959**

The inside right of the dinner menu for January 5, 1959.
Interestingly, it is in both English and German.
Henry Zguda's personal photo album.

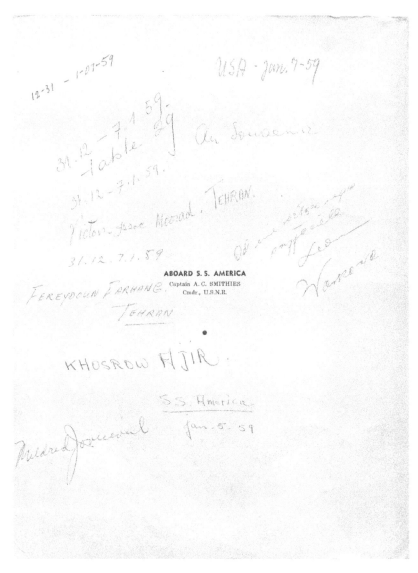

The autographed inside left side of the dinner menu for
January 5, 1959. *Henry Zguda's personal photo album.*

"NOW, I AM A THERAPIST"

Leon and I arrive finally to the New York port. We waved to the Statue of Liberty as we sailed by her. We disembark from the SS *America*. The ship unloads our four valises—two each—and we just stood there on the pier with the water behind us. We are foreign. We stand on the pier with our backs to the ocean, facing our new country. Everyone around us is "Hi, how are you?" and hugs and smiles. All I hear is garbled nonsense—we don't speak any English.

Suddenly, there's a guy that comes with a sign for the Catholic Relief Society and speaks to us in Polish.

"Ahh, good. Welcome. Hello." He looked at his papers. "So, your name is Henryk and your name is Leon? Come on. *Dzien dobry*. Hello. You got a place here to stay at the Hotel Wolcott."

He gives us five dollars each to pay for a taxi, and the address to the Polish Relief Society to go to the next day. Then, he leaves us.

Now, how to get there? We wave our hands and call a taxi. When the taxi gets there we give the driver the address of the Hotel Wolcott.

"How much is it to the Hotel Wolcott?" we ask.

He signaled with hand gestures: "Five dollars each. Two of you, that's ten dollars." Then, he sees our four valises. For four valises you have to take another taxi.

Leon looked at me. I looked at Leon. We have a little money left, but not much more than the five dollars we just got. We are standing next to our valises, our backs to the water. I have one valise that is just shoes and such. Leon the same. So, [he laughed heartily] I just slowly kick one valise back into the water and Leon kicks one back in the water. Now, we have one valise each and we make it to the Hotel Wolcott.

The hotel was very cheap, maybe it was six dollars a week. Just after we got there I heard a cat, scratching, making noise, on the window, like swish, swish. Leon stood there laughing at me.

"Henry, that's no cat. That's a huge rat."

The next day, what to do? The Polish committee, where is it? How far a walk? First, we find the post office. And we look in the book: Polish International Committee. Downtown, 3rd Street. And we are on 31st street. We skip the metro and walk the whole way. We don't see nobody from the Catholic Relief Society again.

We find the Polish Committee, and meet the president of the relief committee. He greets us with a big smile.

"Henyu! How good to see you again. Ah, boys, how are you, how are you? Tell me, how is Kazio?"

Incredulous at Henry's amazing stroke of luck, I had to ask, "Wait. You knew him? The first person you meet in America knew Kazio? And you knew him?"

Sure, sure, sure, Henry replied nonchalantly. Chris Trytko was himself in Cracovia. He was a friend playing water polo with Kazio and our team. Yeah, he knew Kazio. He was one of those guys with us, with our bunch. He was Olympian in basketball and in water polo swimming. Maybe he was not Olympian, but he swim with us and was big champion of Cracovia. I have the Cracovia book with swim scores; his name is mentioned a few times.

He was already here in America. He owned a bar and restaurant in New Rochelle. The next day we call him and he come pick us up. We went there and he treated us to a steak dinner. Very nice. He was very good bartender himself.

He said, "Ah, boys, you don't worry, you gonna live. Don't worry. You gonna make it here. Henry, tomorrow you go see Dr. Sofia Laszewska at St. Barnabas Hospital in the Bronx. She is the director of the physical therapy department."

The next day, I find St. Barnabas Hospital in the Bronx, and I meet with the doctor. I tell her about my swimming, and coaching, and tell her, I study this, and this, and this. Then, she offered me a job.

"All right, come work in my department. You already know the body when you became a trainer."

Dr. Laszewska speak perfect Polish and English. She was a doctor and finished her studies in America. She was the patron saint to many refugees from Poland, helping them in this new country. She and her husband owned a travel agency on Fifth Avenue. Dr. Laszewska knew a friend who was going to Florida for the winter, and convinced her to loan Leon and me her apartment. It was winter and a very cold January.

Now I have a key to apartment here on 10th Street. So very nice. Leon and I went to the apartment on the second floor, on 10th Street, open the door, look inside. It was cold like hell inside. No heat from a fire. No gas turned on. We look on the bed, and no linens, no nothing, only a mattress.

Henry laughs again as he remembered the next part.

And what to do now? Standing, we have a little cover on us. We went outside and I remember in the garbage pail on the corner of the street, there was a Sunday *Times* newspaper. We take it out and take to the apartment and put on the mattress. It was very warm. Paper is the best protector from cold. The paper saved many lives in Auschwitz; prisoners can sneak it and wear under their shirt.

We have the first night. The water work, but it was cold water. We don't care. We're okay now, because we have a place to live for free.

So, I discover I am a therapist. I became a therapist aide first, but I don't care. I started doing a very good job, different than the other therapists there.

The other therapists, mostly ladies, just work the hands and fingers, gentle like. I stretch the arms of patients, make them stretch all the way out. I exercise the whole joint, the whole body. I use more force, like the exercise to work the body with weights heavier than you can stand, so that you stress the muscles. You have to force and stress muscles so they get stronger. It worked in many, many cases.

I was strong, and I used the same exercises from physical education and training. I don't let the patients get away without working. Of course, I check their charts and X-rays first to make sure the body isn't damaged. If they're all right, then we start to work.

The patients liked me. I have many outside clients. I worked with them two to three weeks after they leave the hospital. It was a good deal for me because I made twenty-five dollars an hour back then. That was very good money.

View of St. Barnabas Hospital. Undated.
Henry Zguda's personal photo album.

ST. BARNABAS HOSPITAL FOR CHRONIC DISEASES

Today, St. Barnabas Hospital stands as the oldest continuing healthcare facility in New York City. When it was founded in April 1866, the hospital was the first chronic disease hospital in the United States, and only the second such facility in the world. Originally named the "Home for the Incurables," it welcomed its first thirty-three patients in 1867 at its modest frame house in an incorporated area of New York City.

At the time, there was no known cure for diseases such as tuberculosis, cholera, influenza, pneumonia, and others. Patients with these diagnoses, and other chronic illnesses, could not be cared for in other existing hospitals, so they came to live at St. Barnabas. Many lived there for a long time, some as long as thirty years.

In 1874, the hospital moved to its present site of ten acres on Third Avenue in the Bronx. By 1911, the facility had three hundred beds. One-third of the patients were treated without any compensation, so St. Barnabas relied heavily on donations from wealthy benefactors such as Cornelius Vanderbilt, who also served on the board of managers; John Jacob Astor; Theodore Roosevelt; and Frederic Law Olmstead.

In 1926, a home for nurses opened and, in 1928, a home for elderly patients in need opened on the grounds of the hospital. A new six-story, brick structure opened in 1937, which today stands as the main building. At one point, a tennis court was built on the grounds. It stood where the nursing home stands today. Additionally, there was an outdoor recreation area on the roof.

In 1947, the name was changed to St. Barnabas Hospital for Chronic Diseases, and long-term patients continued to call it home. A tall brick wall that surrounded the grounds gave the impression of a large fortress to residents of the Bronx, some gossiping about what "really" happened behind those strong walls.

In the 1950s and 1960s, the hospital earned a reputation of pioneering medicine, and attracted more colorful and adventurous physicians. Perhaps the most memorable doctor in recent history was Dr. Irving S. Cooper, an innovative spirit who truly pioneered a new surgical intervention in Parkinson's disease, beginning in the 1950s.

In March 29, 1976, *People* magazine wrote an article about his work. The article read in part, *"St. Barnabas has become a sort of shrine for thousands of spastics as a last-resort help."*

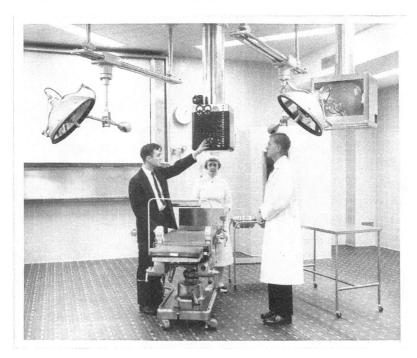

Undated photo of Dr. Irving Cooper in a surgical suite at St. Barnabas Hospital. *Used with Permission of SBH Health System.*

Dr. Cooper (1922–1985) worked at St. Barnabas Hospital as the chief of Neurosurgery from 1954 to 1977, and many of his most advanced techniques were developed during his tenure there. One British scientist of the 1970s referred to Dr. Cooper as "professionally one of the great brain surgeons of the world." *Time, People,* and *Look* magazines all wrote feature articles on Dr. Cooper. He authored many texts himself. He became recognized worldwide for his innovative techniques, dedication, and humanity toward patients with crippling movement disorders such as Parkinson's. His actual technique was to "freeze" or "ligate" a specific artery in the brain to stop tremors. By 1976, the technique he pioneered was used by more than a thousand surgeons in fifteen countries.

So, take this thought one step further. In the early 1960s, there was no Medicare, and who knows what health insurance looked like back then? If Dr. Cooper was the one surgeon in the world to cure your disease, patients and their families needed significant financial resources to fund all travel costs to New York City, the cost of the surgery, the hospital stay, and additional accommodations for themselves and family during recovery.

Accordingly, within weeks of coming to the United States, Henry became good friends with the world-class and renowned neurosurgeon. And who quickly became a favorite physical therapist to the rich and famous patients from around the world? Henry.

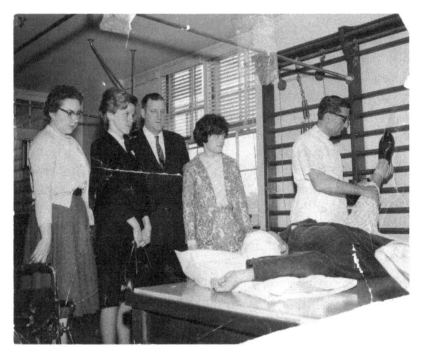

Professional photo of Henry Zguda conducting physical therapy while dignitaries look on. Photo is undated and other people are unnamed. The back of the photo reads "Photographed by Louis Nemeth, TN 7-4355." *Henry Zguda's personal photo album.*

TREMORS AND BRAIN SURGERY

HENRY CONTINUES HIS STORY:

When you have tremors, you can't exercise when you shake so much. You take the cup of coffee and you spill on yourself. So, you don't use the muscles for years. The muscles are stiff and rigid. The surgery stopped the tremors, but after surgery they go for speech and physical therapy.

One week after surgery, the guy is ready to walk. The guys come to me like curled up in a ball with stiff clenched hands.

There was another strong therapist there besides me. Big guy, 220 pounds. The patients come to us and have never been stretched. We work slowly, slowly, slowly, and stretch the muscles. The patients always screamed in pain. But then they scream in joy. "I am straight! I am straight for the first time in ten years!" They were very grateful to me.

In the Warsaw Academy of Sport, I learned how to work muscles, only in Poland I work with healthy people. I used the same techniques I used with athletes, only I go slower because these people are sick.

Dr. Cooper was a sportsman and he liked me. We often played tennis together at the hospital. He was a good tennis player. Soon, I began to assist in brain surgery.

Again, I needed clarification to make sure I heard Henry correctly. "Wait. Did you really just say assist in brain surgery?"

Sure, sure. Dr. Cooper used me during the surgery on the brain. He was operating on the thalamus gland—they called it a thalamectomy. The thalamus gland is the little part of the brain on the bottom. The problem was how close it was to the speech part of the brain, and you could lose that. Patients were awake for the entire surgery.

In the moment of the operation, the patient is lying on the table, with head all covered. The patients don't see what's going on, but I do. I can see only the face, and this top is back, because they open the top and go in the brain, and this is on television screen and everything, how they go in. First, they drill a hole in the skull on one side, and they put the cannula in one side with nitrogen or something to kill the germs or something else. It was Dr. Cooper's invention so we never touch it.

Dr. Cooper needed someone to talk to patients during the surgery. People came from all over the world for Dr. Cooper's surgery, and they spoke many languages. Cooper used me for patients that spoke German, Czech, Russian, maybe French. Talking to them also helped keep them calm.

"Wait. You spoke Czech, too?"

Czech is Slavic. Slavic is almost like Polish. I just asked simple questions. "What's your name? Do you have any sisters? Where are you from?" I have their chart so I know a little about them. Talking to them was important because if they, all of a sudden, started to slur their words or go "aah," then I have to say, "Stop!" Dr. Cooper knew he touched a gland and adjusted.

When Cooper got to the right center of the brain, he'd ask them to raise an arm or leg, whereas they couldn't before. Then, he knew the surgery worked. Cooper did separate surgeries for each side. If the right hand shakes, he operates on the left side of brain. They recover from the first surgery, and then he does surgery on the right side of the brain so the other hand stops shaking. You know the brain reverses sides. The surgery worked, too. The tremors never came back. Rigidity, maybe, but no shake.

HENRY MEETS NANCY

Henry turned back to a file of papers, flipped through them, and pulled out a copy of a *Time* magazine article dated March 25, 1957. The article featured Dr. Charles P. Bailey, a pioneer in heart surgery.

See this doctor? Dr. Bailey was another famous doctor at St. Barnabas. He was a famous promoter of open-heart surgery. He was a maniac. Of course, if you ever watch open-heart surgery, it's like watching a butcher. I knew of him, but I didn't work with him. But I quickly fell in love like nuts with his secretary, Nancy Conforti. She didn't know what was coming to her.

Henry grinned at his own joke, then continued on.

I didn't tell Nancy I didn't have money. Polish men are gentlemen—I always brought flowers.

When he spoke of Nancy, Henry always grinned. His sly humor got us both laughing. Then, he flipped the pages of the photo album and pointed to a lineup of young beautiful women.

See here? Nancy was in a beauty contest in Purling, New York, August 24, 1959. Nancy won. She and her sister were always very cute. When she was young kid, she worked in downtown New York City in the garment district. The owner liked her very much. She loved clothes and she always liked sports.

I taught her to play tennis, and she got pretty good. She had a powerful serve. I liked that she had also been a good baseball player in her younger days. She had the most powerful shot of the girls on her baseball team. She grew up in the Bronx, you know. They had to play in the street. It reminded me of growing up on the Planty in Kraków when we play as boys, too. We both liked sports very much. She was great fun.

At this point in the discussion, Nancy walked out on the patio as if she knew we were talking about her. I had to ask her for her story.

"Nancy, Henry says you were a good tennis player."

Nancy looked directly at Henry and laughed.

"I did learn to be pretty good, didn't I?"

Then she swung an imaginary tennis racket, laughing at her own joke.

I asked her about the beauty pageant. She just scoffed.

"It was nothing. None of them were very good looking. My mother made me enter. I never did that again."

She noticed that Henry had the article on Dr. Bailey out.

"You know, after meeting Henry, Dr. Bailey was always mad at me. The patients were very sick. He operated when they were near the end of life, and many still died even after surgery. The families would be sitting there in the waiting room crying, waiting to see Dr. Bailey. I was supposed to be very quiet and serious because they'd be crying. But Henry wrote me such funny love letters, I'd hold them under my desk, and I could not stop laughing. One time, I crawled under my desk to read them. His English was so bad, I could hardly read any of them without laughing out loud. I'd read them over and over."

• •

The photos in Henry's worn photo album changed after 1960. Instead of bathing suits, swimming events, and groups of teammates, I noticed business suits, albeit the same business suit, and mostly photos of Henry and Nancy. Henry remained easily recognizable from the chiseled angles of his face and lean strong build. But, as with most women, I had to inspect the photos of Nancy more closely. Women's hairstyles declared each decade, and black and white photos hid the color of twinkling blue eyes. The younger Nancy sported dark hair styled in a 1960s bob. More currently, with silver hair, she smiled through a face lined with a few wrinkles.

If I had to choose three words or less for Henry and Nancy, they might be "truly in love." Or perhaps "fun and content." What I recognized in both was the same upturned smiles that still communicated "glad to be alive" through both their eyes.

Nancy had been married before, but it hadn't worked out. Being fairly bold, especially for the time, she had gone to Florida by herself to divorce him. She told me later, her first husband never could leave his mother. When they were newlyweds, he insisted his mother move in with them.

At the time Henry and Nancy met, Nancy was a thirty-nine-year-old Catholic divorcee from a conservative Italian family, living in the Bronx with her family. Henry was a forty-three-year-old Polish immigrant with five dollars to his name who barely spoke English.

In contrast to his stories of growing up, Henry told of living in a rich country. Instead of the horrors of three years in concentration camps, he talked of his life in America as "the best thing I ever did." He laughed frequently through his stories, insisting more than once, "Please write about the good times. They are so many more years than the bad times. That's what I want to remember."

When he spoke of communism, he took on an air of both sadness and anger. In some ways, he'd benefited and held a high position through those connections. But Henry hated communism with a passion and had refused to join the Party. He hated the Russian dominance over his native Poland, a country that would always be a part of his history and soul.

In the 1970s, he traveled back to Poland. Nancy chose not to accompany him. Henry wanted her to come, but there was still an arrest warrant for him as a defector, and he didn't know if he would be held. Nancy avoided the trip because she didn't speak Polish and felt awkward. Since Henry's mother never visited the United States, she and Nancy never met, something she told me later she always regretted. Henry never visited Poland after 1989, the year communism fell.

"See, it's what I tell you. We Poles always come back."

When a humble, politically savvy, Polish bishop became pope in 1978, many more Americans became aware of Poland. Henry's connection to Kraków and Pope John Paul II only added to his Polish pride and gave him more stories to tell to whoever would listen.

Henry reiterated his main regret.

"My mistake was not coming here after the war. I had a choice after liberation: go to America or go back to Poland. Here, there's so many opportunities I never have in Poland. But at that time I didn't know that. I couldn't leave my mother alone after the war."

Years later, when I went through Henry's papers, I found his 1963 letter of congratulations for becoming a US citizen, signed by Nelson A. Rockefeller, governor of New York at that time. One of his proudest moments was becoming a US citizen, and Henry proudly flew the American flag every holiday.

Another mantra he repeated multiple times referenced his two cousins who rose high in the communist government. I never did trace back their history, nor did I feel I needed to. But family is family, and there were many pictures of family reunions in his album. Like Henry and Nancy, I began to recognize the same faces in multiple photos through the years. Politics fade to the background when people and family take priority.

I asked him about a couple of the family photos in which I recognized the same people. He pointed to each man as he spoke about him.

My two cousins were no good—generals in the communist army. Two brilliant men, brilliant brains, and they are nothing. They had to work on orders from Moscow. This one, poor guy, wasted life. He died . . . now he is finally free.

He got him these four children. And, what you say . . . this son becomes a doctor of anesthesiology in Sweden and Warsaw. And this one became another doctor, but he kill himself because he couldn't take the communists, and was so ashamed of his father.

Wedding photo of Henry and Nancy Zguda.
US Holocaust Memorial Museum, gift of Nancy Zguda.

I arrived January 1959, and Nancy and I married in January 1960. Nancy loved New York, and came from a large Italian family. The neighborhood she came from always smell like good provolone cheese and fresh bread. Nancy and I lived close to her mother, which was close to the hospital. Now, I live the good life. I marry a very nice girl, I have a good job, her family likes me and we are happy.

I asked, "Did Nancy ever learn Polish?"

No. I teach her a few words, but I don't think she remembered any. It's so difficult for her. I know for Americans, Polish is very hard, and how it looks in letters and sounds. But English is very hard for a Pole to learn, too. You want a hard name to spell, I give you one. Wladyslaw Zachariasiewicz. He was president of the International Polish Committee.

JERZY KOSINSKI

I had a friend, another Polish refugee, Jerzy Kosinski. Do you remember the book *Being There*? It became a big movie. But, when I know him, he didn't have much and was always hungry, so I help him out and take him for a few dinners at the hospital for free. Then, he became a freelance photographer. He came to our wedding, and took all our wedding photos.

Dr. Lucretia *something*, I can't remember her last name, a daughter of the attaché of Embassy of Poland, was dating Kosinski and liked him very much. She was a beautiful girl, very nice girl. I love her. Nancy loves her. She was my student in the YMCA and I taught her swimming. She was my very good friend and she likes me very much. She and Jerzy were very friendly together and fell in love. Nancy and I visited Kosinski and his girlfriend in his apartment many times.

One day, Mr. Kosinski saw a notice at Columbia University that Mrs. Weir, a wealthy widow of a steel baron, needs someone to coordinate her books, the library in her house. So, they ask

Kosinski to do so. He visits her the Polish way at her Fifth Avenue apartment. He took a bouquet of roses every time he meet her.

Mrs. Weir was beautiful, fragile, and a very rich widow. At that time, Jerzy was twenty-nine, and she was forty-seven. He works on her with flowers and he works on her, too. She was good in English, so in maybe a year he learn English. Maybe he studied English in Poland before he came here, I don't know. But, after meeting Mrs. Weir, he was no longer with my doctor friend. He trade her for someone with money.

In 1962, I am playing tennis with the doctors at St. Barnabas, then comes the Jerzy Kosinski, all excited.

"Henry. Come see my new car."

I go down to the street with him and see a big limousine with chauffeur and everything. I look at him in total surprise. No. Way.

"Yes, I get married to Mrs. Weir."

Nancy and I go to his apartment he live in with Mrs. Weir. It was beautiful. I remember tobacco holders of Napoleon and some beautiful crystal vases. There were garters from Napoleon's mistress, Mrs. Walewska, and many, many other curiosities and curios. This whole flat in the building was hers. You know, her family gave her hell for marrying this unknown Polish Jew with no money, no nothing.

First, he shows me his ski room. He skied. I skied. He shows me six pairs of skis hanging. He has a red telephone with direct connection to the ski lodge in Switzerland.

Then he had a writing room. Already he had written a book. He was dictating his books to three secretaries with three typewriters in a room in his apartment. He was writing these books; I have seven of them. Then, when *The Painted Bird* was published in 1965, he became a big shot.

He and Roman Polanski, another immigrant Pole, both attended the same film school in Lodz before they came to the United States. That's where they became good friends. At that time, Kosinski was all over the world, and served on the committee of Auschwitz. He was recognized by this committee that gave him letters of recognition.

I helped him when he was nobody, but he never helped me when he was somebody. But look who lives longer. I am here writing this story and Kosinski is dead . . . killed himself. He take drugs and alcohol and put plastic bag over his head.

••

Jerzy Kosinski (1933–1991) was born in Lodz, Poland, as Józef Lewinkopf. Following his fortuitous marriage to Mrs. Weir, he went on to great fame, though whether he could have written his books in the first place without marrying a wealthy widow is questionable. In 1979, his novel *Being There* was made into a movie starring Peter Sellers and Shirley MacLaine. His novels appeared on the *New York Times* Best Seller list and have been translated into more than thirty languages. By his suicide in 1991 at the age of fifty-seven, total sales of his novels had reached seventy million.

In June 1982, the *Village Voice* accused him of fakery and plagiarism, claiming *The Painted Bird* was plagiarized from a 1932 Polish bestseller not known in the English-speaking world. They also alleged that he wrote *The Painted Bird* in Polish, and secretly had it translated into English, given his imperfect English at the time.

The book is a fictional account of a boy who wandered through Europe during an unspecified time frame, staying with families who were often cruel and abusive. The book was praised by Elie Wiesel as representative of the Holocaust experience. When published, it was presumed to be autobiographical, and was surprisingly unflattering towards Poles. Kosinski never acknowledged that it was autobiographical, but he never denied it either. The book was banned in Poland until the fall of communism in 1989.

Kosinski's actual experience was quite opposite from the one he portrayed in *The Painted Bird*. As well-to-do Polish Jews, the Lewinkopf family survived World War II because local villagers assisted them at great personal risk. At one point, Jerzy was taken in by a Roman Catholic family, issued a falsified baptismal certificate, and even served as an altar boy while living with this family. He survived the war solely because of their protection. Poles who remembered he was treated well by local Catholic families and remained in one village the entire war questioned and resented Kosinski, who had often regaled himself at parties about his difficult survival and cruel treatment at the hands of Poles. The criticism grew once the novels were published in his native Poland in 1989, after the fall of communism. He never recovered professionally and personally from the accusations and public humiliation.

In August 1969, Jerzy Kosinski was scheduled to be at the home of Roman Polanski, the night that Polanski's wife, Sharon Tate, and everyone else in the house was brutally murdered by followers of Charles Manson. Sharon Tate was eight months pregnant with Polanski's child. Fortuitously, the night before, his flight from New York City was delayed, or he would have been at the same party.

A RICH LIFE

Many, many wealthy people came to St. Barnabas Hospital to have the surgery by Dr. Cooper. I had one senator from California. I straighten him on my therapy table and he was very happy with me. When he go back to California, he tell his friend about me.

Fred Williamson [a pseudonym] came to New York and he had the surgery on his right side. After two weeks of therapy with me, he was so good he almost throw me a basketball. So, we have fun together. Fred took me to dinner in the Bronx and we had a good time.

Then, he recuperate for a month or so, and he had the surgery on his left side. Fred had a plan. He was a millionaire, very high up in an oil company.

"Henry, why don't you come back to California with me? I need therapy every day. I pay for everything. I'll buy a house for you and Nancy. I'll build a therapy room in the house and you tell me what you need. Come to California and work for me."

At that time, I have a good life. It was so perfect. Everything. Nancy's mother is Italian, we live close in to her family, close to the hospital, and I love being part of the family. I hadn't had family like that since Kraków. No way would Nancy leave her mother. We had a big fight. So, I said forget it. I like my wife. I have a good life.

Dr. Cooper is the one who convinced me to go work for Williamson. By then, I was having a hard time working all day because of my war injuries, so this was a good offer in a lot of ways. Nancy's brother-in-law worked on Nancy because she didn't want to leave her mother. Before I make the decision, Williamson, he invite me to California to visit. He pay for everything.

The first time I go to California, he gave me the address, downtown San Diego in a big building. His office took up both the sixteenth and seventeenth floors. So, I go upstairs, ring the bell, and they open the door. His secretary let me in. There's Williamson sitting in the corner at this huge desk. He stood up and came right over to greet me.

"Henry! Come in. Come in. It's so good to see you."

The secretary sees me, smiles big, and says, "So, that's Henry."

Williamson had told everyone about me.

Then, we went down and we went to the parking lot for the building. We stop in front of a brand new 1968 Mustang. Williamson points to it, then looks at me, and smiles and says, "Henry, this is your car. I have a Jaguar, so you need a Mustang. Get in! Then, you can follow me."

I try to get in, but I'm so tall. I remember I laughed so hard I asked him if he had a shoe horn. He laughed at that. I always make them laugh. It was my first time in a Mustang. In my whole life, I never own a car before. In the Bronx we drive Nancy's car. He gets out in traffic, and goes zoom, very fast. I follow him. We stop at a good Mexican restaurant and we have lunch. Finally, we end up at his big house overlooking the La Jolla Country Club. I was very impressed. He had a big pool in the backyard . . . I always like water. It still took some convincing to get Nancy to leave her mother to move across the country. Eventually she said yes, and we made the move.

Sometime after we get to California, Nancy and I go walking on the beach and stop to watch the sunset. We hold hands and Nancy leaned her head on my shoulder. I have a house, a car, a wife, a great life. I'm nobody special, but I survive for two reasons that have been true my whole life: I was lucky, and I know someone.

••

Henry worked exclusively for Williamson before retiring in 1980. Upon retiring, he and Nancy moved to a suburb of Phoenix, Arizona, and bought a modest home near where Nancy's only sister lived. For the remainder of their days, Henry and Nancy stayed involved in the senior community center, and enjoyed a wide circle of friends. At one point, Henry worked at the front desk where he could greet everyone who came in that day. He participated in the Arizona Senior Olympics for many years in tennis. He routinely ranked in the top athletes, beating out many younger competitors. He swam regularly in the nearby community center for the rest of his life.

Undated. *Henry Zguda's personal photo album.*

EPILOGUE

October 2003
Phoenix, Arizona

S ummer vacation had come and gone, school had started up again, and life seemed full of kids, homework, and activities. My own eighty-year-old mother had several unplanned health crises that required my time and attention. While I recorded much of Henry's story on tape, and had spent hours transcribing those sessions, the stories just weren't coming together as I'd hoped. I'd written several pieces, and had taken these drafts to Henry to proofread for names and such. The project loomed far larger than I'd ever envisioned, and larger than my capabilities at the time.

As I got busier, it was getting harder to look Henry in the eye and feel like we were ever going to accomplish a book. An author friend tried to help, and invited me to her writing group. I joined, reading Henry's drafts. No one was impressed with the samples I submitted, but they were impressed with Henry and his story . . . if I could ever figure out how to write it.

Unintentionally, it was now about three months since I'd made any contact with Henry and Nancy. Like so many of my other friends, I adored them, but the busyness of my life always prevailed. And I was embarrassed at how little I'd been able to deliver.

One afternoon, as I was rushing around the house, the phone rang. Henry was on the other line.

"Nancy and I were just wondering are you okay? We haven't heard from you for a while."

"Oh, Henry. I'm so sorry, I've just been busy."

"Nancy and I were worried you were sick or something."

My feelings for this wonderful couple melted, and an instant realization pierced my gut. How foolish I had been to stop meeting with Henry, at his age, then 86. But what almost brought tears to my eyes was his sincere concern. Whereas my mother usually called with an accusatory, daughter-guilt, you-should-know-better voice, Henry's voice dripped true concern. He was actually worried about *me*. I wanted to show up on his doorstep in the next five minutes. I hadn't realized how much I'd missed his voice. Nancy chimed in.

"We miss you, doll." She'd been on the second house extension, so they'd called together.

"Oh, Henry, it's just been the kids, and that I hadn't made any progress on the book. I feel so bad. Tell you what. I want you and Nancy to come over for dinner. Let me cook you dinner and we can sit down as a family."

Busy. It's the American way. I can't remember a time when I wasn't busy, especially after I had children. There was always something to do, some chore around the house, some activity to drive kids to, and lately of course, dealing with my aging mother. My mother's issues weren't constant, but there was always a certain tension in the background, like a slowly turning crank on a toy jack-in-the-box. I never knew exactly when the next illness or mini-crisis would arise. It always did, though, without warning and almost always in direct conflict with plans I'd already made that had to be canceled.

But, oh no! I'd gotten too busy for Henry and Nancy. How could I?

●●

I don't remember what I cooked, but I remember sitting around the white, plastic kitchen table, set with my best china and crystal. This was a time to celebrate and honor Henry and Nancy.

We laughed, had a great time, and my family once again got to meet Henry. I remember it as a wonderful evening.

Henry gifted me a small handcrafted plaque from Poland as a way of thanking me for all the time I'd invested.

I couldn't have known that evening would turn out to be our Last Supper.

Front of Polish plaque given to Katrina. *Author's personal collection.*

Back of Polish plaque given to Katrina.
Author's personal collection.

A short four weeks later, my daughter Jamie and I braved the Thanksgiving shopping crowds at Arizona Mills shopping mall. Naively, I'd hoped by going on Saturday, all the Black Friday shoppers would have been tired. The mall was mobbed. I don't remember what we bought, or where we shopped, I just remember the blue skies and high sun signaled perfect tourist weather. After a relaxing Thanksgiving, I'd just had a great daughter date. After two hours of scouring the holiday sales, we headed out of the mall into the bright sun, for lunch together. What a perfect day.

We exited the mall, found our car, and as we settled in, I turned the ignition and put the car in reverse. Just then, my cell phone rang. I shifted the car back into the parking space and put the car in park. As I dug the phone out from the bottom of the purse, I noticed Rick's number on the caller ID.

"There's a message from Nancy. Henry's in intensive care at St. Luke's Hospital. He collapsed at Thanksgiving dinner and hasn't regained consciousness. I'm sorry."

Stunned, tears began to roll down my cheeks uncontrollably, and I silently hung up. Jamie just stared at me, the mood shattered. Again, why hadn't I made more time for Henry? What's the four-letter American curse word? Busy.

Not Henry. Not yet. Not now. We're not done.

I slowly drove home. Neither Jamie nor I said a word.

When I got home from the mall, Jamie disappeared into her room. I called Nancy right away. She seemed so grateful to hear my voice, but distraught was an understatement. I offered to come over, but she said she was headed over to the hospital.

I paced in the family room, not knowing what to do. I needed to do something, but what? I felt like I knew Henry and Nancy better than some of my family. I wasn't their family, but I couldn't just stand there.

I drove to St. Luke's Hospital, feeling tentative. What was I doing? Shouldn't I just stay home?

I parked my car and headed to the entrance, all the time wondering if I really should be there. I found the entrance to the ICU. There was a phone on the wall and above it a sign: *Immediate family only. Please dial the nurse's station for admittance.*

I picked up the phone. I read the sign again. I set the phone back in its cradle.

When you're sick, it's such a personal thing. Generally, you're at your worst or unconscious, dressed in a hospital gown, tubes dripping medicine into veins, other tubes draining fluids. No, a hospital visit was out of the question.

I debated telling Nancy I was there in the lobby if she wanted company.

I paced for about fifteen minutes, arms crossed, head bowed, not knowing the right thing to do. *Call. Don't call. Call. Don't call.*

Then I decided it was not my place to visit family in such a private situation. I turned around, walked slowly out of the lobby and headed for my car. Constant tears slowly dripped down my cheeks. I made no attempt to wipe them, letting them, instead, drip off my chin onto my collar.

I remembered one of my last conversations with Henry.

"You know, the American healthcare system is so backward from communism. There you take pills to get better, and then you're done with medication. Here they put you on medications for the rest of your life, and they just keep giving you more medicine. The only people winning here are the medicine companies."

Nancy called ten days later. "Henry's gone."

I immediately left and drove the three-minute hop skip to her house. We sat there at the kitchen counter and, over wine, we both cried. We each cried for ourselves in a way. Nancy just lost her best friend of forty-two years, and I knew I would always miss this man. I wanted to do something, anything.

I started talking with Nancy about the funeral arrangements to see if I could help. I'd already been part of two family funerals: my brother's and my father's. I'd learned that people with intact families really don't know what's involved, or where to start. Nancy was on her own. In one sense, Henry had already planned ahead to make things easy for Nancy. He donated his body to science, so Nancy only had to plan the funeral Mass.

She kept asking me if I knew Pat Libby. "You'd really like her. She's just like you."

I shook my head no, knowing I was not part of Nancy's circle of friends, but always accepting that Pat Libby was really Nancy's closest friend.

I offered to help write an obituary. Nancy didn't care about an obituary. She didn't care how many people were at the funeral. She just missed Henry. But there was one thing I *could* do, since I had Henry's history and dates. I composed a program for the funeral. I drafted a timeline of Henry's life, used the book forward Henry had written to Nancy, and placed his photo as a young man on the cover. I only made a hundred copies, and we ran out. I'm told his friends hoarded those programs.

Shortly after we started the project, I asked Henry what he'd like to put in the front of the book. I typed it out, and had him sign it. I used Henry's words in the front of the program:

Thank you America, for being such a wonderful country and for being so good to me.

Thank you, New York, for giving me your wonderful girl, Nancy, as my wife. For 40 years she has survived my broken English, and is always there when I need her. I am truly blessed.

Life can be beautiful!
Henry Zguda
December 4, 2002

Katrina, Nancy, and Henry.
Photo by Pam McBryan. Author's personal collection.

ACKNOWLEDGMENTS

First and foremost, I have to thank my wonderful husband, Rick. You have always been my biggest fan, strongest cheerleader, steadiest supporter, and occasional book widower, as I devoted so much time to this project. To my children, Devin, Jamie, and Derrick, you have enriched and validated my life beyond measure.

Multiple translators through the years have helped make sense of Polish, German, and French documents. For German, I am indebted to Jane Grabowski, Iris Krondorff, and my good friend Uta Behrens, who also helped me with older German words. For French, I thank my good friend Corinne Mayr. For Polish, I remain indebted to my earliest translator and friend, Oana Niculae, who met Henry and became as charmed as I was. To Roman and Lucyna Spychalski, your friendship and unflagging support came unsolicited and have been unwavering since the day we met. Viola Bartosiewicz-Klype, I treasure your friendship and support, and thank you for answering all my Polish questions. Mike Richard of Living Kraków Cultural Pilgrimages, you pointed me in all the right directions when I traveled to Poland in 2013. I salute the work of the Polish-American Congress, Arizona Division, to educate the American public about Poland's historic role and accomplishments and to promote Polish culture. Thank you for your support.

To my writing group, Sande Roberts, Becky Owens, and Wendy Fallon—these stories would not be where they are without your valuable input, questions, comments, and unwavering interest and support. That we became friends is a lasting bonus. To my first editor, Ann Videan, who spent months helping me hone and craft a series of stories into a cohesive narrative, I am grateful and beyond blessed to count you as my editor and my friend. I'm thrilled to have the team and expertise of Köehler Books behind this project. Multiple people have read various portions of this story through the years, and I appreciate each of you for honest, wise feedback I have taken to heart.

Thank you to Lawrence Bell, Ph.D, Executive Director of the Arizona Jewish Historical Society, and to Marcia Fine for previewing sections on Polish-Jewish relations. Marcia, I'm proud to call you my mentor and tireless supporter. Greg Archer, you opened my eyes to what Poland suffered under Stalin, and share the passion for telling Henry's story. Your ongoing support is deeply appreciated.

Thank you to Dr. Wojciech Płosa, Head of the Archives at the Auschwitz-Birkenau State Museum, who has been gracious, helpful, and patient with my questions from the first time we met in October 2013. I am indebted to the International Tracing Service for its assistance in locating, downloading, and thoroughly explaining dozens of documents with Henry's name. Thanks also go to the Buchenwald Memorial in Weimar, Germany, for its assistance. The staff in the Library and Collections departments at the United States Holocaust Memorial Museum has been universally helpful, and careful custodians and protectors of the countless documents, photos, and artifacts like Henry's. As a living memorial to the Holocaust, you inspire people to confront hatred, prevent genocide, and promote human dignity. What you all do does matter.

APPENDIX A: ADDITIONAL CAMP CORRESPONDENCE OF HENRY ZGUDA

H enry possessed nine letters on Auschwitz stationery, two letters on Buchenwald stationery, and two postcards from Buchenwald. Examples of stationery from both camps have been included previously in this book. Due to their unique historical value, the two postcards from Buchenwald are also included below.

Front of Buchenwald postcard, dated June 27.
The year is missing but it would be either 1943, or more likely
1944. *US Holocaust Memorial Museum, gift of Nancy Zguda.*

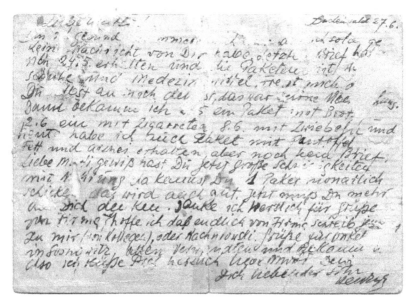

Back of Buchenwald postcard, dated June 27.
The year is missing but it would be either 1943, or more likely
1944. *US Holocaust Memorial Museum, gift of Nancy Zguda.*

Front of Buchenwald postcard, dated January 7, 1945.
US Holocaust Memorial Museum, gift of Nancy Zguda.

Back of Buchenwald postcard, dated January 7, 1945.
US Holocaust Memorial Museum, gift of Nancy Zguda.

APPENDIX B:
POLAND AFTER WORLD WAR II

W hen I first met Henry, I knew very little about Poland, and had never known or interviewed a concentration camp survivor before. What I have learned in the last fifteen years has left me with a lasting respect for Poland, her people, and a far greater understanding of what she has had to endure for centuries, including the devastation wrought by World War II.

Few countries fought harder, lost more, and have received less credit than Poland. The numbers alone are staggering. During nearly six years of war, many Poles fought valiantly until the bitter end. Six million civilian Poles died or were murdered, of which three million were Jewish. That number represents twenty percent of her pre-war population, including ninety percent of her Jewish population. A half million fighting men and women died. The country was left with a million war orphans and a half million invalids. A third of Poland's academics, scientists, and doctors were targeted and murdered. During the war, many Germans had moved to Poland, or lived on German lands that became part of Poland after the war, which led to a mass cross-movement of people to and from Germany after the war. An estimated 3.5 million Germans fled or were ordered out of Poland, while a flood of over two million Poles forced into slave labor and survivors of concentration camps in Germany returned to Poland, many to find their homes destroyed. Even worse, in some remote areas, returned Jews became victims of murder and pogroms. Warsaw lay in ruins, and the country was an economic wreck. The confusion across the country was intense.

Poland was invaded by two powers—Nazi Germany under Adolf Hitler, and Russia under Jozef Stalin. While Henry's story doesn't touch on Stalin, as but one example of Stalin's terrible legacy in Poland, one to two million civilian Poles were deported in 1940 to the frozen depths of Russia and forced into slave labor, horrid living conditions and starvation. Stalin was an ally of Great Britain and the United States during World War II, so very few news stories of those injustices and deaths ever reached the West, and are far less known.

Perhaps the worst betrayal of Poland came after the war. Two of her allies before the war, Great Britain under Winston Churchill, and the United States under Franklin D. Roosevelt, reached an agreement with Jozef Stalin that Poland would fall under Soviet communism after the war. The Polish government in exile was never consulted. Polish men and women who had fought valiantly against the Nazis were later arrested by the Soviets, and executed on false accusations they had cooperated with the Nazis.

Poland would not become a free country until the fall of communism in 1989.

BIBLIOGRAPHY

Adamczyk, Wesley, *When God Looked the Other Way, an Odyssey of War, Exile and Redemption*. Chicago, IL: University of Chicago Press, 2004.

Beattie, Andrew and Tim Pepper, *Cracow*. Derbyshire, England: Landmark Publishing, Ltd, 1999.

Author's note: While this publication may seem dated, it is one of two travel books I used while interviewing Henry. It still contains Henry's handwriting on multiple pages pointing out many things to clarify his stories.

Berenbaum, Michael, ed., *A Mosaic of Victims: Non-Jews Persecuted and Murdered by the Nazis*. New York: New York University Press, 1990.

Berenbaum, Michael and Abraham J. Peck, eds., *The Holocaust and History. The Known, The Unknown, The Disputed, and the Reexamined*. Indiana University Press, Bloomington and Indianapolis, 1998.

Buchenwald Concentration Camp, 1937–1945: A Guide to the Permanent Historical Exhibition. Edited by the Gedenkstätte Buchenwald, Compiled by Harry Stein. Wallstein Verlag 2004. German-English translation: Judith Rosenthal, Frankfurt a.M. 2010 edition.

Davies, Norman, *God's Playground, A History of Poland in Two Volumes*. New York: Columbia University Press, 2005.

Dwork, Debórah, and Robert Jan van Pelt, *Auschwitz, 1270 to the Present*. New York, NY: W.W. Norton & Company, Inc., 1996.

Dydynski, Krzysztof, *Kraków*. Australia: Lonely Planet Publications. 1st edition. 2000.

Höss, Rudolph, *Death Dealer, The Memoirs of the SS Kommandant at Auschwitz*. Edited by Steven Paskuly, Translated by Andrew Pollinger, Buffalo, NY: Prometheus Books, 1992.

Isaszko, Tadeusz, Helena Kubica, Franciszek Piper, Irena Strzelecka, Andrzej Strzelecki, *Auschwitz 1940–1945: Central Issues in the History of the Camp, Volumes I–V*. Translated from Polish by William Brand. Oświęcim: Auschwitz-Birkenau State Museum, 2000.

Księga Pamięci, Volumes I–V; Transporty Polaków Do KL Auschwitz Z Krakówa. Edited by Franciszek Piper, Irena Strzelecka. Warszawa-Oświęcim: Auschwitz-Birkenau State Museum, 2002.

Kochanski, Halik, *The Eagle Unbowed: Poland and the Poles in the Second World War*. Cambridge, MA: Harvard University Press, 2012.

Kogon, Eugen, *The Theory and Practice of Hell: The German Concentration Camps and the System Behind Them*. New York: Farrar, Straus and Giroux. First Revised Edition 2006.

Laks, Szymon, *Music of Another World*, translated by Chester A. Kisiel. Illinois: Northwestern University Press, 1989. First published 1979 in Polish as *Gry Oświęcimski*.

Langbein, Hermann, *Against All Hope; Resistance in the Nazi Concentration Camps 1938–1945*, translated by Harry Zohn. New York: Paragon House, 1994. First published 1980 in German as *nicht wie die Schafe zur Schlachtbank: Widerstand in den nationalsozialistischen Konzentrationslagern 1938–1945*.

Langbein, Hermann, *People in Auschwitz*, translated by Harry Zohn, North Carolina: The University of North Carolina Press, 2004.

Lower, Wendy, *Hitler's Furies: German Women in the Nazi Killing Fields*. New York, NY: Houghton Mifflin Harcourt, 2013.

Lukas, Richard C., Editor, *Out of the Inferno: Poles Remember The Holocaust*. The University Press of Kentucky, 1989.

Lukas, Richard C., *Forgotten Holocaust, The Poles under German Occupation 1939–1944*. New York: Hippocrene Books, 1997.

Lukas, Richard C. editor, *Forgotten Survivors, Polish Christians Remember the Nazi Occupation*. Kansas: University Press of Kansas, 2004.

Metaxas, Eric, *Seven Men: And the Secret of Their Greatness*. Nashville, TN: Thomas Nelson, Inc., 2013.

Naimark, Norman M., *Stalin's Genocides*. Princeton, NJ: Princeton University Press, 2010.

Piotrowski, Tadeusz, *Poland's Holocaust: Ethnic Strife, Collaboration with Occupying Forces and Genocide in the Second Republic, 1918–1947*. North Carolina: McFarland & Company, Inc., 1998.

Piper, Franciszek, *Auschwitz Concentration Camp: How it Was Used in the Nazi System of Terror and Genocide and in the Economy of the Third Reich.*

Piper, Franciszek and Teresa Swiebocka, eds. *Auschwitz. Nazi Death Camp*. Auschwitz-Birkenau State Museum. Translated from Polish. Oświęcim, 1996.

Siedlecki, Janusz Nel (6643); Krystyn Olszewski (75817); Borowski, Tadeusz (119198), *We were in Auschwitz*. Translated by Alicia Nitecki, Welcome Rain Publishers, New York, 2000. First published in Spring 1946 in Polish as *Byliśmy w Oświęcimiu* by Oficyna Warszawska Na Obczyźnle.

Sofsky, Wolfgang, *The Order of Terror; The Concentration Camp*. Trans. William Templer. 1993: Princeton, NJ, Princeton University Press 1997.

The Spanish Inquisition 1478–1614, An Anthology of Sources. Edited and translated by Lu Ann Homza. Indianapolis/Cambridge: Hackett Publishing Company, Inc., 2006.

Swiebocka, Teresa, and Connie Wilsack, eds. *Auschwitz: A History in Photographs*. Oświęcim: Auschwitz-Birkenau State Museum, 1993.

Swimming in Auschwitz: Survival Stories of Six Women. Bala Cynwyd Productions. 2009.

Tyminski, Kazimierz, *To Calm My Dreams: Surviving Auschwitz*. Australia: New Holland Publishers, 2011.

Venezia, Shlomo, *Inside the Gas Chambers; Eight Months in the Sonderkommando of Auschwitz*. Ed. Jean Mouttapa. Translated by Andrew Brown. Cambridge: Polity Press, 2009.

Weigel, George, *Witness to Hope: The Biography of Pope John Paul II*. New York, NY: HarperCollins Publishers, Inc., 1999.

Wetzler, Alfred, *Escape from Hell: The True Story of the Auschwitz Protocol*. Translated from Slovak by Ewald Osers. Edited by Peter Varnai. New York, Berghahn Books, 2007.

Whitlock, Flint, *The Beasts of Buchenwald: Karl & Ilse Koch, Human-Skin Lampshades, and the War-Crimes Trial of the Century*. Brule, WI: Cable Publishing, 2011.

Wiernicki, John, *War in the Shadow of Auschwitz; Memoirs of a Polish Resistance Fighter and Survivor of the Death Camps*. New York: Syracuse University Press, 2001.

Zamoyski, Adam, *The Polish Way, A Thousand-year History of the Poles and their Culture*. New York: Hippocrene Books, 1987.

Websites (Current as of July, 2017)

https://www.ushmm.org/

http://auschwitz.org/en/

https://www.buchenwald.de/en/69/

http://www.ymca.int/where-we-work/ymca-members-profiles/ymca-in-europe/ymca-poland/

http://www.holocaustmemoirdigest.org/Maps/7_Auschwitz.pdf

https://www.olympic.org

Photo Permissions:

The United States Holocaust Memorial Museum, Washington D.C. The views or opinions expressed in this book, and the context in which the images are used, do not necessarily reflect the views or policy of, nor imply approval or endorsement by, the United States Holocaust Memorial Museum.

The Buchenwald Memorial, Weimar, Germany

The Auschwitz-Birkenau State Museum, Oświęcim, Poland

The International Tracing Service, USHMM

Süddeutsche Zeitung Photo, Munich, Germany

National Archives at College Park, College Park, MD

Historical Museum of the City of Kraków

SBH Health System

ADDITIONAL READING

Edsel, Robert M, with Bret Witter, *The Monuments Men, Allied Heroes, Nazi Thieves, and the Greatest Treasure Hunt in History*. New York: Back Bay Books, 2009.

Gelissen, Rena Kornreich, with Heather Dune Macadam, *Rena's Promise: A Story of Two Sisters in Auschwitz*. Boston, Massachusetts: Beacon Press, 1995, 2015.

Frankl, Viktor E., *Man's Search for Meaning*. Massachusetts: Beacon Press, 1959, 1962, 1984, 1992, 2006. First published in German in 1946 under the title *Ein Psycholog erlebt das Konzentrationslager*.

Hart, Kitty, *Return to Auschwitz: the Remarkable Story of a Girl Who Survived the Holocaust*. London, England: Sidgwick and Jackson, 1982.

Karski, Jan, A, *Story of a Secret State: My Report to the World*. Washington, D.C.: Georgetown University Press, 2013.

Author's note: The account was first published in 1944 by Houghton Mifflin. Jan Karski passed away in 2000. This latest edition, in conjunction with the Jan Karski Institute, includes a foreword by Madeleine Albright.

Kirschner, Ann, *Sala's Gift: My Mother's Holocaust Story*. New York: Simon & Schuster, Inc., 2006.

Klein, Gerda Weissman, *All But My Life, A Memoir*. New York: Hill and Wang, 1957, 1995.

Levi, Primo, *The Voice of Memory, Interviews 1961–1987*. Edited by Marco Belpoliti and Robert Gordon, Translated by Robert Gordon, New York, New York: Polity Press, 2001.

Levi, Primo, *Survival in Auschwitz*. New York, New York: Touchstone, 1996. Originally published in 1958 in Italian, as *Se questo è un uamo*.

Wiesel, Elie, *Dawn*. New York: Hill and Wang, 1961, 2006.

Wiesel, Elie, *Night*. New York: Hill and Wang, 1972, 1985.

AUTHOR BIO

 Katrina Shawver wrote hundreds of newspaper columns over eleven years for *The Arizona Republic*, holds a B.A. from the University of Arizona in English/Political Science, and has excelled at the School of Trial and Error. In addition to a variety of previous careers in software support, the paralegal profession, tax preparation, and answering phones for a forensic psychiatrist, she has presented at the community college level on Poland under Hitler and Stalin. She lives in Phoenix, Arizona with her husband, Rick. This is her first book.

Thank you for reading!

Dear Reader:

I hope you enjoyed *Henry – A Polish Swimmer's True Story of Friendship from Auschwitz to America*. I loved the process of learning, and merging history with a meaningful story of survival and ultimate success.

As an author, I love feedback and would love to connect. You can write me at katrina@katrinashawver.com and visit me on the web at katrinashawver.com.

Finally, I need to ask a favor. If you're so inclined I'd love if you could leave a review of *Henry*. Reviews don't have to be long, even a few words help spread the success. All feedback is welcomed.

Thank you so much for reading *Henry – A Polish Swimmer's True Story of Friendship from Auschwitz to America* and for sharing the journey. Always reach for the stars.

In gratitude,

Katrina Shawver

TOPICS FOR DISCUSSION

1. Henry grew up playing on the Planty in Kraków with his friends, mostly unsupervised. How did his experiences growing up differ from today? Has the modern integration of all things electronic into our daily lives restricted the ability to make lasting connections?

2. Much of the story takes place either prior to World War II or during the war when many groups were targeted for discrimination. Are these themes still current today? Have you ever felt targeted for who you are? What power do we have as individuals to stand up to similar events?

3. Yad Vashem in Israel defines the Holocaust as "the murder by Nazi Germany of six million Jews." The US Holocaust Memorial Museum defines the Holocaust as "the systematic, bureaucratic, state-sponsored persecution and murder of six million Jews by the Nazi regime and its collaborators." Neither definition recognizes or includes Henry Zguda, Christian Poles, and millions of others who perished under the Nazi regime and in German concentration camps. How can we recognize and honor other victims of the larger Nazi genocide?

4. What did you learn about Poland that you didn't know before reading this story?

5. Henry and his friend Wilik Tomaszczyk stood only 100 yards away from the Germans who "sorted" an entire trainload of Jews into lines of the living and those doomed to an immediate death in the gas chamber. They could do nothing to help anyone. Can you describe a time you watched something terrible happen that you truly were unable to stop? How did that make you feel?

6. Were you surprised at the differences between Auschwitz and Buchenwald? Can you think of three main ways they differed?

7. What factors or traits contributed to Henry's survival?

8. Friendship is a recurrent theme from Henry's life and the retelling of his story. Have you ever met the right person at the right time? Can you describe an unexpected friendship with someone who was different than you?

9. Henry sometimes refers to food at different stages of his life as charactistic of the time and place. Can you think of favorite foods in your life that have symbolism, or that evoke strong memories? Do you have a favorite example from Henry's life?

10. Katrina Shawver met Henry on a random phone tip, yet after one meeting with Henry, his story resonated with her. Have you ever met someone who made a lasting impression on you?

11. Have you ever told someone they have such a unique story they "should write a book?" If so, what made that story worth sharing with the world?

12. Henry stayed friends with the communists in Buchenwald, and served in the communist government after the war, but never believed in communism. Have you ever kept your own beliefs quiet in order to survive or to keep a job? Have you ever been threatened for your beliefs?

13. What would you say to someone who claims the Holocaust never happened? What would you say to someone who claims there were no Poles in the camps?

14. Do you think a war like World War II could happen again? Do you think your country would win?

15. What will you remember most about this story?